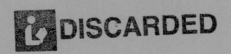

GOSSIP in the first decade of VICTORIA'S reign

Lord Melbourne.   *The Queen.*   *Lord Palmerston.*

SUSANNAH AND THE ELDERS.

GOSSIP

IN THE FIRST DECADE OF

VICTORIA'S REIGN

By

John Ashton

AUTHOR OF

" Social Life in the Reign of Queen Anne "

ILLUSTRATED BY REPRODUCTIONS FROM CARTOONS
AND OTHER DRAWINGS

With an Introduction and Bibliography
by
LESLIE SHEPARD

LONDON

HURST AND BLACKETT, LIMITED

13, Gt. Marlborough St., W.

1903

Now Reissued by
Singing Tree Press
1249 Washington Blvd., Detroit, Michigan 1968

Library of Congress Card Number: 67-23942

INTRODUCTION

John Ashton compiled some thirty works, mainly in the fields of social history and folklore, but never received proper biographical notice. There are stray bibliographical notes in Allibone's *Critical Dictionary of English Literature* and Cousin's *Short Biographical Dictionary of English Literature* (Appendix to 1910 edition) but there are no details of his life, and even his death was not recorded in any standard reference work. The present reissue of a group of his books is a good opportunity to list the few facts it has been possible to discover about this interesting author.

John Ashton was born in London, September 22, 1834, son of Thomas and Isabella Ashton. Thomas Ashton was a shipbroker in the city of London and his wife followed the specialized trade of gun maker in the Goodman's Fields area. In addition to John Ashton there were two sisters and one brother. Thomas Ashton died in 1851 at his residence in Lewisham, Kent, and Isabella Ashton in 1875. We have no details of the early education and employment of John Ashton, but by the age of 40 he had settled down to regular research at the British Museum, London. In 1882 he published three books: *The Earliest Known Printed Ballad. A ballade of the Scottysshe King* (a facsimile of the first printing of Skelton's ballad, with introductory notes), *Chap-books of the Eighteenth Century*, and *Social Life in the Reign of Queen Anne*—the latter book was the first of a series of valuable compilations on social history. Ashton read steadily at the British Museum for more than thirty years, producing a new book about once a year.

In 1895 he lived at 4 Middleton Road (now Grove), Islington, in north west London, a rather dreary area near Camden Road. It was in this district that novelist

George Gissing lodged his character Alfred Yule in *New Grub Street*, and John Ashton must have been one of many struggling authors contemporary with Gissing, living frugally in a furnished room and making his way each day to the British Museum by omnibus, studying under the great glass dome of the Reading Room. It is doubtful whether Ashton made much money out of his books. Although they sold well, the rewards of authors in those days were modest, especially for non-fiction books. But clearly Ashton studied the kind of subjects that interested him—curiosities of history, and manners, modes and customs of past times. Living in an uninspiring district of endless rows of houses, he plodded away at his books, living in a romantic past. He had some skill in sketching, and embellished his books with many copies of old prints. Two of his books—*The Old Bailey and Newgate* [1902] and *Old-Time Aldwych, Kingsway and Neighbourhood* [1903] were published under the pseudonym "Charles Gordon", possibly to avoid complications on a publishing contract.

Ashton wrote little in his last few years and his death on July 29, 1911 seems to have passed unnoticed. Between 1906 and 1913 *Who's Who* had noted his works and it continued to list him until 1913 (though he does not appear in *Who Was Who*).

Ashton did not claim to be more than a compiler, but his compilations were thorough and entertaining, avoiding the extremes of heavy scholarship or over popularisation. He was a typical dedicated researcher with a keen delight in the everyday customs and traditions of ordinary people of former times. His books are not dated, and more than half a century after his death they remain as interesting and instructive as when they were first published.

London, England   Leslie Shepard
1967

BIBLIOGRAPHY OF WORKS WRITTEN OR EDITED
BY JOHN ASHTON

(Publication dates are for British editions; American editions sometimes vary.)

Chap-books of the Eighteenth Century; with facsimiles, notes, and introductions. 1882.

[SKELTON, John] *The Earliest known printed English Ballad. A ballade of the Scottysshe King* (facsimile reprint without introduction). 1882.

Social Life in the Reign of Queen Anne, taken from original sources. 1882.

The Adventures and Discourses of Captain John Smith, sometime President of Virginia. 1883.

Humour, Wit, and Satire of the Seventeenth Century. 1883.

Lord Mayor's Show in the Olden Times [Drawings by F. C. Price] [1883].

English Caricature and Satire on Napoleon I 2 vols. 1884; new edition 1888.

Old Times: a picture of social life at the end of the Eighteenth Century. 1885.

The Dawn of the XIXth Century in England. A social sketch of the times. 1886 [1885]; Popular edition 1886.

The Legendary History of the Cross. A series of sixty-four woodcuts from a Dutch book published by Veldener, A.D. 1483. Introduction by J. Ashton; Preface by S. Baring-Gould. 1887 [1886].

Romances of Chivalry told and illustrated in facsimile. 1887. [1886].

A Century of Ballads . . . Edited, and illustrated in facsimile of the originals. 1887.

[MANDEVILLE, Sir John] *The Voiage and Travayle of Sir John Maundeville* (Edited, annotated and illustrated by J. Ashton). 1887.

The Fleet: its River, Prison, and Marriages. 1888. [1887].
Eighteenth Century Waifs [essays]. 1887.
Modern Street Ballads. 1888.
Men, Maidens and Manners a Hundred Years Ago. 1888.
Curious Creatures in Zoology. 1890. [1889].
Social England under the Regency, 1890; New edition 1899.
[HOOD, Thomas] *The Poetical Works of T. Hood* [with memoir and notes by J. Ashton] [1891].
Real Sailor-Songs. Collected and edited. 1891.
[with MEW, James] *Drinks of the World.* 1892.
A History of English Lotteries. 1893.
Charles Letts's Date Book and Chronological Diary, or record of important events in English history [1893].
A Righte Merrie Christmasse!!! The story of Christmastide [1894].
Varia [essays]. 1894.
Hyde Park from Domesday-Book to date. 1896 [1895].
When William IV was King. 1896.
The Devil in Britain and America. 1896.
The History of Gambling in England. 1898
Florizel's Folly. George IV and Brighton. 1899.
[under pseudonym of GORDON, Charles] *The Old Bailey and Newgate.* 1902.
[under pseudonym of GORDON, Charles] *Old-Time Aldwych, Kingsway and Neighbourhood.* 1903.
Gossip in the First Decade of Victoria's Reign. 1903.
The History of Bread from prehistoric to modern times. 1904.

PREFACE.

I HAVE written this Gossip not only for the edification of those
to whom a portion, more or less, may be news, but for those who,
like myself, have lived through the whole of Queen Victoria's reign,
to whom the remembrance of things, almost forgotten, may bring
pleasure and excite interest. The items, herein displayed, have
been gathered from many sources, and their authenticity is
guaranteed by giving the name of the authority whence they were
taken, in very many instances *ipsissima verba*, as paraphrasing
would rob them of their freshness and individuality. All the
illustrations are contemporaneous, and, good or bad, belong to
the text and should not be altered.

JOHN ASHTON.

CONTENTS.

CHAPTER V.

CHAPTER VI.

CHAPTER VII.

1839]   CHAPTER VIII.

CHAPTER IX.

CHAPTER X.

CHAPTER XI.

1840]   CHAPTER XII.

ILLUSTRATIONS.

CHAPTER I.

The Queen's Accession—Proclamation—Funeral of the King—The Queen and
social functions—Mr. Montefiore—Amusing letter—Electric telegraph—
Knocker wrenching—Amusements of the young aristocracy.

KING WILLIAM THE FOURTH was as sincerely fond of his
niece, Alexandrina Victoria, as he cordially detested her
mother, and he earnestly hoped that she might obtain her
majority, which took place on the 24th of May, 1837, before
he died, for he had a horror of the Duchess of Kent having
even the shadowy power of a Regent. Greville, in his
Memoirs, writing on 23rd of May, says: " The King prayed
that he might live till the Princess Victoria was of age, and
he was very nearly dying just as the event arrived. He is
better, but supposed to be in a very precarious state. There
has been a fresh squabble between Windsor and Kensington
about a proposed allowance to the Princess."

The old King lived but a very short time after the desired
event, for he expired at 2.12 on the morning of the 20th of
June, 1837, and how the sad news was broken to the young
Sovereign may best be told in the words of that mine of
anecdote, Miss Frances Williams Wynn, the daughter of Sir
Watkin Williams Wynn (the fourth baronet):

" On Monday we were listening all day for the tolling of
the bells, watching whether the guests were going to the
Waterloo dinner at Apsley House. On Tuesday, at 2½

I

a.m., the scene closed, and in a very short time the Archbishop of Canterbury and Lord Conyngham, the Chamberlain, set out to announce the event to their young Sovereign. They reached Kensington Palace at about five; they knocked, they rang, they thumped for a considerable time before they could rouse the porter at the gates; they were again kept waiting in the courtyard, then turned into one of the lower rooms, where they seemed forgotten by everybody. They rang the bell, desiring that the attendant of the Princess Victoria might be sent to inform H.R.H. that they requested an audience on business of importance. After another delay, and another ringing to enquire the cause, the attendant was summoned, who stated that the *Princess* was in such a sweet sleep, she could not venture to disturb her. Then they said, 'We come to the *Queen* on business of State, and even her sleep must give way to that.' It did; and, to prove that *she* did not keep them waiting, in a few minutes she came into the room in a loose white night-gown and shawl, her nightcap thrown off, and her hair falling upon her shoulders, her feet in slippers, tears in her eyes, but perfectly collected and dignified."

Lord Melbourne was summoned to Kensington Palace by the Queen at 9 a.m., and a Privy Council was called for 11 a.m., but the notice was so short that several of the Privy Councillors had no time to put on their official costume, and were obliged to attend in undress. Amongst others who made their appearance at Court in this novel fashion were the Duke of Cumberland (then, by the fact of the King's death, King of Hanover) and Lord Glenelg.

The Queen was proclaimed the next day, but there is no need to detail the ceremony, as we have all experienced a similar scene lately. The existing ministry was retained, and things settled down in their places, yet not quite all at once, for *The Western Luminary*, a paper long since defunct, says, " In one writ which came down to this city, a ludicrous mistake was made in the date, as follows : ' In the year of Our Lady 1837,' instead of ' Our Lord.' " And the Royal Arms had to be altered from those borne by Her Majesty's five predecessors. Being a female, they had to be borne on a lozenge, instead of a shield; the crest of a lion surmounting a crown was discontinued, as was also the escutcheon of pretence bearing the arms of Hanover, surmounted by the crown of that country.

The preparations for the funeral of the late King were at once commenced; and, in connection therewith, I cannot help quoting from *The Times'* Windsor Correspondent (28 June): "In the platform erected for the interment of George IV., there were more than 70,000 superficial feet of boarding, and 49,000 feet of quartering. The quantity of black cloth used for covering the floor of, and the roof over, amounted to more than 10,000 yards. I understand that, after the interment, it becomes the perquisite of the clergy of the chapel, as do, also, many of the decorative ornaments placed on, and suspended over, the coffin. You will, perhaps, recollect what some people would willingly have you forget—I mean the squabbling which occurred respecting the velvet cushion upon which the coronet of the late Princess Charlotte rested at her funeral, and the scramble which took place for the real or supposed baton of the Duke of York, on the occasion of his burial. Care was taken to prevent the occurrence of any such indecent proceedings at the funeral of George IV., and, hence, I do not anticipate any such scenes on the present occasion."

The King was buried with great pomp on the night of the 8th of July, the Duke of Sussex being chief mourner, and Queen Adelaide occupying the Royal Closet. At the close of the ceremony, the members of the procession, who were much fatigued by the toil they had undergone and by the sultry heat of the chapel, proceeded to quit as quickly and as quietly as possible, but nothing like order was observed in the return to the Palace. In fact, it was, for a considerable time, a scene of indescribable confusion. Arrangements had been made, by orders of the Earl Marshal, for the places at which the carriages of those who had to take part in the procession were to set down and take up; but, owing to the immense number of the carriages, the ignorance of many of the coachmen as to the prescribed regulations, and the obstinacy of others, the rules very soon became a dead letter, and every man seemed disposed to take his own way. This, as might be expected, caused such confusion that it was long past midnight before anything like order was restored. There were smashed panels and broken windows in abundance, but no serious accidents were recorded.

The Queen soon had plenty of business on her hands, and on 30th June she gave her assent to forty Bills, one of which (a remarkably short one), the 7 Gul., iv. and i. Vic., c. 23, enacted : " That from and after the passing of this Act, Judgment shall not be given and awarded against any Person or Persons convicted of any Offence that such Person or Persons do stand in, or upon the Pillory." Owing to the recent change in Sovereigns, there were a few slips in " Her Majesty," and " La Reine le veult." On the 13th July the Queen and her mother left Kensington Palace and took up their residence in Buckingham Palace. On the 17th, the Queen dissolved Parliament in person, dressed in white satin, decorated with gold and jewels, wearing the Order of the Garter and a rich diadem and necklace of diamonds. She bore the function remarkably well, although one evening paper said that " Her emotion was plainly discernible in the rapid heaving of her bosom, and the brilliancy of her diamond stomacher, which sparkled out occasionally from the dark recess in which the throne was placed, like the sun on the swell of the smooth ocean, as the billows rise and fall " ! On the 19th July she held her first levée, and on the 20th her first drawing room.

Having dutifully chronicled the doings of Royalty, let us do the same by meaner folk. On 24th June, Mr. Moses Montefiore, the celebrated Jewish philanthropist, who lived over one hundred years, was elected Sheriff of London, and, on the 9th Nov. following, he received the honour of Knighthood. He was the first Jew who ever served the office of Sheriff, or who had been made a Knight, in England.

Of course, there were no Board Schools in those days, and education was somewhat lax, but it will do no harm to note a piece of orthography, which will show the standard at which the middle lower class had then arrived. It is copied from

The Times of 29 June, 1837.   "*(From an Evening Paper)*—
Last autumn, Mrs. C——, of London, during a visit to ——
House, in the West of Scotland, called one day, along with
some other ladies, in the family carriage, at the Golden Arms
Inn, of a sea bathing place on the coast, and stopped for about
an hour.   Some time after the party had returned to D——
House, Mrs. C—— discovered that she had lost a very fine
boa, which she supposed she must have left at the Inn.   On
enquiry, no trace of the boa could be found ; but, about two
months after Mrs. C——'s return to London, she received a
parcel with a boa somewhat torn, accompanied by the accompanying *(sic)* epistle, which we give as rather a curiosity of
its kind : —

"Golden Arms Inn—29 Oct., 1836.
   " Mrs. C——, London,
      " MADUM,—I was sorry to heer that when you lost
your Bowa in my huse, that the Bowa was stole by my sarvant
lasses ; and the sarvants at D—— House spred a report
against my huses karakter, which no person ever questioned
afore.   My wiffe, Peggy, was muckle vexed at the report, and
sershed the trunks of all the lasses, but did not find your
Bowa ; she fund in Jenny McTavish's kist half a pund of tea
which Jenny had stole from my wiffes cupboard.   Jenny
denied taking your Bowa ; but not doubting that you would
tell a lee, and as Jenny tuke the tea, my wife thocht she must
have taken your Bowa too, so I turned off Jeny for your
satisfaction.   She went home to her mithers house in ——,
and four Sundays after, wha should be cocken in the breist
of the laft, all set round with ribbons in her heed, but Miss
Jeny with your Bowa on her shoulders, like a sow with a
saddle on its back.   I stopped her coming out of the kirk.
So So, Miss Jeny (says I) hae ye stumped the cow of her tale,
or is this the ladies Bowa ye have on your sholders ?   The
brazen faced woman had the impudence to deny the Bowa
was yours, and said her sweetheart had bot it for her in a
secondhand shop in the Salt Market of Glasgow.   But I cut
matters short wi' Jeny ; I een, as if by your authority, tuke

the law in my own hand, and tore the Bowa from her sholders;
it was torn a little in the scuffle wi' Jeny and me afore the
congregation in the kirk yard, but I carried it off in spite of
her, and now send it to you, hopping you will put a letter
in the newspaper of Lundon cleering the karacter of me and
my wiffe Peggy, and my Inn of the Golden Arms. As for
Miss Jeny ye may mak her as black as auld nick, for over
and above Peggies half pund of tea, and your Bowa, Jeny
(I hae good reason to believe) is no better than she should
be. I am, Madum, your vera humbel sarvint,

"JOHN ———."

It will hardly be credited that at the commencement of
1837 there was only one railway running out of London, and
that was the Greenwich railway, which, however, only went
as far as Deptford, where it deposited its passengers in the
midst of market gardens, leaving them to walk or ride to
Greenwich. But there were several running in the midlands
(six railways in all England), and what was then called " The
Grand Junction Railway," from Liverpool to Birmingham,
was opened on the 4th July of this year. Cognate with
railways is the practical working of the Electric Telegraph,
now so necessary to their being. On 12 June, 1837, a patent
was granted (No. 7390) to William Fothergill Cooke, of Breeds
Place, Hastings, and Charles Wheatstone, of Conduit Street,
Hanover Square, for their invention of " Improvements in
giving signals and sounding alarums at distant places by
means of electric currents transmitted through metallic
circuits." This hitherto scientific toy was first tried on 25
July by permission of the London and North Western Railway (then in progress) between Euston and Camden Town
stations, and its successful operation was witnessed with
delight by Fox and R. Stephenson, amongst many others.

A great feature in this year was the " Tom and Jerryism "
(so called from Pierce Egan's " Life in London," 1821) that
existed, especially among the upper class of young men.
Foremost of all was the Marquis of Waterford, whose delight
was in the company of prize fighters, *et hoc genus omne*, and

whose idea of amusement consisted in visiting the lowest public houses, and treating everybody with liquor, even pails full of gin being distributed to whoever would partake of it—being never so happy as when the debauch ended in a fight. Knocker wrenching and similar pranks were his delight, and *Punch*, at the very commencement of vol. i., gives a suggestion for a monument to him. His pranks would fill a volume, and in August of this year (during a yachting trip),

Punch, vol. I., p. 14.   July, 1841.

whilst at Bergen, he received a blow on the head from a stalwart watchman that nearly killed him.

Here is a specimen police case. *Times*, 10 *July*, 1837:

BOW STREET.—On Saturday (8th July) three persons were brought before Mr. Minshull, charged with twisting knockers off hall doors, assaulting the police, and other dis- orderly conduct; and, it having been rumoured that one of the parties charged was the Marquis of Waterford, a great crowd of persons assembled in front of the Office to catch a glimpse of his Lordship. It proved, however, that the gentleman alluded to was not the noble Marquis himself, but his brother, Lord William Beresford, who gave the name of Charles Ferguson. Two other persons were placed in the dock besides his Lordship, one of whom gave the name of Edward Hammersley, of 41, St. James's Street, and the other, who was equipped in the garb of a waterman, said his name was George Elliott, and that he was his Lordship's coxswain.

William Dodds, a police constable of the E division, No. 9, then stated that he was on duty in Museum Street, between 1 and 2, on the previous night, when he saw the two gentlemen at the bar go up to the house, No. 49, and wrench the knocker from the door. Witness expostulated with them, and, seeing another knocker in the hand of the prisoner Elliott, he took him by the collar, upon which the prisoner Hammersley dropped the knocker which he had just carried off. The prisoner Ferguson then came up, and said, "It's all right, old boy," and offered him money, which witness refused to take. The two gentlemen then ran away, but were soon apprehended, witness still retaining hold of Elliott. They were then conveyed to the police station, where Ferguson refused to be searched, declaring that he would not submit to such a rascally degradation, and, having said so, he struck witness. The prisoners were then locked up.

Mr. William Gibson, of 49, Museum Street, proved that one of the knockers produced belonged to him, and had been wrenched off his street door.

Ferguson, in his defence, said he had been up the river on a boating excursion, and had taken "rather too much wine." The other two prisoners also pleaded having taken a drop too much.

Mr. Minshull observed that there were two charges against Ferguson, whom he should consider as the principal offender, and should fine him £5 for unlawful possession of one of the knockers, and £5 for assaulting the police constable in the execution of his duty. He should not fine the other two.

Ferguson said he had no objection to pay £5 for the knocker, but, as he denied the assault, he should appeal against the fine.

Mr. Minshull informed him that there was no appeal in the case, but he intimated that Mr. Ferguson might go to prison, if he pleased, instead of paying the fine.

Ferguson: Oh, there's no occasion for that; I shall pay the fine.

Mr. Minshull then desired him to come round in front of the bench, and said to him: "I dare say, Sir, you have money enough at your disposal, but I pray you not to entertain the notion that you can therefore do as you think fit in the streets of this metropolis, either by night, or by day. You were brought before me, recently, for a similar offence, when I fined you £5, and I now warn you, that if you should again appear before me, under circumstances like the present, I shall, most assuredly, feel it to be my duty, not to inflict a pecuniary fine upon you—for that is no punishment to a person in your station—but I shall send you, at once, as I am authorized to do, to hard labour in the House of Correction, and you will then see that neither rank, nor riches, can entitle you to the privilege of committing depredations upon the property of peaceable and industrious persons, or of disturbing the peace and quiet of this town with impunity."

The noble Lord was then handed over to the custody of the gaoler, and his two companions were discharged. It appeared that he had not sufficient money about him to pay the fines, but his brother, the Marquis of Waterford, after visiting him in " durance vile," released him from his ignoble captivity by paying the fines.

On the same day, his brother, Lord James Beresford, was arrested for disgusting behaviour, and two " young men of genteel appearance," who gave false names, were taken in custody by the police for maliciously upsetting a shell-fish stall.

One more illustration of the amusements and behaviour of the *jeunesse dorée* of that period will suffice. *Times, 25 Nov.* 1837:

MARLBOROUGH STREET.—Lord Harley, of Chester Place, Capt. W. E. Reynolds, of Jermyn Street, and Mr. Charles Lushington, of Tavistock Hotel, were on Thursday (23 Nov.) brought before Mr. Chambers, charged with having practised the fashionable amusement of ringing door bells.

Mr. Young, surgeon, Piccadilly, said, about 5 o'clock that morning he was roused by a violent ringing at his bell. He answered the summons immediately.

Capt. Reynolds: It's a —— lie. You have committed perjury.

Mr. Lushington (to the complainant): You are a —— liar. The fact is, I hurt my fingers and wanted some diachylum plaister, and I therefore rang the bell of the first surgeon I came to. This is the truth. So help me, God.

Mr. Young continued: When he got to the door, he found that all the three defendants had gone away; and he immediately followed them, and demanded their reason for disturbing him. The defendants turned upon him, and made use of language and epithets which he would not pollute his lips by repeating.

Capt. Reynolds (shaking his stick at the witness): I wish I had you elsewhere.

Mr. Lushington: I'd roll you in the kennel, if it was worth while.

Mr. Young continued: The altercation attracted the notice of the police, and witness gave them into custody. When they got to the station house, and witness was proceeding to make the charge, the defendants repeated their disgusting epithets and language.

It is impossible to do more than to remark that the language was of a description hitherto presumed to be confined to the vilest class of the community.

Mr. Young added that all the defendants appeared to be intoxicated.

Lord Harley: I beg pardon, I was sober.

Inspector Beresford was sworn to the fact.

Inspector: His Lordship was more intoxicated than the others.

Mr. Lushington (falling on his knees, and holding up his hands): I was not drunk this night—so help me, C——t.

The Inspector swore that none of the defendants were sober.

Mr. Lushington: The case shall be carried to a higher court.

Mr. Chambers: Then, to give you an opportunity of taking your case elsewhere, I shall make you all find bail; and Mr. Young, if he pleases, may prefer an indictment against you.

Mr. Chambers asked Mr. Lushington if he was a relative of Dr. Lushington,* and received a reply in the affirmative.

Capt. Reynolds said, if his language had been offensive towards the bench, he was sorry for having used it.

Mr. Chambers said, personally, he was indifferent to the language used to him.

The parties having left the box, Mr. Young told Mr. Chambers that he had no wish to press the case further. He wished an arrangement could be made, so that the bench could decide the matter summarily.

The defendants were acquainted with this very handsome conduct on the part of the complainant, and, after some discussion, Capt. Reynolds and Mr. Lushington agreed to pay £5 each to a charity.

Lord Harley was fined 5/- for being intoxicated.

When Mr. Chambers was inflicting the latter fine, he said to Lord Harley that he hoped he would exert his influence, if he had any, with some members of the Legislature, to get the fine for drunkenness increased to £1 where the party was a gentleman.

The defendants paid the fines, and went away.

* Then a very active M.P.; afterwards Judge in the Admiralty and Probate Courts, Dean of Arches, &c.

CHAPTER II.

Thames Tunnel flooded—First mention of the Nelson column—Moustaches—Sale
of the King's stud—Marriage by Registrar—Commencement of New Houses
of Parliament—Lunatics and the Queen—The Queen's visit to the Guildhall
—Lord Beaconsfield's maiden speech.

NOWADAYS very little is thought of making a tunnel under
the Thames, but the first one, designed and carried out by
Sir Marc Isambard Brunel, was regarded, and rightly so, as
a most wonderful feat of engineering. One was proposed
in 1799, and a shaft was sunk in 1804, but the work went
no further. The one now spoken of was approved by Act
of Parliament 24 June, 1824, and the shaft was begun and the
first brick laid on 2 March, 1825. It suffered several times
from irruptions of water; one, on 18 May, 1827; another, in
which six lives were lost, on 12 Jan. 1828. In 1837 there
were two irruptions, the first taking place on 23 August, and
it is thus described by one of Brunel's assistants: "We were
at work about two o'clock on Wednesday, when we found the
water coming in faster than usual. At first, we observed a
quantity of loose sand falling near the gallery, which changed
to thin, muddy drops. This convinced us that the *stratum* in
which the men were working was bad, loose soil. The
increase of water made it necessary to withdraw the men,
which was done by a passage under the crown of the arch,
made for their safety in case of accidents. No injury was
sustained by any of the men. I was not satisfied, at the time,
of the real extent of the bad soil, and I ordered a boat to be
brought, with a rope of sufficient length to enable us to float
to the shield. The boat was brought, but the rope attached

to it, and by which we were to be hauled into the shaft, was shorter than we had ordered it. This deficiency probably saved our lives. We had not proceeded far in the boat when I perceived, by the twinkling of the lights in the tunnel, and other indications of inundation, that the waters came in with increased rapidity. I then gave the signal to be hauled into the shaft, and had scarcely done so when I observed the ground above give way, and the water descending in a thousand streams, like a cascade, or the Falls of Niagara. We were rescued, but, had the rope by which we were relieved from our perilous situation been of a length to allow the boat to go to the extremity of the tunnel, in all probability we should have been drowned. This happened about four o'clock, and, soon after five, the tunnel was entirely filled. No lives were lost. The only injury done is the suspension of the works. The steam engine, when the leak is stopped, will throw out a ton of water per minute ; and, in three days and nights, the whole of the tunnel may be pumped dry."

The second irruption, on 3 Nov., also filled the Tunnel, but on this occasion one man lost his life.

In the *Times* of 9 Sep. of this year I find the first suggestion of a monument to Nelson, in Trafalgar Square :

" Sir, I observe in your paper of Tuesday last, that a correspondent has commented upon the proposed plan for laying out Trafalgar Square.

" Allow me to suggest through your columns the favourable opportunity and most appropriate situation, now afforded, of erecting in the centre of the Square some worthy trophy, or statue, commemorating the glorious victories of the immortal Nelson. Whilst other great commanders and statesmen are honoured with suitable public monuments to their fame, surely the British nation would be eager, if called on, to pay this tribute to the valour, intrepidity and success of this illustrious hero. Yours, etc.—J. B."

In those days every man went clean shaven, or only had side whiskers, a full beard being unknown, and moustaches were confined to foreigners and to a few cavalry regiments, so that for a working man to sport them (although now so exceedingly common) would probably lead to derision and persecution, as in the following police case reported in the *Times* of 21 Sep. :

MARLBOROUGH STREET.—Yesterday, a young man, "bearded like the pard," who said he was a carpenter employed on the London and Birmingham Railroad, applied to Mr. Rawlinson, the sitting magistrate, for an assault warrant, under the following ludicrous circumstances :

Mr. Rawlinson : What do you want the warrant for ?

Applicant : I'll tell your worship, and you'll say it's the most haggrawating and provoking thing as ever was heard on. Vell, then, I goes to my vork, as usual, this 'ere morning, ven one of my shopmates said to me, " Bill, you arn't shaved your hupper lip lately." " Don't mean it," says I. " Vy ? " says he. " 'Cos," I replied, " I intends vearing mustachios to look like a gentleman." " Vell, then," says he, " as you intends to become a fashionable gentleman, p'raps you'll have no objection to forfeit half-a-gallon of ale, as it's a rule here that every workman vot sports mustachios, to have them vetted a bit." Vell, has I refused to have my mustachios christened, they made game of them, and said they weren't half fledged ; and, more nor all that, they hustled me about, and stole my dinner out of the pot, and treated me shameful, and so I want your advice respecting my mustachios.

Mr. Rawlinson : My advice is, to go to a barber and have them shaved off without loss of time.

Applicant : Can't part with a single hair.

Mr. Rawlinson : You want to look like a grenadier, I suppose ?

Applicant : My granny-dear (God bless her old soul !), she never had such a fashionable and warlike appendage in her life.

Mr. Rawlinson : What business has a carpenter with a quantity of long hair hanging from his lip ?

Applicant : The reason vy I vears it is 'cos it's fashionable, and makes me look like a man of some courage.

Mr. Rawlinson : Fashionable, indeed ! I wish, with all my

heart, that the fashion was discontinued. Why need an Englishman make a Jew of himself? It is disgusting to see persons strutting through the streets with mustachios, and, sometimes, a fringe of hair round the face and chin, which is dignified by the name of whiskers. As you won't take my advice, I can't assist you.

Applicant: Vot! not for striking me on the hupper lip?

Mr. Rawlinson: Then your mustachios must have saved you.

Applicant: No, they didn't.

Mr. Rawlinson: How's that?

Applicant: 'Cos the hair ain't long and thick enough; they're only young 'uns as yet. There was no occasion to strike me.

Mr. Rawlinson: And there's no occasion for you to wear mustachios. You may have a warrant, if you like, but I think you had better not.

The man with mustachios then withdrew.

The late King's stud at Hampton was doomed to be sold, and the sale thereof created something of a sensation. On this subject there is, in a little twopenny weekly magazine, called *The Torch*, 9 Sep., '37 (vol. i., p. 19), a periodical now long forgotten, a poem by Tom Hood, which I have not seen in any collection of his poems. It is a

PETITION TO HER MAJESTY FOR PRESERVING THE ROYAL STUD AT HAMPTON COURT.

BY THOMAS HOOD.

I.

LIEGE LADY, all the nation's in high dud-
  geon that Lord Melbourne's brains should be so muddy
As to advise you sell your royal *stud*,
  Which to preserve, should be your royal study.

II.

Poor nags you would not in your stable find,
  Like cavalry of Evans called De Lacey,
No! I do rather hope your royal mind
  Is naturally fond of something racy.

III.

Pray, what has Hampton done that you should trounce ill-
  naturedly its prancers and its sport ?
You have a breed of *asses* in the *Council*,
  Do keep a breed of *horses* in the *Court*.

IV.

His truth who says that you should sell them, fails.
  Believe me, Lady liege, he tells a crammer ;
You'll set your people biting all their *nails*,
  If you put up your horses to the *hammer*.

V.

I like these money-turning Whigs, indeed ;
  Who, into coin, change everything they're able.
You're just installed, and they would sell *the steed*,
  It doesn't make me think they're very *stable*.

VI.

I daresay they believe they're very knowing,
  I think they're close to their official shelves :
And, when they set the horses "Going, going,"
  It's nearly time they should be gone themselves.

VII.

The nation quite in Hampton Court rejoices,
  What ! sell its stud of steeds beyond all praise !
Nay, shout the people with indignant voices,
  And the stud echoes with a hundred *neighs*.

VIII.

Then sell them not, dear lady, I implore ye ;
  Of tears 'twill set your people shedding floods ;—
I tell ye what will make 'em all adore ye,—
  Kick out your ministers and keep your bloods !

But Hood must have laboured under a misapprehension,
for the horses were the private property of the late King,
and his executors had no option but to sell them. It was said
that William IV. in his lifetime wished the country to take the
stud over, at a valuation, and, after his death, it was offered
to Queen Victoria for £16,000. The sale took place on
Oct. 25, and there were 80 lots, which did not fetch particularly high prices, the highest being " The Colonel," who was
bought, after winning the St. Leger, by George IV. for 4,000

guineas; but the horse broke down after running a dead heat at Ascot in 1831. He only realised 1,150 guineas, and was bought by the auctioneer, Mr. Tattersall. The next highest price given was for "Actæon," which fetched 920 guineas. The total proceeds of the sale was 15,692 guineas.

In October a great change was made in the matter of marriage, which had, hitherto, been a purely ecclesiastical affair, but by the 6 & 7 Gul. iv., cap. 85, Registrars of births and deaths were empowered to marry couples, and it became a purely civil contract. This Act was to have come into force on the first day of March; but a subsequent Act postponed it to the last day of June, and it really only became effective in October. It surprised people by its simplicity, and the gist of the Act is in Section xx.: "And be it enacted, That, after the expiration of the said Period of Twenty-one Days, or of Seven Days, if the Marriage is by Licence, Marriages may be solemnized in the registered Building stated as aforesaid in the notice of such Marriage, between and by the Parties described in the Notice and Certificate, according to such form and ceremony as they may see fit to adopt: Provided nevertheless, that every such Marriage shall be solemnized with open doors, between the Hours of Eight and Twelve in the Forenoon, in the Presence of some Registrar of the District in which such registered Building is situated, and of Two, or more, credible Witnesses; provided also, that in some Part of the Ceremony, and in the Presence of such Registrar and Witnesses, each of the Parties shall declare:

"'I do solemnly declare, That I know not of any lawful Impediment why I, A. B., may not be joined in Matrimony to C. D.'

"And each of the Parties shall say to the other:

"'I call upon these Persons here present to witness that I, A. B., do take thee, C. D., to be my lawful wedded Wife [or Husband].'

"Provided also, that there be no lawful Impediment to the Marriage of such Parties."

The old House of Commons was destroyed by fire on 16 Oct., 1834, and it was not until September, 1837, that the

first contracts for the commencement of the construction of
the new works, in connection with the present building, were
entered into.   They were for the formation of an embankment
886 feet in length, projecting into the river 98 feet further
than that then existing, to be faced with granite, and a terrace
673 feet long next the river, and 35 feet wide, in front of the
new Houses, with an esplanade at each end 100 feet square,
with landing stairs from the river 12 feet wide.   The whole
surface of the front building was to be excavated, and filled
in with concrete 12 feet thick, thus forming a permanent and
solid foundation for the superstructure.

Towards the end of this year, the Queen was somewhat
pestered with lunatics.   On Nov. 4, as she was going through
Birdcage Walk on her return from Brighton, a man of respectable appearance went near the Queen's carriage, held up
his fist, and made use of most insulting language towards Her
Majesty and the Duchess of Kent, declaring that the Queen
was an usurper, and he would have her off her Throne before
a week was out.   He was afterwards arrested, and turned
out to be Mr. John Goode, a gentleman of large property in
Devonshire, who had been previously in custody on 24th of
May (Her Majesty's birthday) for creating a disturbance and
forcibly entering the enclosure of Kensington Palace.   He
was taken before the Privy Council, and when examined,
declared that he was a son of George IV. and Queen Caroline,
born at Montague House, Blackheath, and that, if he could
but get hold of the Queen, he would tear her in pieces.   He
was told to find bail, himself in £1,000, and two sureties of
£500 each ; but these not being forthcoming, he was sent to
prison.   On entering the hackney coach, he instantly smashed
the windows with his elbows, and screamed out to the
sentinels : " Guards of England, do your duty, and rescue
your Sovereign."   He was, after a very short imprisonment,
confined in a lunatic asylum.

The other case was a German baker, but he only uttered
threats against the Queen and her mother, and he, too, was
put in an asylum.

A great event, and a very grand sight, was the Queen's

visit to the City of London on 9 Nov., when Alderman Cowan inaugurated his mayoralty. The Queen went in State, attended by all her Court, her Ministers, the Judges, etc. The procession started from Buckingham Palace soon after 2 p.m. and reached Guildhall about 3.30.

The interior of the Guildhall was "exceeding magnifical." There was a canopy of carved gilt, with draperies of crimson velvet and gold fringe and tassels, its interior, being also of crimson velvet, was relieved by ornaments in silver and a radiated oval of white satin with golden rays. The back was fluted in white satin, enriched with the Royal Arms in burnished gold. The State chair was covered with crimson velvet with the Royal Arms and Crown, with the rose, thistle and shamrock tastefully interwoven.

At each end of the Hall, the walls were covered with immense plates of looking-glass. The window at the eastern end of the Hall, above the throne, having been removed, a gigantic wooden framework was substituted, on which was erected a gorgeous piece of gas illumination. Above the mouldings of the windows, and over the City Arms, waved the Royal Standard and the Union Jack. Above was the Royal cypher, V.R., in very large characters, surmounted by the appropriate word "Welcome," the whole being encircled by an immense wreath of laurels, which terminated, at the lower extremity of the framework, with the rose, thistle and shamrock. Over the clock at the western end, and reaching nearly the whole breadth of the Hall, with Gog and Magog on the right and left, was placed an immense stack of armour, with upwards of 30 furled flags as an appropriate background. Immediately above was the magnificently radiated star of the Order of the Garter, surrounded by crimson drapery, and the scroll "God save the Queen" entirely composed of cut glass, which, when lit up, seemed, literally, one continued blaze of diamonds. The whole was surmounted by the imperial crown and wreaths of laurel, intermingled with the rose, thistle and shamrock, covering the entire outline of the window. Where, formerly, was the musicians' gallery, on the opposite side, was occupied by three stacks of armour; complete

2*

coats of mail were, likewise, suspended in other parts of the Hall; two knights in complete armour guarded the entrance of the Hall and Council Chamber, which latter was fitted up for the Queen's reception room, and hung throughout with crimson fluted cloth, finished with gold mouldings and festoons of red and white flowers. Upon a platform stood a chair of state, splendidly gilt and covered with crimson velvet, and there was no other chair nor seat of any kind in the apartment. The Queen's retiring-room was the Aldermen's Court, and was superbly decorated, having a magnificent toilet table covered with white satin, embroidered with the initials V.R., a crown and wreath in gold, and looped with gold silk rope and tassels.

After the Queen's arrival at the Guildhall, and having spent some little time on her toilet, her Majesty was conducted to the Council Chamber, where—seated on her throne, and surrounded by Royal Dukes and Duchesses, etc.—she listened to a dutiful address read by the Recorder, and, at its conclusion, she was graciously pleased to order letters patent to be made out conferring a baronetcy on the Lord Mayor and knighthood on the two Sheriffs, John Carroll and Moses Montefiore, Esquires, the latter, as before mentioned, being the first Jew who had received that honour.

At 20 minutes past 5 the Queen entered the Hall, in which was the banquet, wearing a rich pink satin dress, ornamented with gold and silver, a splendid pearl necklace, diamond ear-rings, and a tiara of diamonds. She occupied the centre of the Royal table, having on her right the Duke of Sussex, the Duchess of Gloucester, the Duchess of Cambridge, Prince George of Cambridge and the Duchess of Sutherland; and on her left, the Duke of Cambridge, the Duchess of Kent, the Princess Augusta of Cambridge and the Countess of Mulgrave. As a specimen of the magnificence of this banquet, it may be mentioned that at the Royal table the whole of the service was of gold, as were the candelabra, epergnes, soup tureens, cellarets, etc.; one firm furnished gold plate for the Queen's table and sideboard to the value of £115,000, and another firm nearly the same amount, whilst the value of plate lent by various gentlemen was assessed at £400,000, besides which there was the Civic plate. The china dessert plates at the Queen's table cost 10 guineas each, and all the glass decanters and china were specially made for the occasion.

At 20 minutes past 8, the Queen left the Hall, and in her retiring room was served with tea from a splendid gold service made for the occasion, and she reached Buckingham Palace about half-past 9—highly delighted with her entertainment.

There is nothing more of interest in this year, if we except the maiden speech of Lord Beaconsfield, in the House of Commons, which took place on 7th Dec. Mr. Disraeli (as he then was) had the disadvantage of following O'Connell, in a noisy debate on the legality of the Irish Election Petition Fund. He was not listened to from the first, and, in the middle of his speech, as reported by *Hansard*, after begging the House to give him five minutes, he said: "He stood there to-night, not formally, but, in some degree, virtually, as the representative of a considerable number of Members of Parliament (*laughter*). Now, why smile? Why envy him? Why not let him enjoy that reflection, if only for one night?" All through his speech he was interrupted, and this is its close, as reported in *Hansard*. "When they recollected the 'new loves' and the 'old loves' in which so much passion and recrimination was mixed up between the noble Tityrus of the Treasury Bench, and the learned Daphne of Liskeard—(*loud laughter*)—notwithstanding the *amantium ira* had resulted, as he always expected, in the *amoris integratio*—(*renewed laughter*)—notwithstanding that political duel had been fought, in which more than one shot was interchanged, but in which recourse was had to the secure arbitrament of blank cartridges—(*laughter*)—notwithstanding emancipated Ireland and enslaved England, the noble lord might wave in one hand the keys of St. Peter, and in the other—(*the shouts that followed drowned the conclusion of the sentence*). Let them see the philosophical prejudice of Man. He would, certainly, gladly hear a cheer from the lips of a popular opponent. He was not at all surprised at the reception which he had experienced. He had begun several things many times, and he had often succeeded at last. He would sit down now, but the time would come when they would hear him. (*The impatience of the House would not allow the hon. member to finish his speech; and during the greater part of the time the hon. member was on his legs, he was so much interrupted that it was impossible to hear what the hon. member said.*)."

CHAPTER III.

Destruction of Royal Exchange—Sale of the salvage—Spring-heeled Jack and his pranks—Lord John Russell's hat.

As a sad pendant to the Civic festivities at the close of 1837 comes the destruction by fire of the Royal Exchange on the night of the 10th of January following.

It was first noticed a little after 10 p.m., when flames were observed in Lloyd's Coffee Room in the north-east corner of the building, opposite the Bank, the firemen of which establishment were soon on the spot, as well as many other of the metropolitan engines. But, before any water could be thrown upon the building, it was necessary to thaw the hose and works of the engines by pouring hot water upon them, as the frost was so very severe; so that, by 11 p.m., all Lloyd's was a mass of flame. Nothing could be done to stop the conflagration, it having got too great a hold, and great fears were entertained that it would spread to the Bank and surrounding buildings, the which, however, was fortunately prevented. The Lord Mayor was present, and a large body of soldiers from the Tower assisted the Police in keeping the crowd away from the immediate scene.

It must have been a magnificent sight, and somewhat curious, for amidst the roar of the flames, and until the chiming apparatus was destroyed, and the bells dropped one by one, the chimes went on pealing " There's nae luck about the house,"* " Life let us cherish," and " God save the Queen." The fire was not completely got under until noon the next day, but, practically, the building was destroyed by 5 a.m., and,

* It is said that this was the last chime rung.

so bright was the conflagration, that it was visible at Windsor
—twenty-four miles off, and at Theydon, in Essex, a distance
of eighteen miles ; whilst from the heights of Surrey on the
south, and Highgate and Hampstead on the north, the progress of the fire was watched by crowds of people.

The following account of the Exchange after the fire is
taken from the *Times* of 13 Jan. :

" Yesterday afternoon the ruins of the Exchange were
sufficiently cooled to allow the firemen and a party of gentlemen, amongst whom we noticed the Lord Mayor, Mr. Alderman Copeland, several members of the Gresham Committee,
and other persons connected with the mercantile interest, to
inspect them. In consequence of the loose fragments of
stone work belonging to the balustrades and ornamental parts
of the building being covered over with ice, the difficulty of
walking over the ruins was very great, and the chief magistrate fell more than once, receiving sundry bumps. The lofty
chimnies standing appeared to be in such a dangerous condition, that they were hauled down. with ropes, to prevent
their falling on the people below. The iron chests belonging
to the Royal Exchange Assurance Company could be
distinctly seen, from the area, inserted in the walls. Ladders
were raised, and they were opened, when it was discovered
that their contents, consisting of deeds and other papers
connected with the Company and their insurances, were uninjured. This afforded much satisfaction to the directors.
Another iron safe, belonging to Mr. Hathway, whose office,
under the tower, was consumed, which was also in a recess
in the wall, was opened at the same time, and a considerable
sum in francs and bank-notes was taken out.

" The walls of the west wing of the building, which seemed
to bulge outward, were shored up in the afternoon, and they
are not, now, likely to fall. Cornhill presented a most desolate
appearance, the shops, from Finch Lane to the termination of
the street near the Mansion House, were all closed, and the
place presented a deserted and desolated appearance ; which,
contrasted with the bustle hitherto observed during business
hours, and the sight of the ruins, forced very unpleasant

reflections on the mind. Barriers were placed at the Mansion House end of Cornhill, and across that part of the street between Finch and Birchin Lanes, and no person was allowed to pass except the firemen and persons on business. All the avenues leading to Cornhill were also blocked up in like manner; and, at each barrier, police officers and ward constables were placed to prevent people passing. Various schemes were devised, by numerous individuals, to pass these barriers, and sums were, occasionally, offered to the police to be allowed to visit the ruins, but without effect. The City police kept the thieves away by their presence and activity, and the conduct of the people was, yesterday, very quiet, forming a contrast with the disorder got up by the swell mob on Thursday last. Those who viewed the ruins at a distance appeared to wear an air of melancholy, and no fire has occurred, for centuries, which has caused more universal regret.

"On searching the ruins under the Lord Mayor's Court Office, the great City seal was picked up, with two bags, containing £200 in gold, uninjured. On this discovery being communicated to the Lord Mayor and Aldermen, it caused much gratification, it having been rumoured that the Corporation would lose their Charter by the loss of the seal, but we did not hear it explained how this could be.

"Owing to the great body of fire underneath the ruins at the north-east angle of the Exchange, it was impossible for the firemen to ascertain, until a late hour, whether any injury had been done to Lloyd's books, which were deposited in a large iron safe inserted in the wall. Two engines had been playing on it during the latter portion of the day. In the presence of several of the Committee it was opened, when it was discovered that the fire had reached the books, and partially consumed them. In the drawers were cheques on the Bank of England to a large amount, and also Bank of England notes to the amount of, it is said, £2,500. The notes were reduced to a cinder, and, on the drawers being opened, the air rushing in on the tender fragments blew them over the Exchange. They were, however, very care-

fully collected, and the cinders of the notes were, with much
trouble and caution, put into a tin case, which was taken
to the Bank, and the words 'Bank of England,' with the
numbers and dates, were distinctly traced.   The amount will,
in consequence, be paid to the owners.   From what information could be obtained from the gentlemen who took possession of the box, and who were understood to be underwriters,
it was the usual custom of the secretary not to leave any
money or notes in the safe, but to deposit the money in the
Bank, which was done on the evening the fire took place.
The money and notes above mentioned, and which were found
in the safe, belonged to a subscriber who, on the afternoon
of Wednesday, asked permission to deposit his money in the
safe until the next day, which was acceded to by the secretary.
Some idea may be formed of his state of mind on arriving
at the Exchange on the following morning, to see it on fire,
and he was in a state of distraction until the finding of the
cinders of the notes yesterday, which has, in some measure,
calmed his feelings.   The underwriters are severe sufferers,
having left sums of money, to a large amount, in their desks,
which, no doubt, will never be recovered.

"During the confusion on the discovery of the fire, in removing some books from a room in the north-east corner,
in addition to £500 in Bank of England notes, which were
taken to St. Michael's Church, twenty sovereigns, in a bag,
were thrown out of the windows.   The bag broke, and the
sovereigns rolled about the pavement; they were all picked
up by the mob, who appropriated them to their own use.

"It is firmly believed that the overheating of the stoves
caused the disaster which the nation has now to deplore.
Wednesday was an exceedingly cold day, and large fires had
been kept up from morning till night in the building.   There
is no doubt the fire had been spreading, to some extent, in
Lloyd's rooms, long before it was seen in the street.   Some
few months back, two watchmen were on the premises all
night, but, on the miserable plea of economy, they were discharged, and the sacrifice of one of the finest buildings in
the Kingdom has been the consequence.   We believe that

most of our cathedrals and large public buildings are left without watchmen during the night, and we hope that the fate of the Royal Exchange will bring about a change in this respect."

The merchants, who used to congregate " on 'Change," were accommodated in the Guildhall, and the members of Lloyd's met at the Jerusalem Coffee House—but these arrangements were, afterwards, modified. The Royal Exchange Insurance Coy. took Sir James Esdaile's house, in Lombard Street.

Times, 4 Ap., 1838 :—" THE ROYAL EXCHANGE.—Yesterday, the first day's sale of the materials of the Royal Exchange took place. It produced nearly £2,000. The porter's large hand-bell (rung every day at half-past four p.m. to warn the merchants and others that 'Change ought to be closed), with the handle consumed, and valued at 10/-, was sold for £3 3/-; the two carved griffins, holding shields of the City arms, facing the quadrangle, £35 ; the two busts of Queen Elizabeth, on the east and west sides, £10 15/-; the copper grasshopper vane,* with the iron upright, was reserved by the Committee ; the alto relievo, in artificial stone, representing Queen Elizabeth proclaiming the Royal Exchange, £21 ; the corresponding alto relievo, representing Britannia seated amidst the emblems of Commerce, accompanied by Science, Agriculture, Manufactures, etc., £30 ; the carved emblematical figures of Europe, Asia, Africa and America, £110. The sale of the remainder of the materials, etc., it is understood, will take place in about a month."

In the Mansion House Police Court, on 10 Jan., the Lord Mayor announced that he had received five letters relative to an individual who was going about the metropolitan suburbs frightening females to such an extent that they were afraid to go out at night, as they were met by a man, who, under different disguises, would suddenly appear before them, and as suddenly disappear with terrible bounds, which earned him the name of " Spring-heeled Jack," and he inspired such

---

* Still in use on the Royal Exchange.

terror, that the recital of the victim had to be taken with caution. Whoever he was, or why he so acted, was never known, as he was never taken; but, certainly, robbery had no part in his escapades, for he was quite content with paralysing the poor women with fright.

The first facts I can gather about Jack are at the latter end of 1837, at Barnes, where he appeared as a large white bull; at East Sheen he was a white bear; he then visited Richmond, and after having terrorised that town, he went to Ham, Kingston and Hampton, where he was clad in brass armour, with large claw-like gloves. Teddington, Twickenham and Hounslow were all visited by him, and at Isleworth we hear of him wearing steel armour, in which he seems to have been attired when seen at Uxbridge, Hanwell, Brentford and Ealing. At Hammersmith he took the form of a huge baboon, and as such was seen in the moonlight, dancing at Kensington Palace, ever and anon climbing over the forcing houses. He varied his localities frequently, one day being at Peckham, another at St. John's Wood, and anon at Forest Hill.

This about brings up to the time of its being mentioned by the Lord Mayor, the consequence of which was that a Committee was formed at the Mansion House for the purpose of receiving subscriptions and deciding upon the best means of capturing this erratic genius. Probably feeling that he had sufficiently terrorised the districts before mentioned, he turned his attention to the East end of London, and particularly favoured Bow. A case is given in the *Times* of 23 Feb. A gentleman named Alsop, living between Bow and Old Ford, appeared before the police magistrate at Lambeth Street (then the Thames Police Office) accompanied by his three daughters, one of whom stated that at about a quarter to nine o'clock on the evening of the 21st February, 1838, she heard a violent ringing at the front gate of the house, and, on going to the door to see what was the cause, she saw a man standing outside, of whom she enquired what was the matter. The person instantly replied that he was a policeman, and said, " For God's sake bring me a light, for we have caught Spring-heeled Jack here in the lane." She returned to the house, and brought a candle, and handed it to the man, who was enveloped in a large cloak. The instant she had done so, he threw off his outer garments, and, applying the lighted candle to his breast, presented a most hideous and frightful appearance, vomiting forth a quantity of blue and white flame from his mouth, his eyes resembling red balls of fire. From the hasty glance which her fright enabled her to get at his person, she observed that he wore a large helmet, and his dress, which appeared to fit him very tightly, seemed to her to resemble white oilskin. Without uttering a sentence, he darted at her, and catching her partly by her dress and the back part of her neck, placed her head under one of his arms, and commenced tearing her clothes with his claws, which she was certain were made of some metallic substance. She screamed out as loud as she could for assistance, and, by considerable exertion, got away from him, and ran towards the house to get in. Her assailant followed, and caught her on the doorstep, when he again used considerable violence, tore her neck and arms with his claws, as well as a quantity of hair from her head; her story was fully corroborated by her parents and sisters, and her injuries, which were very considerable, bore unmistakable testimony to the truth of the assault.

At the same police court, on 8 Mar., 1838, a Miss Scales deposed that as she and her sister were walking in Lime-house, about half-past eight in the evening, on coming to Green Dragon Alley, they observed some person standing in an angle in the passage. She was in advance of her sister at the time, and just as she came up to the person, who was enveloped in a large cloak, he spirted a quantity of blue flame right in her face, which deprived her of sight, and so alarmed her, that she instantly dropped to the ground, and was seized with violent fits, which continued for several hours. In this case no violence to the person was done.

He had a literature of his own. I know of three pamphlets on the subject; one, from which is taken the accompanying illustration, is entitled "Authentic particulars of the awful appearance of the London Monster, alias Spring-heeled Jack, together with his extraordinary life, wonderful adventures and secret amours. Also an account of his horrible appearance to Miss N—— and his singular letter to the Lord Mayor of London."

Spring-heeled Jack.   Awful representation of the London monster.

There is much more to be related of Jack, but space will not permit; but, whether too much attention was beginning to be paid to him with a view to his capture, or whether his love of mischief had died out, cannot be told; but certain it was that nothing was known publicly of this singular being after April, 1838, having kept London in a ferment of excitement and terror for about six months.

There is an amusing police case anent Lord John Russell's hat.—*Times*, 8 Feb. :

THAMES POLICE COURT.—Yesterday, a poor woman, named Mary Ann Blay, who stated that she resided at Limehouse, applied to Mr. Ballantyne and Mr. Broderip, the magistrates, to request their interference under very odd circumstances. The applicant stated that, about three or four months ago, she was on her way home from Poplar, where she had been purchasing some vegetables, when she saw something black lying on the ground. She first supposed it was a piece of coal, but, on stooping to pick it up, discovered it was a hat. She walked onward, with the hat in her right hand, until she reached the Commercial Road, when she was met by a policeman, who asked her where she had got the hat. She informed him that she had picked it up at the corner of the New Road, and the policeman looked at it, and saw the name of Lord John Russell in the inside. He demanded the hat of her, and, on her refusing to give it up to him, he seized the hat, and took her into custody. She was locked up in the station house, and, on the following morning, was brought before the sitting magistrate at that office. The justice, after hearing the policeman's statement, directed her to be discharged, and gave orders that the hat should be detained for a certain time, in the station house ; and, if no owner was discovered, that it should be given up to her. She had, since, made repeated inquiries of the police, but could obtain no information from them, nor any redress for the false imprisonment she had suffered.

Mr. Ballantyne asked the applicant if she was sure the hat belonged to Lord J. Russell.

The woman said there had been a whitebait Cabinet dinner at Mr. Lovegrove's, West India Dock Tavern, Blackwall, on the night she found the hat, and Lord John Russell was one of the party.

Mr. Ballantyne : Well, I don't understand how his Lordship could lose his hat at the corner of the New Road.

The woman said it was supposed that Lord J. Russell had put his head out of the carriage window, and looked back to see if his friends were following him, when his hat fell off his head, and, as he was a Lord, he would not stop until it was picked up again (laughter).

Mr. Ballantyne : What do you want me to do in the matter?

The applicant said she wanted to know to whom the hat belonged.

Mr. Ballantyne : Why, I should say it belonged to Lord John Russell.

The woman said the hat was worth a guinea, and that if she had accepted 5/- from the policeman, and given it up to him, he would not have taken her into custody.   She thought it was very hard to be subject to such tyranny because she had picked up Lord John Russell's hat, for she had done no harm to the crown of it.   She supposed Lord John Russell was in liquor, or he would have ordered his carriage to stop, and picked up his hat. (Roars of laughter, in which the magistrates could not help joining.)   " You may laugh," said the woman ; " but it's all true what I say ; you may depend upon it, the Ministers don't eat whitebait without drinking plenty of wine after it, you may be sure. (Increased laughter.) I don't know why the gentlemen laugh, I am sure.   I was locked up all night away from my husband and children."

Mr. Ballantyne said it was very singular the woman could not recollect what night it was she picked up the hat, and the number and letter of the policeman who took her into custody.

The applicant said she was too much alarmed at being locked up in the station house, and brought before the magistrate, to recollect what night it was, or the policeman's identity.

Mr. Ballantyne said it was a very odd affair, and he would direct the books to be searched to ascertain when the woman was brought before the magistrate.

Soon afterwards, the woman was again brought up.

Mr. Ballantyne said, it appeared from the minutes that she was brought before him on Tuesday, the 3rd of October last, on suspicion of stealing a hat, and that the policeman said that he had stopped her at two o'clock in the morning with the hat in her possession.   It appeared that he had discharged her, but no mention was made of the hat belonging to Lord John Russell.   If that fact had been mentioned to him, he would have ordered the hat to be restored to his Lordship immediately.

The Applicant : I am sure it is his Lordship's hat.   There is Lord John Russell inside of it, quite plain ; it's a new one.

Mr. Ballantyne : Very well ; an inquiry shall be made about the hat, and you can attend here to-morrow, and we will let you know what has become of it. I think Lord John Russell has the best claim to the hat, if he has not already got it.

The sequel :

Times, 10 Feb. :—On Thursday, Mary Ann Blay again appeared before Mr. Ballantyne upon the subject of Lord John's hat. She adhered to her old story, that the hat had the noble Home Secretary's name in it when she picked it up, but it had, subsequently, been torn out, after it was taken out of her possession. Mr. Ballantyne examined the hat, and said it was a dirty, greasy hat—a boy's hat, and that he would not give 6d. for it. The policeman who took the woman in custody declared that the woman's statement was, altogether, a fabrication, and that the hat never had the name of Lord John Russell in it. Mr. Ballantyne said he would make no order about the hat ; and, if the woman thought she had been wrongly imprisoned, she might seek her remedy elsewhere.

CHAPTER IV.

I MUST give another police case, as showing the manners and customs of the *jeunesse dorée* of this period.

Times, 19 Feb. :

MARLBOROUGH STREET.—On Saturday, Samuel Evans, better known as " Young Dutch Sam," a pugilist, was brought before Mr. Conant, charged with having committed an unprovoked and violent assault on policeman Mackenzie, C 182, and Lord Waldegrave was also charged with attempting to rescue Evans from the police.

The defendant Evans, when sober, is civil and well-conducted, but, when drunk, is one of the most dangerous ruffians connected with the prize-fighting gang. Lord Waldegrave is a very young nobleman, with a fund of native simplicity in his countenance, rendered the more conspicuous by the style of dress he had adopted, namely, a large coloured shawl round his neck, and a rough pilot coat. Both parties exhibited unquestionable proofs of the effect of their previous night's potations.

Policeman Mackenzie, who had his arm in a sling, made the following statement: About a quarter-past six that morning, after he had come off duty, he went to the Standard public house, in Piccadilly, for the purpose of getting some refreshment, but, on perceiving some of the saloon frequenters there, to whom he was personally obnoxious, in consequence of having taken disorderly persons of their acquaintance into custody, he was about to go back, when he found himself suddenly pushed into the house, with sufficient violence to cause his cape to fall off. While engaged in folding up his cape, the defendant Evans said, "Will any gentleman like to see a policeman put on his back?" Complainant had not exchanged a single word with anybody; he, however, found himself suddenly and quite unexpectedly seized by the defendant, who had come behind him, and then thrown with violence upon the floor; the defendant Evans fell upon him at the same time; and, as complainant lay almost stunned and unable to rise, some persons called out "Shame!" Complainant was then helped up and assisted out of the house. He went immediately to the station house, and mentioned what had occurred to Inspector Beresford, who instantly sent a sufficient force to take the offenders into custody. Complainant went and pointed out Dutch Sam to his comrades, and the defendant was taken into custody. Lord Waldegrave, who was in the pugilist's company, declared the police should not take his friend, and he attempted to prevent the police from doing their duty. Complainant, feeling his shoulder pain him very much, went to the surgeon, and, by that gentleman's advice, proceeded to the Charing Cross Hospital. When he was examined, it was ascertained that one of the bones of his shoulder was broken.

Another policeman stated that Lord Waldegrave was very drunk, and, when his Lordship attempted to resist the police, he was, accidentally, thrown down on the pavement, and witness picked him up.

Lord Waldegrave: He! he! he! Picked me up, did you? Oh! He! he! he!

Mr. Conant: This is no laughing matter, I can tell you; and it is quite improper of you to make it a subject of merriment.

Lord Waldegrave: He! he! he! I beg pardon, but I can't help laughing.

Mr. Conant asked Evans what he had to say in his defence?

Evans: Why, you see, Lord Waldegrave and me had been supping together—hadn't we, my Lord?

3*

Lord Waldegrave: Yes, we had.

Evans: And when we went into the public house there, we saw the policeman, who was drunk, and who had been drinking purl in the house. The policeman asked me to wrestle with him, and, as I thought I could throw him, I accepted the challenge.

The Inspector proved that there was not one word of truth in Evans's defence as far as regarded the sobriety of Mackenzie. The assault took place within a few minutes after Mackenzie had come off duty, and, certainly, before he could have time to get refreshment.

The policeman declared what the defendant asserted was entirely false. He had taken nothing to drink; and, as to challenging a man like the defendant to wrestle, the assertion was improbable.

Inspector Beresford, on being asked if he was certain Evans was drunk, answered that he was decidedly drunk.

Evans: Silence, sweep, let a gentleman speak. I can get a dozen oaths for half-a-crown.

Mr. Conant said the assault on the policeman was wanton and unprovoked, and the matter was further aggravated by the fact that a person of the defendant's well-known pugilistic powers had chosen to attack an unoffending party. He should, therefore, call on the defendant Evans to put in good bail.

Evans: Serve his Lordship the same; for I like to have such a pal.

Mr. Conant directed that Lord Waldegrave should be put back until a second magistrate arrived.

Mr. Dyer having, soon afterwards, taken his seat on the bench, Lord Waldegrave was placed at the bar.

Policeman Filmer, C 130, stated that he went with others to the Standard public house, and took Evans into custody. Lord Waldegrave threw his arms round his friend, and swore he should not be taken. Witness swung his Lordship away, and, in doing so, his Lordship fell down. Witness picked him up, and would have let him go had his Lordship abstained

from repeating his conduct.   As he would not allow the
police to do their duty, he took him into custody.

Mr. Conant asked his Lordship what he had to say?

Lord Waldegrave : I have nothing to say.   Perhaps I had
taken too much that night.

Policeman : His Lordship was very drunk.

Lord Waldegrave : Not very.

Mr. Conant : There has been no complaint of your conduct
at the station house, and I daresay your Lordship feels hurt
at being in the company of a person of the other defendant's
description.   Taking into consideration the violence of the
outrage committed by Evans, as a warning, we must inflict
a heavy fine.   You must, therefore, pay £5 to the Queen.

Mr. Dyer : And because—in our summary jurisdiction—
we cannot go beyond that sum, we inflict it as being the
highest penalty in our power.

The sum was paid, and the noble defendant discharged.

The whole social tone was low, from the highest to the
lowest, and if the police court gives us occasional glimpses
of aristocratic amusement, so it affords us a view of the enter-
tainments provided for the lower classes.   Let us take one.

Times, 10 March :

HATTON GARDEN.—For some time past, numerous complaints have been made to the magistrates of this office of two
penny theatres, one in Mortimer Market, Tottenham Court
Road, and the other in a field adjacent to Bagnigge Wells
Road, where gangs of young thieves nightly assembled.   On
Wednesday last, several inhabitants of Mortimer Market attended at the Office to complain of the former establishment,
when Mr. Rogers granted a warrant to apprehend the whole
of the parties concerned, and on Thursday night, Duke, Baylis
and Halls, of this Office, in company with Inspector Jenkins
and a body of constables, proceeded to the theatre, and
captured the manager, performers, and musicians, and the
whole of them were, yesterday, brought to the office, and
placed at the bar, when the office was excessively crowded.

There were twelve prisoners, some of whom were attired in their theatrical habiliments, with their countenances painted, which made a very grotesque appearance.

Duke being sworn, stated that, in consequence of a warrant, on Thursday night last, about 9 o'clock, he proceeded, with other officers, to a penny theatre in Mortimer Market, St. Pancras, where he found the whole of the prisoners, some of whom were engaged in performing their parts, whilst Ewyn, the manager, was employed in taking money at the doors, and the woman, Green, was acting as check taker. Campbell and Lewis were enacting their parts upon the stage, and Joseph Burrows was in his theatrical dress between them, with his face painted and wearing a huge pair of moustaches. John Pillar was in a temporary orchestra with a large violoncello, scraping away most melodramatically, whilst the players were endeavouring to humour the sounds, and to suit their action to the word, and the word to the action; and just at that part of the performance when Burrows had to exclaim, "The officers of justice are coming," witness and his brother officers rushed upon the stage, and apprehended the whole of them.

Mr. Rogers: What description of audience was there?

Duke: A dirty, ragged set, principally consisting of boys and girls; two of them were barefooted, and had scarce a rag to cover them, and did not seem to have been washed for a month. The theatre was of the most wretched description; there was a temporary stage, and bits of scenery. The boys said they were errand boys and servants. Brierly and Smith said they were country actors out of an engagement, and had visited the place out of curiosity.

Mr. Mallett: Had they an inscription that they were "Licensed pursuant to Act of Parliament"?

Duke: They had not. On the gates was written up, "For this evening's performance The Spectre of the Grave; after which, a comic song by Mr. Ewyn; to conclude with The Key of the Little Door." They found various theatrical dresses and other properties, with stars, swords, etc., now produced.

Baylis proved having paid 1d. for admission. He paid the money to the woman Green. Ewyn was at the door, and he confessed that he was the manager. He took him into custody, and, subsequently, he apprehended Lewis and Campbell, at the back of the stage, in their theatrical dresses.

Mr. Rogers: Have you got "The Spectre of the Grave" here?

Inspector Jenkins: No, your Worship, he vanished. The other male performers were dressed in sandals and armour, with their helmets up.

Hall and the other officers corroborated the above evidence. Several inhabitants of Mortimer Market proved that they were, every night, alarmed by firing off guns, cries of "Fire," clashing of swords, the most boisterous ranting and shrieks from the voices of the ladies of the *corps dramatique*, and the place was a perfect nuisance to the neighbourhood.

The owner of the place stated that, on the 24th of January, he let the place to a person named Summers, for chair making, when it was turned into a theatre.

Ewyn said he had engaged with Summers to divide the profits of the theatrical speculation. Summers agreed to take the place, and he (Ewyn) to provide the scenery and wardrobe; "and proud I am to say, that I have conducted the consarn respectably, which some of the neighbours can testify. This is the head and front of my offending—no more."

Inspector Jenkins said that, about a month ago, he called on Ewyn and cautioned him, but he said that the magistrates had nothing to do with the matter.

Mr. Rogers, addressing the prisoners, said they had received a warning which they did not heed. He should not order them to find bail, but would discharge them; and, if they dared to repeat their performances after this admonition, he would grant a warrant for their apprehension, and every one of them should find bail, or be committed. They held out temptation to the children of poor persons, some of whom, it appears, were without shoes and nearly naked, who robbed their parents, or others, for the purpose of procuring the penny for admission. He would order their paraphernalia to be restored to them, but, on condition that they would remove their fittings, and desist from any future performances.

Ewyn: You must give me time to take down the seats and decorations.

Mr. Rogers: You must take them down this day.

Ewyn (with a start): What! this day? Impossible.

Mr. Rogers directed Inspector Jones to see the mandate obeyed.

The month of April is famous for the inauguration of steam traffic between England and America. A vessel named the *Savannah* had in 1819 crossed from America to England, but her steam was only intended to be auxiliary to her sailing power, for her boilers had only a pressure of 20 lbs. to the square inch. She sailed from New York on 28 Mar., 1819, reached Savannah on 7 Ap., and anchored at Liverpool on 19 June; on her return home her engines were taken out, and she was finally lost off Long Island. In 1836 the Great Western Railway founded the Great Western Steam Co., whose vessels were intended to run from Bristol in co-opera-tion with the railway, and the first ship built was the Great Western, the largest steamer then afloat. She was 236 feet long and her engines showed 750 indicated horse power, her registered tonnage being 1,300. She was intended to be the pioneer ship, and was ready for sea in April, 1838; but competition was as keen then as now, and the St. George's Steam Packet Coy. started their s.s. Sirius, for the voyage to New York, from London, on the 29th March. She had a tonnage of 700 tons, and her engines were of 320 horse-power. She was elegantly fitted-up, and started with 22 passengers, whose number was increased at Cork, and, being intended solely for a passenger boat, carried no cargo. On going down the Thames, she encountered her rival, the Great Western, which had a pleasure party on board, and a trial of speed took place between the two, resulting in favour of the Sirius. She sailed from Cork on 9th April. The Great

Western sailed from Bristol on the 12th April, and both reached New York on the same day, the Sirius being first. The Great Western made, in all, 64 passages between the two countries, her fastest passage occupying 12 days, 7 ½ hours. At the present writing, the record voyage for an English steamer (the *Lucania*) is 5 days, 7 hours, 23 minutes.

The *Manchester Guardian* of 14th April gives an account of a woman living in that city, who for many years passed as a man, which has occurred before, but the extraordinary part of this story is that she *married another woman.*— "Subsequent inquiries confirm the truth of the statements made in the *Guardian* of Wednesday last, as to this singular case. This woman man, who, for probably more than 25 years, has succeeded in concealing her sex, and in pursuing a trade of more than ordinarily masculine and hazardous description, with a degree of skill and ability which has led to her establishment in a good business in this town, bound herself apprentice, at the age of 16 or 17 years, to a Mr. Peacock, a bricklayer and builder, at Bawtry, a small market town in the West Riding of Yorkshire. She did not remain with Mr. Peacock during the whole period of her apprenticeship, but was 'turned over,' as it is called, to another person in the same business. It was during her apprenticeship that she met with her present wife; and they were married at the old parish church of Sheffield, in the year 1816, when the wife was only 17 years old. Since the investigation and disclosure of the circumstances, on Thursday week, the wife and husband have separated. She was, for many years, a special constable in the 13th division of that body, acting for this town; and we are assured that, on all occasions when the services of the division were required, as at elections, Orange processions, and meetings of trades' unions, turn-outs, etc., so far from absenting herself from what, as in the case of well founded apprehension of a riot, must have been, to a woman, a post of some unpleasantness, she is remembered to have been one of the most punctual in attendance, and the most forward volunteer in actual duty, in that division. We understand that she is no longer a special constable, because she did not, on the last annual special session, held for that purpose at the New Bailey, present herself to be resworn. She was not discarded or discharged; there was no complaint against her; and, probably, the extension of her own business was her only motive for not resuming the duties of this office. Altogether, this is the most singular case of the kind which has ever reached our knowledge."

The following is an advertisement which appeared in the *Times* of 27th April:—"NELSON MONUMENT.—The Committee for erecting a Monument to the Memory of Lord Nelson hereby give notice that they are desirous of receiving from architects, artists, or other persons, DESIGNS for such a MONUMENT, to be erected in Trafalgar Square.

"The Committee cannot, in the present state of the subscriptions, fix definitely the sum to be expended, but they recommend that the estimated cost of the several designs should be confined within the sums of £20,000 and £30,000. This condition, and that of the intended site, are the only restrictions to which the artists are limited."

In the same newspaper of 16 May, we read of a punishment which might, occasionally, be revived with advantage, as being less dangerous than the ducking stool, and, probably, quite as efficacious, although we have the authority of St. James, "For every kind of beasts, and of birds, and of serpents, and of things of the sea, is tamed, and hath been tamed of mankind, but the tongue can no man tame." It relates how, "at the Mayor's Court, Stafford, last week, Mary, wife of Thomas Careless, of the Broad Eye, a perfect termagant, was ordered to pay 1/- penalty, and 7/6 costs, for an unprovoked assault on Mary, the wife of Lewis Bromley. During the investigation, her garrulity was so incessant that the mayor was under the necessity of sending for the 'scold's bridle,' an iron instrument of very antique construction, which, in olden times, was occasionally called into use. It is formed of an elliptical bow of iron, enclosing the head from the lower extremity of one ear to the other, with a transverse piece of iron from the nape of the neck to the mouth, and completely covers the tongue, preventing its movement, and the whole machinery, when adjusted, is locked at the back of the head. The bridle is to be put in thorough repair, and hung *in terrorem* in the Mayor's office, to be used as occasion may call it forth."

These "scold's bridles," or "branks," as they are sometimes called, are not uncommon. The earliest dated one is preserved at Walton-on-Thames, and bears the date 1633, with the inscription:

> "Chester presents Walton with a bridle,
> To curb women's tongues that talk to idle."

Brayley, in his "History of Surrey," says that it was given by a gentleman named Chester, who lost a valuable estate through a gossiping, lying woman; but, as there are several examples of branks in the Palatinate, one being kept in the gaol at Chester, some people think it was a present from that city. There is one at Leicester, and another at Newcastle-on-Tyne, which used to hang in the mayor's parlour, and tradition has it that many cases of disputes between women have been speedily and satisfactorily settled on his worship's pointing to these branks.

There is one in the Ashmolean Museum at Oxford, which is very tender as far as the gag is concerned, but which has a leading chain fastened between the eyes. Hainstall, Ridware, Lichfield, Morpeth, Shrewsbury, Holme, Kendal, Altrincham, Macclesfield, Congleton (where it was last used in 1824), all have examples, whilst Chester has four! There are several in Scotland, and there are some in private hands, notably one which used to be in the Mayer Museum, Liverpool, which came from Warrington, where, however, the brank formerly used at Carrington is preserved, and there are several places—Newcastle-under-Lyne (now in the Mayer Collection), Manchester, and others—where they have existed. There is a very grotesque one in Doddington Park, which is a mask, having eyeholes, and a long funnel-shaped peak projecting from the mouth; and there are some very terribly cruel ones,

with fearful gags ; but these can scarcely come under scold's
or gossip's bridles.   There was one at Forfar, with a spiked
gag, which pierced the tongue, and an even more severe one
is at Stockport ; whilst those at Ludlow and Worcester are,
also, instruments of torture.

CHAPTER V.

Thom, the religious fanatic—His riots and death—Delusions of his followers.

FROM the earliest ages of Christianity *pseudo-Christoi*, or false Christs, existed. Simon Magus, Dositheus, and the famous Barcochab were among the first of them, and they were followed by Moses, in Crete, in the fifth century; Julian, in Palestine, *circa* A.D. 530; and Screnus, in Spain, *circa* A.D. 714. There were, in the 12th century, some seven or eight in France, Spain and Persia; and, coming to more modern times, there was Sabbatai Zewi, a native of Aleppo, or Smyrna, who proclaimed himself to be the Messiah, in Jerusalem, *circa* 1666. A list of religious fanatics would be a long one, but the *pseudo-Christos* of modern times was, certainly, John Nicholl Thom, of St. Columb, Cornwall, *alias* Sir William Percy Honeywood Courtenay, Knight of Malta, and King of Jerusalem; who also claimed to be Jesus Christ, in proof of which he shewed punctures in his hands, and a cicatrice on his side.

He was first introduced to public notice in Michaelmas, 1832, when he paid a visit to Canterbury, and took up his abode, for some time, at the "Rose Inn," where he was remarkable for his eccentric behaviour, passing under the name of Rothschild. His countenance and costume denoted foreign extraction, while his language and conversation showed that he was well acquainted with almost every part of the kingdom. He often dressed in a fine suit of Italian clothing, and, sometimes, in the gayer and more imposing costume of the east. In December of the same year, he surprised the inhabitants of Canterbury by proposing himself as a candidate for the representation of that city in Parliament, under the name of Sir W. P. H. Courtenay. His canvass proceeded with extraordinary success; and, such were his persuasive powers, that people of all ranks felt an interest in his society; some, however, considered him insane, while others were of a contrary opinion, and he did not succeed in his ambition.

He next got mixed up in a smuggling affair, H.M. sloop *Lively* having captured a smuggling craft (the *Admiral Hood*) off the Goodwin Sands. He attended the examination of the smugglers before the magistrates at Rochester, attired in a fancy costume, and having a small scimitar suspended from his neck, by a massive gold chain. He defended one of the men, who, despite his advocacy, was convicted. He then offered himself as a witness, swore that he had seen the whole transaction, that there was no smuggling, and that the *Lively* was to blame. This the prosecution could not stand; he was indicted for perjury, and was tried at Maidstone on 25 July, 1833. The sentence of the Court was imprisonment and transportation, but, being proved to be insane, this was commuted to confinement in the lunatic asylum, at Barming Heath. After about four years spent in this establishment, he was released, on security being given for his future good behaviour. He then went to live at the residence of Mr. Francis, of Fairbrook, in the neighbourhood of Boughton, near Canterbury. Owing to some misunderstanding with the family, he removed to an adjoining cottage, and, at the time of which I write, he lived at a farm-house, called Bossenden farm, occupied by a person named Culver.

The influence obtained, by this maniac, over the small farmers and peasantry in his neighbourhood, is most astonishing. They believed in all he told them; first that he should be a great chieftain in Kent, and that they should all live rent free on his land, and that if they would follow his advice, they should have good living and large estates, as he had great influence at Court, and was to sit at the Queen's right hand, on the day of her Coronation. It would seem as if his madness, then, was personal and political, but the religious mania speedily developed itself. He told his deluded

Death of Sir Wm. Courtenay. (Thom). 1838.

followers that they were oppressed by the laws in general, but more particularly by the new poor law; and called upon them to place themselves under his command. Nearly 100 at once joined him, and as they marched through the neighbouring parishes their numbers increased. It was then that he proclaimed his divinity—assuring them that both he and they were not only invincible, but bullet proof, and that they could never die.

The following account, which appears to me to be the most succinct of those I have seen, is from the *Times* of 1 June:

" On Monday (28 May) they sallied forth from the village of Boughton, where they bought bread, and proceeded to Wills's house, near Fairbrook. A loaf was broken asunder, and placed on a pole, with a flag of white and blue, on which was a rampant lion. Thence they proceeded to Goodnestone, near Faversham, producing throughout the whole neighbourhood the greatest excitement, and adding to their numbers by the harangues occasionally delivered by this ill-fated madman. At this farm Courtenay stated that ' he would strike the bloody blow.' A match was then taken from a bean stack, which had been introduced by one of the party. They next proceeded to a farm at Herne Hill, where Courtenay requested the inmates to feed his friends, which request was immediately complied with. Their next visit was at Dargate Common, where Sir William, taking off his shoes, said, ' I now stand on my own bottom.' By Sir William's request, his party went to prayers, and then proceeded to Bossenden farm, where they supped, and slept in the barn that night. At 3 o'clock, on Tuesday morning they left, and proceeded to Sittingbourne to breakfast, where Sir William paid 25s.; they then visited Newnham, where a similar treat was given at the ' George.' After visiting Eastling, Throwley, Selwich Lees and Selling, and occasionally addressing the populace, holding out to them such inducements as are usually made by persons desirous of creating a disturbance, they halted, in a chalk pit, to rest, and, on Wednesday evening, arrived at Culver's farm, called Bossen-

den, close to the scene of action. Mr. Curling, having had
some of his men enticed from their work, applied for a warrant
for their apprehension.   Mears, a constable, in company with
his brother, proceeded to Culver's house, when, on application
being made for the men alluded to, Sir William immediately
shot the young man who accompanied his brother in the
execution of his duty. Such was the excitement, and the
desperate menaces of Sir William and his party, that it
became necessary for the magistrates to interfere to put a
stop to the proceedings, by the capture of the ringleader of
the party, from whose advice to his followers the most serious
consequences were likely to ensue.   At 12 o'clock, they
assembled at a place called the Osier Bed, where every means
were resorted to, to quell the disturbance, but without success.   Sir William defied interruption to his men, and fired
on the Rev. William Handley, of Herne Hill, who, with his
brother, was assisting to take him into custody.   They then
made their way to Bossenden Wood, where they lay in
ambush ; but, as no means appeared to present themselves,
by which the ringleader could safely be secured, he being
evidently mad, and in possession of loaded firearms, threatening to shoot the first man who interfered with him, it became necessary to apply for the assistance of the 45th regiment, stationed in Canterbury barracks.   On the arrival of
a detachment of this regiment, they proceeded to the wood,
where the party was awaiting their arrival.

" A few minutes previous to the attack, Sir William loudly
halloed to his companions, supposed for the purpose of
getting them prepared for the fight.

" Sir William, on perceiving his opponents, advanced with
the greatest *sang froid*, and deliberately shot Lieutenant
Bennett of the regiment, before his own men. This occasioned a return from the man covering his officer, who
advanced, and shot Sir William, who fell, and died instantly.
The excitement, at that period, occasioned by each party
losing its commander, caused a desperate attack, which terminated in the death of ten persons, besides the brother of
the constable shot in the morning, and several others seri-

4

ously wounded, of some of whom little hopes are entertained of their recovery. The weapons in the hands of the followers of Sir William, were chiefly, if not altogether, heavy bludgeons."

The following, from a correspondent, goes far to show the delusions shared by this maniac and his followers :

" The mention of this lad's name, reminds me that his mother is said to have done more than any other person in the parish to foster and encourage the belief which she herself entertained, that Thom was our blessed Redeemer and Saviour. So steadfast was she in her belief, that when, after the battle in the wood, a neighbour went to tell her ' the awful news,' that Thom was killed, and her own son wounded, she would not credit the information. ' Sir William killed ! ' said she, ' no, no, you can't kill him ; it is not the truth, it is not possible.' The reply to her was : ' It is the truth, and it is possible.' She again asserted that it was not possible. Again the reply was : ' It is possible, and it is as true as that your poor boy has got a shot in his thigh.' Then, and not till then, would she credit that her son was hurt. But as to Sir William, she still remained incredulous, saying : ' Mind, three days will show you and all the world what Sir William is. When that time is elapsed, you will see whether he is not that which he professes to be.'

" Of the general belief in the neighbourhood that he was the Saviour, I saw a strong proof in some writing which I found on the parsonage barn at Herne Hill. It has been there for the last ten days, and is said to be in the handwriting of Wills. On the left side of the door is written, in one long line, these words, with spelling and capitals just as I have copied them :—' If you newho was on earth your harts Wod turn ' ; then in another : ' But dont Wate to late ' ; and then, in a third, ' They how R.' On the right side of the door is the following : ' O that great day of gudgment, is close at hand ' ; in another : ' it now peps in the dor every man according to his woks ' ; and in a third : ' Our rites and liberties We Will have.' I mentioned some of them in a former communication. At one of the places where he

ordered provisions for his followers, it was in these words:
'Feed my sheep.' To convince his disciples of his divine
commission, he is said to have pointed his pistol at the
stars, and told him that he would make them fall from their
spheres. He then fired at some particularly bright star; and,
his pistol having been rammed down with tow steeped in oil,
and sprinkled over with steel filings, produced, on being fired,
certain bright sparkles of light, which he immediately said
were falling stars. Again, in the early part of his progress
on Monday, he went away from his followers with a man
named Wills, and two of the other rioters, saying to them,
'Do you stay here, whilst I go yonder,' pointing to a bean
stack, 'and strike the bloody blow.' When they arrived
at the stack, to which they marched with a flag, the flag bearer
laid his flag on the ground, and knelt down to pray. The
others then put in, it is said, a lighted match; but Thom
seized it and forbade it to burn, and the fire was not kindled.
This, on their return to the company, was announced as a
miracle worked by the Saviour. There is another of his acts,
which he mentioned as one of the proofs of his Divinity,
that I confess myself at a loss to understand. After he had
fired one shot at the constable, Mears, and subsequently
chopped at him with his dirk, he went into the house, seized
a loaded pistol, and on coming out, said: 'Now, am I not
your Saviour?' The words were scarcely out of his mouth,
when he pulled the trigger of his pistol, and shot Mears a
second time."

He administered a parody on the blessed Sacrament, in
bread and water to his followers, before the encounter and
harangued them. He told them on this occasion, as he did
on many others, that there was great opposition in the land,
and, indeed, throughout the world, but, that if they would
follow him, he would lead them on to glory. He told them
he had come to earth on a cloud, and that, on a cloud, he
should some day be removed from them; that neither bullets
nor weapons could injure him, or them, if they had but
faith in him as their Saviour: and that if 10,000 soldiers
came against them, they would either turn to their side, or

4*

fall dead at his command.   At the end of his harangue, Alexander Foad, a respectable farmer, and one of his followers, knelt down at his feet and worshipped him; and so did another man named Brankford.   Foad then asked Thom whether he should follow him in the body, or go home and follow him in heart.   To this Thom replied : " Follow me in the body."   Foad then sprang on his feet in an ecstasy of joy, and, with a voice of great animation, exclaimed : " Oh, be joyful!   Oh, be joyful!   The Saviour has accepted me. Go on—go on, till I drop, I'll follow thee! "   Brankford was also accepted as a follower, and exhibited the same enthusiastic fervour, while Thom uttered terrific denunciations of eternal torture in hell fire against all who should refuse to follow him.

With the death of Thom and his deluded followers, the excitement calmed down, and entirely subsided after the trial of nine prisoners, which took place at Maidstone, on the 9th of August, before Lord Denman.   They were charged on two counts : first, with aiding and abetting John Thom, *alias* Courtenay, in the murder of Nicholas Mears, on the 31st of May, and second, with being principals in the murder. Lord Denman charged the jury that, if they were of opinion that Thom was of unsound mind, so that, if he had been put upon his trial, he could not have been convicted of murder, the principal being acquitted, the accessories must also be acquitted, and the prisoners could not be found guilty on the first count.   This, the jury acquiesced in, and brought in a verdict of " guilty" on the second count, with a strong recommendation to mercy on account of the infatuation under which they were led astray by Courtenay.   Lord Denman pronounced sentence of death upon the prisoners, but added, that their lives would be spared.   Two were sentenced to transportation for life ; one to transportation for ten years ; and the remainder to be imprisoned for one year, and kept to hard labour in the House of Correction, one month in solitary confinement.

CHAPTER VI.

THE next event which occupied the public attention was the
Queen's Coronation, which took place on the 28th of June.
It was, like the " Half Crownation " of William IV., a much
plainer affair than that of George the Magnificent, the walking
procession of all the estates of the realm, and the banquet in
Westminster Hall, with all the feudal services thereunto belonging, being wholly dispensed with. The day began badly,
with a cold shower about 8 a.m., but it cleared off, and the
sun shone out fitfully, throughout the time the ceremony
occupied—the head of the procession starting from Buckingham Palace at 10 a.m., and the Queen reaching Westminster
Abbey at half-past eleven. Next to the Queen herself, the
principal attraction in the procession was the equipages and
liveries of the Ambassadors Extraordinary, chief among which
was the carriage of Marshal Soult (who represented France),
which had formerly belonged to the last great prince of the
House of Condé, the father of the Duc de Bourbon, and
which, by its superior magnificence, eclipsed all other vehicles.
Besides which, it held the Duke of Dalmatia, Wellington's
old foe, who had now come to visit, in peace, the country he
had so manfully fought against.

Of the ceremony itself, I say nothing—everything was done
decorously and in order. It took a long time, for it was a
quarter to four when the royal procession reformed and took
its way through the nave of the abbey. The Queen entertained a party of 100 at dinner ; and, in the evening, witnessed,

from the roof of her palace, the fireworks discharged in the Green Park. The Duke of Wellington gave a grand ball at Apsley House, for which cards of invitation were issued for 2,000 persons.

As an indication of the numbers of people set down at the Abbey, I may mention that the carriages which were ordered to proceed (after setting down) to the south side of Westminster Bridge, occupied a line from the bridge to Kennington Cross (more than a mile). The carriages which were to proceed, after setting down their company, to the west side of London, formed a line nearly to Kensington (a mile and a half). Those ordered to wait in the Strand extended, in double lines, to St. Mary le Strand, and those directed to wait in Bird Cage Walk, St. James's Park, occupied (in double rows) the whole line to Buckingham Palace.

There was a balloon ascent from Hyde Park, which was a comparative failure, for it descended in Marylebone Lane, quite done up with its short journey, and another sent up from Vauxhall, which was more successful. There were grand displays of fireworks in the Green and Hyde Parks, and all London was most beautifully and brilliantly illuminated.

But the great thing was the Fair in Hyde Park, which had official leave to exist for two days—but which, in fact, lasted four. The area allotted to it comprised nearly one third of the Park, extending from near the margin of the Serpentine to within a short distance of Grosvenor Gate. The best account I know of this Fair is in *The Morning Chronicle* of 29 June, and I here reproduce it:

" Of all the scenes which we witnessed, connected with the Coronation, probably this was the most lively, and that in which there was the least confusion, considering the mass of persons collected together. Our readers are already aware that the Fair was permitted to take place by the Government, on the petition of the present holders of the show which formerly belonged to the celebrated Richardson ; and it was to their care, together with that of Mr. Mallalieu, the Superintendent of Police, that its general management was entrusted. In justice to those gentlemen, we must say that the arrange-

ments made for the accommodation of the public were
admirable, while they were carried out with the very greatest
success. The booths were arranged in a square form, and
covered a space of ground about 1,400 feet long and about
1,000 feet broad.

"They were arranged in regular rows, ample space being
allowed between them for the free passage of the people;
and they consisted of every variety of shape, while they were
decked with flags of all colours and nations. One portion
of the fair was set apart exclusively for ginger-bread and
fancy booths, while those rows by which these were surrounded
were appropriated to the use of showmen, and of persons
who dealt in the more substantial articles of refreshment.
Of the latter description, however, the readers would recognize
many as regular frequenters of such scenes; but, probably,
the booth which attracted the greatest attention, from its
magnitude, was that erected by Williams, the celebrated boiled
beef monger of the Old Bailey. This was pitched in the
broadest part of the fair, and immediately adjoining Richardson's show; and, at the top of it was erected a gallery for
the use of those who were desirous of witnessing the fireworks
in the evening, and, to which, access was to be procured by
payment of a small sum.

"While this person, and the no less celebrated Alger, the
proprietor of the Crown and Anchor, were astonishing the
visitors with the enormous extent of the accommodation which
they could afford the public, others set up claims of a character
more agreeable to the age in the exceedingly tasty mode in
which they had decorated their temporary houses. Of these,
that which struck us as most to be admired, was a tent erected
by a person named Bull, of Hackney, the interior of which,
decorated with fluted pillars of glazed calico, had a really
beautiful appearance. It would be useless, however, to
attempt to particularize every booth, for each held out its
alluring attractions to the gaping crowd with equal force,
and each appeared to be sufficiently patronized by the friends
of its proprietor.

"Not a few, in addition to the solid attractions of eating

and drinking, held out those of a more ' airy ' description, and,
in many, it was announced that a ' grand ball ' would be
held in the evening, ' to commence at six o'clock ' ; whilst, in
others, bands of music were heard ' in full play,' joining their
sweet sounds to the melodious beatings of gongs and shouting
through trumpets of the adjoining shows.   In attractions of
this kind we need only say that the fair was, in most respects,
fully equal to any other at which we ever had the good fortune
to be present, whether at Greenwich, or Croydon, or in any
other of the suburban or metropolitan districts.   Beef and
ham, beer and wine, chickens and salad, were all equally
plentiful, and the taste of the most fastidious might be pleased
as to the quality, or the quantity, of the provisions provided
for him.   In the pastry cooks' booths, the usual variety of
gingerbread nuts, and gilt cocks in breeches, and kings and
queens, were to be procured ; while, in some of them, the
more refined luxury of ices was advertised, an innovation
upon the ancient style of refreshment which we, certainly,
had never expected to see introduced into the canvas shops
of the fair pastry cooks.

"While these *marchands* were holding out their various
attractions to the physical tastes of the assembled multitude,
the showkeepers were not less actively employed in endeavouring to please the eye of those who were willing to enjoy
their buffooneries, or their wonders.   Fat boys and living
skeletons, Irish giants and Welsh dwarfs, children with two
heads, and animals without any heads at all, were among the
least of the wonders to be seen ; while the more rational
exhibition of wild beasts joined with the mysterious wonders
of the conjuror and the athletic performances of tumblers,
in calling forth expressions of surprise and delight from the
old, as well as from the young, who were induced to contribute
their pennies ' to see the show.'

"Nor were these the only modes of procuring amusement
which presented themselves.   On the Serpentine river a
number of boats had been launched, which had been procured
from the Thames, and watermen were employed, during the
whole day, in rowing about those who were anxious to enjoy

the refreshing coolness of the water after the turmoil and heat of the fair. Ponies and donkeys were, in the outskirts of the fair, plentiful, for the use of the young who were inclined for equestrian exercise, while archery grounds and throw sticks held out their attractions to the adepts in such practices, and roundabouts and swings were ready to gratify the tastes of the adventurous. Kensington Gardens were, as usual, open to the public, and not a few who were fearful of joining in the crowd, contented themselves here, in viewing the gay scene from a distance. Timorous, however, as they might be, of personal inconvenience, they did not fail to enjoy the opportunities which were afforded them of looking into the book of fate ; and we observed many of the fairest parts of the creation busily engaged in deep and private confabulations with those renowned seers, the gypsies.

"With regard to those persons who visited the fair, we must say we never saw a more orderly body. From an early hour the visitors were flocking in ; but it was not until Her Majesty had gone to Westminster Abbey that the avenues approaching Hyde Park became crowded. Then, indeed, the countless thousands of London appeared to be poured forth, and all seemed to be bound for the same point of destination. Thousands who had taken up their standing places at Hyde Park Corner, poured through the gate ; whilst many who had assumed positions at a greater distance from the Parks, passed through the squares and through Grosvenor Gate. Every avenue was soon filled, every booth was soon crammed full of persons desirous of procuring refreshment and rest after the fatigue of standing so long in the crowd to view the procession.

"These, however, were not the only persons who joined the throng. Every cab, coach, or omnibus which had been left disengaged, appeared to be driving to the same point, full of passengers. Fulham, Putney, Mile End and Brixton alike contributed their vehicles to carry the people to the Parks, and thousands from the very extremity of the City were to be seen flocking towards the Fair. All seemed bent on the same object, that of procuring amusement, and work seemed to have been suspended, as if by common consent. While the East-end thrust forth her less aristocratic workmen, the West-end was not altogether idle in furnishing its quota to the throng, and we noticed many really elegantly dressed ladies and gentlemen alight from their carriages to view the enlivening scene ; and many of them, who were, apparently, strangers to such exhibitions, were, evidently, not a little amused at the grotesque imitations of those amusements in which the aristocracy delight.

"Carriages of every description were admitted into the Parks, and the splendid carriage of an aristocrat was not unfrequently followed by the tilted waggon of some remover of furniture, with its load of men, women and children, who had come to ' see the fun.' All seemed, alike, bent on amuse-ment ; all, alike, appeared to throw aside those restraints which rank, fashion, or station had placed upon them, and to enter fully into the enjoyment of the busy scene in which they were actors. The delightful locality of the Fair, the bright sunbeams playing upon the many-coloured tents, the joyous laughter of the people, untouched by debauchery, and unseduced by the gross pleasures of the appetite ; the gay dresses of the women, all in their best ; joined in making the scene one which must live long in the recollection of those who witnessed it. All appeared to remember that this was the day of the Coronation of a Queen, so youthful, so beautiful, so pure, and all appeared to be determined that no act of insubordination or of disorder on their part should sully the bright opening of a reign so hopeful, and from which so much happiness is to be expected.

"We have already said that the arrangements of the fair were excellent ; but, while these called forth our admiration, the exceeding attention paid to the public by the police force appeared to prevent the possibility of accident or robbery. All gambling booths and thimble riggers had, of course, been necessarily excluded, but we fear it was not possible to shut out all those persons whose recollection of the laws of *meum* and *tuum* was somewhat blunted. We heard of numerous losses of small sums, and of handkerchiefs and other trifles, but, throughout the day, we gained no information of any robbery which was of sufficient extent to produce more than a temporary inconvenience to the person robbed. A temporary police station was erected in the grounds, in which Mr. Mallalieu and a considerable portion of his men were in attendance during the day; but, although there were, necessarily, some cases in which slight acts of intemperance were visible, nothing of any serious importance occurred during the whole of the early part of the day.

" The orderly conduct of the people, which we have already described as having been observable during the morning, was maintained through the rest of the day. Notwithstanding that the crowd, at three o'clock, had increased tenfold, no disturbance nor riot occurred. The return of Her Majesty attracted a few from the crowd, but nearly every one returned, and all remained for the grand attraction of this part of the day's amusement—the fireworks. As evening closed in, the fatigue of the people rendered rest, as well as refreshment, necessary, and every booth was, in a short time, crowded with eager inquiries for eatables and drinkables. The dancing booths were crowded to suffocation, and the viands of the purveyors of grog were soon put into requisition."

The next day was stormy and wet at first, but afterwards turned out fine, and the Fair was crowded. On the third day, a booth caught fire, but no great damage was done. On the fourth, and last day, the Queen drove as close to it as she well could do, and all the booths were cleared away that night.

The Marquis of Waterford still continued his mad pranks, and he was brought before Mr. Dyer, the Magistrate at Marlborough Street, on 30 June, charged with being drunk and disorderly in Piccadilly at 5 o'clock in the morning.

Policeman Ellis, C 91, saw the Marquis, with two or three other persons and a woman in his cab, driving down the Haymarket, and committing the insane freak of making the foot pavement his road. The policeman had no hope of overtaking the Marquis, from the speed at which his lordship was driving; he, however, followed as fast as he could, and, when the Marquis turned into Piccadilly, he saw his lordship again pull his horse on the pavement, and drive on, to the imminent danger of foot passengers. The cab went against some posts, and this brought the horse to a standstill. The policeman ran up, and after much difficulty and opposition on the part of the Marquis's friends, he succeeded in lodging his lordship in the station house. His lordship was too drunk to allow his being enlarged on bail.

In explanation, the Marquis said he had a young horse in his cab, which was very difficult to drive. The animal, having a heavy load behind him, became unmanageable, and went, in spite of all he could do, on the pavement.

The policeman, in the most positive manner, said he saw the Marquis pull his horse upon the foot pavement, and whip the animal to make him go the faster.

The Marquis declared, " upon his honour," he did not go more than five yards upon the pavement.

The policeman declared the Marquis drove about 100 yards on the pavement in the Haymarket, and about 100 yards more upon the pavement in Piccadilly. The concussion against the post was so great, that the woman was thrown six yards out of the cab.

Marquis: I was thrown out myself. The fact is, I consider this charge to be quite unwarranted. No one was hurt, and the policeman exceeded his duty in taking me to the station house.

Mr. Dyer: The policeman states you were intoxicated.

Marquis: Why, I had been about all night, and I don't think I was very sober.

Policeman: You had your collar and shirt open, and your chest was quite exposed.

Marquis: I was dressed just as I am at present.

Policeman: Your coat is now buttoned up; it was not so when I took you in charge. You said, when I took you, you would defy your brother to drive your horse.

Marquis: I might have said so because none of my brothers are in town. But the horse is only four years old, has never had a collar on before, and I'll defy any man to drive him the length of this street.

Mr. Dyer: It was the more imprudent on your lordship's part to bring such an unsafe animal into the public streets, especially at the present time, when the streets are more than usually thronged. Have you any witnesses?

Marquis: Yes, I can bring them, but I had rather not.

Mr. Dyer: If they can allege anything in contradiction of the charge of wilful driving on the footpath, I am willing to hear it.

Marquis: No. It will be a fine, I suppose, and I had rather pay it than trouble my friends to come forward   I'll call my horse, if your Worship thinks proper.

Mr. Dyer then inflicted a fine of 40s.

The Marquis paid the money, and, turning to the policeman, made some unhandsome remarks on his evidence.

Mr. Dyer said the policeman bore an excellent character, and, as far as the magistrates could judge, had always done his duty fairly and respectably.

The Marquis took the arm of his friend, the Earl of Waldegrave, and left the office.

We hear of him again very shortly afterwards, for on 31 July, at Derby assizes, came on an indictment charging the Marquis of Waterford, Sir F. Johnstone, Hon. A. C. H. Villiers, and E. H. Reynard, Esq., with a riot and assault. On the 5th April were the Croxton Park races, about five miles distance from Melton Mowbray. The four defendants had been dining out at Melton on the evening of that day; and about two in the morning of the following day, the watchmen on duty, hearing a noise, proceeded to the Market Place, and near Lord Rosebery's house saw several gentlemen attempting to overturn a caravan, a man being inside; the watchmen succeeded in preventing this, when the Marquis of Waterford challenged one of them to fight, which the watchmen declined. Subsequently, hearing a noise in the direction of the toll bar, they proceeded thither, and found the gate keeper had been screwed up in his house, and he had been calling out " Murder! "

On coming up with the gentlemen a second time, it was
observed that they had a pot of red paint with them, while
one carried a paint brush, which one of the constables wrested
from the hand of the person who held it ; but, subsequently,
they surrounded the man, threw him on his back, and painted
his face and neck with red paint.   They then continued their
games, painting the doors and windows of different persons ;
and, when one of their companions (Mr. Reynard) was put
in the lock up, they forced the constable to give up the
keys, and succeeded in getting him out.   The jury found
the defendants (who were all identified as having taken part
in the affray) guilty of the common assault, and they were
sentenced to pay a fine of £100 each, and to be imprisoned
till such fine be paid.

Motor cars are not the modern invention we are apt to
imagine them, except as regards the power used—which, until
lately, was always steam.   As far back as 1769, a Frenchman,
named Cugnot, made a steam carriage which carried four
people, and attained a speed of two and a quarter miles an
hour!   But it was unfortunate to its inventor—for it came
to grief in a street in Paris, and the unhappy man was imprisoned.   In England our engineers exercised their inven-
tive power in making steam carriages—Murdock in 1782,
Watt in 1784, Symington in 1786—and others made models,
but the first which actually ran in England was made by
Trevithick and Vivian in 1803, and this, in the streets of
London (which were very far from being as good as they are
now), attained a speed of eight or nine miles an hour.   Between the years 1827-34 there were numerous steam carriages
built and tried, proving more or less successful.   One made
by Sir Goldsworthy Gurney ran for three months in 1831
with passengers between Cheltenham and Gloucester, while
Hancock's steam omnibuses (carrying 14 to 16 passengers)
ran in London pretty constantly during the years 1833-36,
and often at a speed of 10 or 12 miles an hour ; some of his
coaches ran long journeys, such as from London to Brighton,
and he was the most successful of all inventors in this line,

unless we except Scott Russell, who, in 1834, ran six steam coaches between Glasgow and Paisley.

We read in the *Standard* of 21 June, 1838, that " Yesterday afternoon, Hyde Park presented a more than usually gay appearance, in consequence of a crowd of fashionables being assembled to witness the trial of a newly-constructed steam cab.   Among the many splendid equipages were observed those of the Dowager Duchess of Sutherland, the Marquis of Salisbury, the Marquis of Northampton, the Earl of Winchilsea, Lord Howick, Lord Holland, and many other distinguished personages.   About 3 o'clock the object of attraction moved forward at a slow pace from the old Foot Guard Barracks, Knightsbridge, and threaded its way through the various vehicles into the Park, passing through the centre gate of the triumphal arch, and making, in the open space opposite the statue, several turns within its own length.   The vehicle after the date hereof, will render themselves liable to be hours round the Park, and, from the slight noise it made, the horses passing did not appear to be frightened.   The average speed of the cab was about twelve miles an hour   The vehicle was guided by Mr. Hancock, the inventor."

But, if mechanical science had advanced as far as motor cars, we were, in other ways, still as backward as Belgium and Germany are at the present, in using dogs as draught animals. This practice had increased to such an extent that it was found necessary to placard the walls of the metropolis with the following notice.   " Notice is hereby given, that all persons using dogs under carts or trucks, as beasts of burden, after the date hereof, will render themselves liable to be prosecuted, and fined £2, according to the provisions of an obsolete Act lately discovered. London, 18 Aug., 1838." This scandal did not last long, for in " an Act for further improving the Police in and near the Metropolis," 2 and 3 Vict., c. 47 [17 Aug., 1839], we find that Section LVI. says, " And be it enacted, That after the First Day of *January* next, every person who, within the Metropolitan Police District, shall use any Dog for the purpose of drawing, or helping to draw any Cart, Carriage, Truck, or Barrow, shall be liable to a penalty of not more than Forty Shillings for the first offence, and not more than Five Pounds for the Second, or any following offence." This act was extended to all parts of the Kingdom by the 17 and 18 Vict., c. 60.

On the 13th July the Corporation of the City of London gave a grand banquet, at the Guildhall, to the foreign Princes, Ambassadors extraordinary, and *Corps Diplomatique*, then in the metropolis, in honour of the Queen's Coronation ; and in order to completely divest the occasion of anything like a political aspect, care was taken to invite, besides the Ministers, an equal number of the *élite* of both parties in the State. The principal guests went in their state carriages, and the streets were crowded with sightseers who especially welcomed the Duke of Wellington and Marshal Soult. The arrangements and decorations in the Hall were almost the same as those used for the Royal banquet in the previous November, the tables and sideboards were ablaze with plate lent by the various City Companies, and the General Bill of Fare was as follows :

One hundred and twenty tureens of turtle soup, of five pints each ; 17 dishes of fish, consisting of salmon, turbot, whitings, tench and eels ; 40 haunches of venison ; 80 dishes of fowls, capons and pullets ; 40 cherry, gooseberry and currant tarts ; 30 strawberry tarts ; 40 dishes of potatos ; 60 dishes of French beans ; 30 French pies ; 30 pigeon pies ; 30 hams ; 30 tongues ; 2 barons of beef ; 37 Chantilly baskets ; 30 dishes of peas ; 10 sirloins, ribs and rumps of beef ; 45 dishes of shell fish ; 30 ribs, chines and legs of lamb ; 40 dishes of ducklings ; 20 turkey poults ; 80 jellies ; 20 creams ; 40 salads and cucumbers ; 20 dishes of cauliflowers. DESSERT.—Seventy-five pine apples of 2lbs each ; 100 dishes of hothouse grapes ; 20 melons ; 30 dishes of cherries ; 100 dishes of strawberries ; 40 dishes of currants and gooseberries ; 120 cream and water ices, various ; 40 dishes of dried fruit ; 35 ornamented Savoy cakes ; 30 dishes of preserves, biscuits and olives.

Marshal Soult stopped for some time in England, and visited many of the manufacturing towns.

CHAPTER VII.

Genesis of "The Charter"—L. & N. W. Railway opened to Birmingham—
   Overland route to India—A bold smuggler—Bull baiting—Visitors to the
   Queen—"The Boy Jones."

PROBABLY nearly all my readers have heard of the "Chartists," but it is equally probable that few know when the agitation commenced, and the reason for its existence. The "Charter," as it was called, was the Radical outcome of the Reform Bill of 1832. For a time, after the passing of that Bill, the land had peace, for all reasonable reforms had been granted, but the demagogues were not going to be quietly annihilated, and an agitation for more trenchant reform was got up, and a mass meeting in its favour was held at Birmingham, on the 6th of August, and at it were inaugurated the principles of "The People's Charter," as it was called. It is currently reported that this "Charter" was drawn up by William Lovett, a carpenter and cabinet maker, who took an active part in getting rid of the stamp tax upon newspapers; and it is very likely that it was so, for he drew up most of the petitions and addresses for the movement, and, in connection with it, he, the following year, suffered 12 months' imprisonment. He died Aug. 1877. The demands of this "Charter" were six, and they were familiarly known as the six points. They were:

> Universal Suffrage.
> Vote by Ballot.
> Annual Parliaments.
> Payment of the Members.
> Abolition of the Property Qualification.
> Equal Electoral Districts.

5

The meeting was got up by T. Atwood, Esq., M.P., and
the site chosen for it was a large vacant piece of ground,
at Birmingham, on the north-west side of the town, and there
drinking booths galore were erected. The morning began
very wet, and the different divisions from the neighbouring
country marched bemired and bedraggled to the rendezous.
There they soon filled the drinking booths, in which they
abode ; hence, probably, the very diverse statements as to
the numbers present at the meeting, which vary from 10,000
to 200,000. The ground chosen was a natural amphitheatre,
and, if the weather had been finer, it would have been a
pretty sight, enlivened by the bright banners of the different
Trades' Societies. However, Mr. Atwood read the Petition,
which embodied the above six points, and moved its adoption.
Feargus O'Connor, a well-known firebrand, seconded it in a
violent speech, in which occurred the following balderdash.

> "On with your green standard rearing,
>   Go, flesh every sword to the hilt ;
> On our side is Virtue and Erin,
>   On yours is the *parson* and guilt."

Of course the Motion was enthusiastically carried, and then
a very heavy shower of rain terminated the proceedings. The
petition was afterwards presented to Parliament by Mr.
Atwood on the 14th of June, 1839.

On 17th Sept. the London and North Western Railway
(then called the London and Birmingham Rly.) was opened
throughout to Birmingham ; the first train, containing Directors and their friends, leaving Euston at 7.15 a.m. The times
of this train are useful for comparing with the present time.
"The train left Euston at 15 minutes past 7, but did not
take on locomotive until 20 minutes past   It arrived at Tring
station at 25 minutes past 8, where there was five minutes'
delay. Arrived at Wolverton at 6 minutes past 9, where the
directors alighted and changed engines. The train arrived
at Rugby at 11 o'clock, where the Duke of Sussex and his
suite alighted, and proceeded by carriage to the place of
his destination. The directors remained at Rugby 10 minutes,

and arrived at Birmingham 3 minutes past 12, having performed the whole journey, including stoppages, in 4 hours
48 minutes, and, exclusive of stoppages, in 4 hours 14 minutes.
This is, unquestionably, the shortest time in which the journey
from London to Birmingham has ever been performed, being
upwards of two hours less than the time occupied by Marshal
Soult and attendants a few weeks ago."

" The fare for one person from London to Birmingham, or
back, by the ' four inside ' carriages, by day, or the first class,
' six inside ' by night, will be £1 12s. 6d. ; by the second-class
carriages, open by day, which is the cheapest, it will be £1.
The intermediate fares will be £1 10s. and £1 5s."

It is not generally known that the two lodges at the
entrance of Euston Station, were the original ticket office and
waiting room.

People were beginning to wake from the torpor in which
they had hitherto slumbered, with regard to locomotion, and
on 12th October an influential meeting of merchants and
others was held at the Jerusalem Coffee House to hear a
Captain Barber unfold his scheme for a quicker communication with India. This was that passengers and goods
should be taken by steam to Cairo, and thence, by omnibuses
and vans to Suez—as was afterwards done by Waghorn, who
was already forming an Overland Mail (see *Times*, 29 Nov.,
1838).

With the very heavy duties on foreign goods, of course
smuggling was very rife, and the Inland Revenue was de-
frauded on every possible occasion by the sharp wits opposed
to it ; and the difficulty of conviction, unless the smuggler was
caught red-handed, was very considerable. The following is
a case in point, and for sheer impudence, it bears the palm.
17 Oct. :

MANSION HOUSE.—A Scotchwoman, named Frances
Bodmore, the wife of a Frenchman, who has been engaged
in smuggling, appeared to answer for her husband, on a charge
of having two two-gallon bottles of French brandy in his
possession, without having paid the duty thereon.

Child, the constable, said he went into the house of the Frenchman, in Sugarloaf Court; and, while searching for other things, found the bottles under the pillows of the bed.

The Lord Mayor: Why don't your husband attend?

Woman: Why, because he knows nothing at all about the business. I think he'd be a great fool to come here without knowing for what.

The Lord Mayor: How do you get your living?

Woman: Why, as well as I can. I don't get it without running some risk for it, you may depend.

The Lord Mayor: We know you to be a consummate smuggler.

Woman: Whatever my business may be, I generally get through it like a trump. There's no nonsense about me.

The Lord Mayor (to the Revenue officer): She is constantly backward and forward between this and France, I daresay.

Woman: Yes, my Lord, I travel a good deal for the benefit of my health, and I always come back stouter than I go. (Laughter.)

Officer: She's perfectly well known, my Lord, as one of a number that are commissioned by parties in London. They are all very clever, and elude us in every possible way, and the steamers afford them great facilities.

The Lord Mayor: I can't send this woman to prison, and she knows it well, but I shall punish every experienced smuggler I catch as severely as I can. They cheat the fair trader, they endanger the vessel in which they come over, and they cheat the Government.

Woman: Ay, my Lord, that's the cleverest thing of all. Only think of cheating the Government! Well, well, I wonder where the villainy of man will end! (Laughter.)

The Lord Mayor: Take care of yourself. You think you are secure. You may go now.

Woman: Good morning, my Lord. Although you are so kind, I hope I shall never have the pleasure of seeing your face again.

The Lord Mayor was informed that great quantities of

lace were brought over by women. Some had been found
stitched up in the skins of wildfowl, and there was scarcely
an article, dead or alive, that was not suspected of being a
depository of contraband goods. It was but a short time
ago, that a wretched-looking object was discovered to be the
carrier of a large stock of lace. He had an old bedstead,
which, in his trips to Boulogne, he used to take with him.
At last, somebody on board expressed his surprise, why a
ricketty piece of furniture, which looked as if it was the
tenement of living animals, should be so frequent a passenger.
Upon close examination, it was found that the several pieces
of the bedstead had been hollowed and stuffed with lace.

The cruel old English sport of bull baiting was still continued at Stamford, in Lincolnshire, where it is said to have
existed since the year 1209, in the reign of King John. The
story goes that, in that year, William, Earl Warren, lord of
the town, standing on the walls of his castle, saw two bulls
fighting for a cow, in the castle meadow, till all the butchers
dogs pursued one of the bulls (maddened by the noise and
multitude) clean through the town. This sight so pleased
the Earl, that he gave the castle meadow, where the bulls'
duel began, for a common, to the butchers of the town, after
the first grass was mown, on condition that they should find
a mad bull the day six weeks before Christmas Day—for the
continuation of that sport, for ever.

But the time had come for putting an end to this barbarous
practice, and it was this year put down by direct interference
of the Secretary of State. At Stamford, and elsewhere, it
was believed that this bull baiting was legal, being established
by custom ; but the Society for the Prevention of Cruelty to
Animals, with a view of setting the question at rest by the
decision of the Court of Queen's Bench, caused an indictment
to be preferred against several of the ringleaders. The indictment was tried at Lincoln, before Mr. Justice Park and a
special jury, when several of them were found guilty ; and,
upon their being brought up for judgment in the Court of
Queen's Bench, the Court unanimously declared the practice

to be illegal; the Chief Justice, in particular, said: "It was supposed there was some matter of law—at first, there was a supposed old Charter—for the future, it must be considered as an illegal practice."

In consequence of this decision, a troop of the 14th Dragoons, together with 12 Metropolitan policemen, were sent into the town of Stamford. Placards, apprising the public of the illegality of the bull baiting, were posted in the town and neighbourhood, and the threatened and attempted repetition of this barbarous scene was prevented without any loss of life or serious injury. The *bullards* (as they were called) mustered in strong numbers. They had provided two fierce bulls to be hunted and tormented; but the bulls were seized and pounded by the police; and, although the ruffian mob remained in considerable numbers, no serious breach of the peace took place. But they were determined not to be altogether baulked of their *sport;* for a bull calf, enclosed in a cart, and followed by its lowing mother, entered the town, and was immediately seized on as a substitute for a bull. It was taken out, and hunted through the town for some time, until rescued by the police.

Every lunatic seems to have wanted to say something to the young Queen, and visitors to Buckingham Palace were very frequent, although the object of their wishes was never attained. To show the nuisance involved by these fools let me give one paragraph out of the *Times*, 19 Dec. :

VISITORS TO HER MAJESTY.—On Saturday night, about 9 o'clock, a very respectably dressed young man rang the bell at the tradesmen's entrance of the new Palace, and, upon being asked the nature of his business, he said he had come for the direction of his house, as he was tired, and wished to go home. Upon being asked to explain himself, he said he had just come from Sydney, and had been desired to call at the Palace by the Queen, who told him he should have a house to live in, and £150 a year, for some very important spiritual communication he had made to her. The young man, whose every action showed he was a lunatic, was then told the Queen was not in town, when he turned away, observing that he would go immediately to Lord Hill, and lay his case before him. Visits of the preceding kind are very frequent at the Palace, and the tales told by the visitants are of the very strangest nature. It is only a few weeks since, an elderly man, having the appearance of a farmer, called at the Palace, and handing to the porter the certificate of his birth, requested him to let Her Majesty sign it. From inquiries made concerning this man, it was discovered that he was a respectable farmer in the neighbourhood of Exeter, from which distant place he had wandered on so strange an errand.

But of all visitors to the Royal Palace, THE BOY JONES was the most frequent and successful. Who, in this generation, knows anything about THE BOY JONES? Yet his escapades were very daring and his story is very true—but so strange is it that, in order to be believed, I must, at least, in part, give the chapter and verse for it:

The Times, 15 Dec. :

QUEEN SQUARE.—Yesterday, a lad about 15 years of age, who gave his name as Edward Cotton, whose dress was that of a sweep, but who was stated to be the son of a respectable tradesman in Hertfordshire, was charged with being found in the Marble hall of Buckingham Palace, under circumstances of an extraordinary nature. It should be stated that Buckingham Palace, even during the absence of the Queen, is guarded by the gentlemen porters of the establishment, two inspectors of the A division of police, and sentries from the Foot Guards. In spite of this, a number of cases have lately occurred at this office, where persons have been found in the interior of the Palace under unaccountable circumstances.

George Cox, one of the porters, having been sworn, said, that at five o'clock yesterday morning he saw the prisoner in the Marble hall. The latter endeavoured to make his escape into the lobby, but he pursued him, and he then took

a contrary direction, across the lawn at the back of the Palace.
Witness called for the sentry at the gate, and a policeman
of the B Division who was on duty in James Street, caught
the lad, after a long chase over the lawn. Mr. Cox added,
that he found, in the lobby, a regimental sword, a quantity
of linen, and other articles, all of which had been purloined
from the Palace. The sword was the property of the Hon.
Augustus Murray, a gentleman attached to the Queen's establishment. Witness went into that gentleman's bedroom, and
the bedding was covered with soot. The prisoner had,
evidently, endeavoured to get up the chimney, in order to
effect his escape; there was a valuable likeness of Her
Majesty, in the Marble hall, which was broken, and covered
with soot; and it was supposed that the lad, in the first
instance, had descended from the top of the building, and
had endeavoured to make his way back again in the same
manner.

James Stone, 31 B, deposed that he was called upon by
the last witness to secure the prisoner. There were marks of
soot in several of the bedchambers, as well as in one of the
corridors of the Palace, and the Grand (or Marble) hall. He
found upon him two letters, one addressed to Her Majesty,
and the other to the Hon. Mr. Murray. These letters had
been placed underneath Her Majesty's portrait, and had, no
doubt, been taken by the prisoner at the time the picture
was destroyed. Part of the scabbard of the sword was discovered in one of the beds, and a quantity of bear's grease,
part of which he had placed upon his flesh, was taken from
him—it belonged to one of the servants of the Palace. Upon
being taken to the station house, he said he came from Hertfordshire, and that his father was a respectable man.

Mr. White, the sitting magistrate, observed that it was a
most extraordinary thing that persons could get into the
Palace under such circumstances.

Several persons belonging to the Palace said that every
inquiry had been made, but it could not be accounted for.

Mr. White (to the prisoner): Where do you come from?

Prisoner: I came from Hertfordshire 12 months ago,

and I met with a man in a fustian jacket, who asked me to
go with him to Buckingham House. I went, and have been
there ever since. I got my victuals in the kitchen, and I
thought myself very well off, because I came to London to
better myself.

Mr. White: Well, you could not go to a higher place.

Prisoner: I declare it to be the case, and I lived very well.
To be sure, I was obliged to wash my shirt now and then.

Mr. White: You fared, then, altogether, pretty well?

Prisoner: Very well indeed, Sir, and I was always placed,
when the Queen had a meeting with the Ministers, behind a
piece of furniture in the room; but I, certainly, did live well.

Mr. White: Indeed! And which was your favourite
apartment?

Prisoner: The room in front of the gardens; but I was
always in the secret when the Ministers came.

Mr. White: Do you mean to tell me that you have lived
in the Palace upwards of 11 months, and been concealed
when Her Majesty held a Council?

Prisoner: I do.

Mr. White: Were you hid behind a chair?

Prisoner: No. But the tables and other furniture concealed me.

Mr. White: Then you could hear all Her Majesty said?

Prisoner: Oh, yes! and her Ministers too.

The prisoner's answers to the questions of the magistrate
were given in the most shrewd manner possible, and he
evidently appeared to be a lad of some education, but nothing
further could be elicited from him.

Mr. White said it was a most singular affair, and that it
should be strictly inquired into. For the present, he should
remand the prisoner until Wednesday next.

The magistrate also told Cox that, as he should be sitting
there every day, he should be glad to receive any information upon the subject.

The letters found upon the prisoner were directed to be
sent to the Palace, under seal of the Office, the prisoner having broken them open.

The case excited great interest, and, in the first instance, was sent to Bow Street; but Sir Frederick Roe being out of town, it was ordered to be heard at this office.

The Times, 20 Dec.—Yesterday, the lad found in Buckingham Palace, who had given his name as Edward Cotton, and described himself as the son of a respectable tradesman living in the town of Hertford, was brought before Messrs. White and Gregorie for final examination. It will be recollected that he had purloined, amongst other articles, two letters, which were immediately sealed up, and sent back to the Palace. The prisoner turns out to be the son of an industrious tailor, named Jones, residing in York Street, Westminster; and, it appears, had frequently expressed his intention to enter the Palace, under any circumstances. He had often stated that he wished to see the grand staircase, in order to take a sketch of it, and had often expressed his determination to see the Queen, and to hear her sentiments when Her Majesty and her Ministers were assembled in Council.

Frederick Blume now deposed that he was valet to the Hon. Mr. Murray, and that a sword, a quantity of linen and other articles, had been stolen from that gentleman's apartments in the Palace.

Mr. White: When were they stolen?

Witness: I can't recollect.

Mr. White: Was it a week, a month, or three or four months ago?

Witness: I cannot say.

Mr. White: Where was your master's sword at the time you saw it last?

Witness: When I went to Windsor.

Mr. White: When was that?

Witness: I cannot exactly recollect, and then he added, that about a week since, he had sent from Windsor to the Palace, a portmanteau containing his linen, and three pairs of trousers, four of stockings, and three cravats were missing. The padlock of the portmanteau had been forced by the sword having been applied to it. The sword had broken in the attempt. He had also lost five 10 sous pieces, which had been found upon the prisoner.

Mr. White: What is the value of the articles you have lost?

Witness: I don't know; but I should like to give three guineas to get them back.

Mr. White: Can you swear to the French coin found upon the prisoner as being yours?

The witness was then shown the coin, and he said that he certainly could. They had been taken from his bed-room.

.   .   .   .

Mr. White: Can any information be given as to the manner in which the prisoner gained access to the Palace? Cox, one of the porters to the Palace, said that the principal entrance door was always locked, and the key in his possession. At 5 o'clock on Saturday morning, just as he was about to get out of bed, the prisoner opened the door of his room, as witness considered, to obtain the key; his face and hands were disguised with soot and bear's grease, and he was asked whether he came to sweep a chimney: he did not make any answer, but endeavoured to escape.

Inspector Steed, A division, said that upon examining the gates of the principal entrance of the Palace, he found that, at the Marble Arch, there was a vacuum sufficient to admit a boy into the Palace, without any inconvenience.

Mr. White: And is there no sentry at this gate?

Witness: There are two.

The inspector said that he had examined the boy's boots, and the gravel upon them corresponded with that lately laid down close to the Marble Arch. The boots had been taken off by the prisoner, and left in one of the apartments appropriated to the use of the porters of the Palace.

Mr. Griffiths, builder, Coventry Street, said that the lad had been in his employment for a few months; he had always expressed his intention to get into the interior of the Palace by some means or other; he was a clever lad, and had made a sketch of the exterior, and a view of the enclosure fronting the Palace. He had left his service two days since, and witness was very much distressed, as were his parents, to know what had become of him. Upon reading the accounts in the newspapers, he immediately went to Tothill Fields, and identified him, much to the gratification of his father, who supposed that he had drowned himself, the latter having, on account of his son's bad conduct, turned him out of doors.

The Magistrate, after telling the boy that he would, most likely, be committed for trial, asked him what he could say in his defence.

Prisoner: I wished to see the Palace, and I went in with a man in a fustian jacket. I had the whole range of the Palace for a day or two, but the money found upon me I picked up in one of the rooms.

Mr. White: Tell me the truth, for I am about to send you for trial.

Prisoner: Oh, very well; with all my heart.

He was fully committed to the Westminster Sessions, and all parties bound over to prosecute.

He was tried on 28 Dec., and was most ably defended by his Counsel, Mr. Prendergast, who turned everything to ridicule, and the jury returned a verdict of Not Guilty, regarding the escapade in the light of a youthful folly, and being, also, mindful of the fact that the boy did not enter the Palace for the purpose of theft.

But we shall hear of THE BOY JONES again.

CHAPTER VIII.

Death of Lord Norbury—Birth of photography—Experimental street pavements—
Forecast of the Queen's marriage—Sad story of Lady Flora Hastings—Story
of a climbing boy—Van Amburgh—Embanking the Thames—Victoria Park
—Robbery of gold dust.

In a book, professedly of Gossip, politics should be strictly
kept in the background—but at this time Ireland was seeth-
ing with sedition. Still I should hardly have adverted to
it, had not the deliberate and brutal murder of the Earl of
Norbury, on 1 Jan., set all tongues wagging. His Lordship
was walking in the shrubbery, near his own house at Kil-
beggan, in the county of Meath, talking to his steward, and
pointing out to him some trees he wished to have cut
down, when some miscreant, behind a hedge, fired a blunderbuss loaded with swan shot at him, and he fell, mortally
wounded. He lived for 43 hours afterwards—but his assassin
ran away and escaped; nor, in spite of large rewards offered,
was he ever discovered.

Photography may be said to have been practically born
early in this year, for, on 7 Jan., the French Academy reported on the invention of M. Daguerre, by which the pictures
of the camera lucida were rendered permanent. All former
attempts may be regarded as scientific dilletanteism and nothing more. The earliest known pictures caused by light on
a sensitive surface were made by Thomas Wedgwood (a
son of Josiah, the famous potter), whose researches were published in 1802 in the *Journal of the Royal Institution,* under
the title : " An account of a Method of copying Paintings upon
Glass, and making Profiles by the agency of Light upon
Nitrate of Silver : with Observations by H. Davy." After-

wards, came Nicephore Niepce, of Châlon sur Saône, who
produced permanent light pictures in 1814, and he and
Daguerre went into partnership in this matter, in 1829. Fox
Talbot was the first to invent a negative photograph, and he
read a paper on " Photogenic Drawings " before the Royal
Society, on 31 Jan., this year ; and that scientific investigation of the new wonder excited the attention, even of
amateurs, is shown by a letter in the *Times* of 21 Feb. :

   " SIR,—Seeing in a newspaper, last week, that a German
had found out M. Daguerre's secret, I was so impressed with
that testimony to the possibility of *seizing a shadow*, that I
thought over all the little I knew of light, colours and
chymistry. The next day, I took a piece of writing paper,
hastily prepared by myself, placed it behind the lens of a
camera obscura, made on the spur of the moment, and obtained a satisfactory result ; for the trees, in front of my
house, were produced, but not the parts agitated by the wind.
Since that, I have obtained, progressively improving, several
landscapes, which may be called, most appositely, ' lucigraphs.'
I mention my humble effort as corroborative of the reality,
or feasibility of M. Daguerre's beautiful discovery ; and I
can readily conceive that, in a very short time, the traveller's
portmanteau will not be complete without the very portable
means of procuring a lucigraph at pleasure.—Yours, etc.,
CLERICUS, Welney, Wisbeach." This gentleman's prophecy
has, long since, been verified, as the " Kodakers " all over the
world can testify.   But the first public experiment in England
(if we exclude Wedgwood's) was made, on Sept. 13, 1839,
when M. St. Croix exhibited the whole process of Daguerreo-
type, in presence of a select party of scientific men and
artists.   He also succeeded in producing a picture of the place
of meeting ; No. 7, Piccadilly.

   People were beginning to wake up as to social improvements, and the better paving of, at least, the most public
thoroughfares, was loudly called for. Hitherto people had
been content with the old cobble stones, and wide kennels,

or gutters—but henceforth there was to be inaugurated a
newer and better *régime*, as we learn from the *Observer* of
6 Jan. :

"EXPERIMENTAL PAVEMENT OF OXFORD STREET.—This,
doubtless, the most extraordinary and novel undertaking
which has ever been attempted in the annals of road making,
is, to the gratification, not only to the respectable inhabitants
of Oxford Street, but to a curious public, at last, completed.
On Friday (4 Jan.) at 2 o'clock, the line of this great thoroughfare, occupied by the various specimens of paving, extending
from Charles Street to Tottenham Court Road, presented a
most animated spectacle, being thronged by thousands of
spectators anxious to witness its opening to the public.
Shortly after 2 o'clock, the Paving Committee appointed by
the Marylebone Vestry to superintend the arrangement of
this work of art, headed by the parish beadles, in full uniform,
with their maces ; and accompanied by the respective projectors and the parochial authorities, arrived on the spot in
procession, and passed over the ground, followed by 21 omnibuses, after which, the road was thrown open to the public.
From time to time, during the progress of the work, many
erroneous statements have gone the rounds of our daily con-
temporaries, with respect to the extent of ground allotted to
the experiments, and on other matters connected with the
arrangements.   The following, however, being obtained from
an official source, may be fully relied upon as correct : The
whole space between Charles Street and Tottenham Court
Road is occupied by 12 different specimens, which are completed in the following order, commencing at Charles Street :
viz.—40 feet of Robinson's Parisian bitumen—24 feet laid
in straight courses, and 16 feet diagonally : 74 feet of parish
stone paving, 54 feet of which is laid in straight courses, the
stones 9 inches deep, and the interstices filled up with
Claridge's asphalte ; the remaining 20 feet consisting of stones
only 4½ inches deep, but laid diagonally, and filled up with
the same composition : 60 feet of the Bastenne and Gaujac
bitumen, partly laid in straight courses, and partly diagonally :

135 feet of parish stone paving, divided into three sections, in the following order—1st, 70 feet of dressed Aberdeen granite, with concrete bottom, and the joints grouted with lime and sand; 2nd, 40 feet of the same, laid diagonally; and 3rd, 25 feet of dressed Aberdeen granite, without concrete bottom, the joints filled in with fine gravel; this is followed by 50 feet of the Scotch asphaltum, which is entirely the produce of this country, laid down in straight courses : 60 feet of Mr. Stead's pavement, of wooden blocks, of a sexagonal form, 12 inches deep, divided into three compartments, one prepared with Kyan's patent, part dipped in, and joints run with asphalte, and part without any preparation whatever: the last specimen, at Tottenham Court Road, is 60 feet of the Val de Travers bitumen, a portion of which consists of square blocks, laid in straight courses, and the remainder consisting of a layer of clean Guernsey chippings cemented together by boiling asphalte, run among them nearly to the surface, and a face made with asphalte, merely showing the chippings, here and there, in patches. The whole work presents a most even and beautiful road, and, yesterday, during the day, attracted the notice of many hundreds of persons. The portion, however, it is but justice to add, to which attention was more particularly directed, was that of the wooden blocks, the noiseless tendency of which, made the vehicles passing along, appear to be rolling over a thick carpet or rug. The time allowed by the Vestry of St. Marylebone for the test of these experiments, is until the last Saturday of June next, when the official report of the surveyors will be laid before that body, and upon which the fate of Oxford Street depends."

People began to feel that it was high time that the Queen should marry—but, as yet, no signs of such a thing, and no speculations, as far as I can see, were hazarded as to who her future consort should be. At length, one newspaper, the *Sun*, seems to have been inspired, by authority, and is thus quoted in the *Times* of 24 Jan:—"'MARRIAGE OF HER MAJESTY.—The country will learn with delight that the most interesting part of the speech from the throne* to both Houses of Parliament, and the country at large, will be the announcement of Her Majesty's intended marriage. The happy object of Queen Victoria's choice is Prince Albert, son of the reigning Duke of Saxe Coburg, and cousin of Her Majesty. Prince Albert is handsome, and about 22 years of age. He has resided, for some time, in this country, on a visit to his Royal relatives. How soon the happy event is to take place, we are not prepared to say, but our readers may depend upon the authenticity of our information.'—*The Sun.* Has not some wag been hoaxing the editor? We suspect so, though, at the same time, we do not profess to have any knowledge on the subject."

Indeed, it was about time that the Queen married, and got out of the leading strings of the women folk who surrounded her. Had she been married, we should, probably, have never heard of the sad episode of Lady Flora Hastings.

This lady, who was highly accomplished, and the authoress of some pretty poems,† which were published after her death, was the eldest daughter of Francis, Marquis of Hastings, and Flora, Countess of Loudon, and was lady of the bedchamber to the Duchess of Kent. Two old busybodies, the Ladies Portman and Tavistock, spread the vile and unfounded rumour that the unfortunate lady was *enceinte*, and the Queen forbade Lady Flora to appear at Court until she had submitted to the indignity of a medical examination. The case called forth some very strong feeling—and a vast quantity of correspondence was published on the subject, especially the indignant letters of the poor lady's mother to the Queen ; but, perhaps, the most temperate account of the whole affair, is in a letter from Lady Flora's uncle, Mr. Hamilton Fitzgerald, which

---

* It is needless to say that the Queen's Speech to Parliament on 5th Feb. was absolutely silent on the matter ; indeed, the Queen did not inform her Prime Minister, Lord Melbourne, of her choice until October of this year.

† Poems by the Lady Flora Hastings, edited by her sister. Edinburgh, 1841, 8vo.

was published in the *Examiner* of Sunday, 24th of March, and, afterwards, copied into all the daily papers.

"SIR,—Many false and contradictory reports of the deplorable insult which has been lately offered to my niece, Lady Flora Hastings, at Buckingham Palace, having appeared in the public papers, I, as her ladyship's nearest connection, feel it my duty to request of you to publish the following account of the transaction, for the correctness of which I vouch.

"Lady Flora arrived, some weeks since, from Scotland, very unwell. She immediately consulted Sir James Clark, the physician to both Her Majesty and the Duchess of Kent. One symptom of her complaint was a swelling of the stomach. By dint of exercise and medical treatment, she was getting better; the swelling had considerably subsided, and she had every hope of a speedy recovery; when, on or about the 1st of March, Sir James Clark went to her room, and announced to her the conviction of the ladies of the Palace that she was pregnant. In answer to all his exhortations to confession, 'as the only means of saving her character,' Lady Flora returned an indignant, but steady denial that there was anything to confess. Upon which, Sir James Clark told her, 'that nothing but her submitting to a medical examination would ever satisfy them, or remove the stigma from her name.' Lady Flora found that the subject had been brought before the Queen's notice, and that all this had been discussed, arranged and denounced to her, without one word having been said on the subject to her own mistress, the Duchess of Kent; who had no suspicion of what was going on, and whose sanction was not sought for the humiliating proposition which had been made to Lady Flora. On leaving Lady Flora's room, Sir James Clark went to the Duchess of Kent, and announced his conviction that Lady Flora was with child; and was followed by Lady Portman, who conveyed a message from Her Majesty to her mother, that the Queen would not permit Lady Flora to appear till the examination had taken place. Lady Portman (who, with Lady Tavistock, are mentioned as most active against Lady Flora) expressed to the Duchess of Kent, her conviction of Lady Flora's guilt.

"'Her beloved mistress' never, for a moment, doubted Lady Flora's innocence. She said that she knew her, her principles, and her family too well to listen to such a charge. However, the edict was given; and, the next day, Lady Flora having obtained the Duchess of Kent's very reluctant consent —'for Her Royal Highness could not bear the idea of her being exposed to such a humiliation'—but, Lady Flora, 'feeling it her duty to Her Royal Highness, to herself, and to her family, that a point blank refutation should be instantly given to the lie,' submitted herself to the most rigid examination; and now possesses a certificate, signed by Sir James Clark, and also by Sir Charles Clark, stating, as strongly as language can state it, that there are no grounds for believing that pregnancy does exist, or ever has existed. Lord Hastings, though, at the time very ill from influenza, went to London immediately, and demanded, and obtained, from Lord Melbourne, a distinct disavowal of his participation in the affair; and demanded, and obtained, an audience of Her Majesty, in which, while he disclaimed all idea that the Queen had any wish to injure his sister, he plainly, though respectfully, stated his opinion of those who had counselled her, and his resolution to find out the originator of the slander, and bring him, or her, to punishment. Lady Flora is convinced that the Queen was surprised into the order which was given, and that Her Majesty did not understand what she was betrayed into; for, ever since the horrid event, Her Majesty has shown her regret by the most gracious kindness to Lady Flora, and expressed it warmly, with 'tears in her eyes.'

"The Duchess of Kent's conduct was perfect; 'a mother could not have been kinder.' 'She immediately dismissed Sir James Clark from her service, and refused to see Lady Portman'; and has crowned her goodness by a most beautiful letter she has written to the Dowager Lady Hastings, from whom the accounts were kept, till all hope of avoiding publicity was impossible."

6*

Her brother, the Marquis of Hastings, was indefatigable in trying to unearth the promoters of the scandal, but, from the published letters, without much result ; but the unfortunate affair involved the whole Court, for a time, in unpopularity— Lady Loudon, her mother, demanded from the Queen, Sir James Clark's dismissal, but was not successful. Meantime, the object of all this agitation, after resuming, for a time, the duties of her situation, grew gradually worse, and, at length, expired, on the 5th July, at the age of 33. By the desire of Lord Hastings, a *post mortem* examination of the body took place, the particulars of which, attested by five of the most eminent surgeons of the metropolis, were published in the papers, and fully established the unfortunate lady's complete innocence of the charge brought against her, the cause of death being clearly shown to be enlargement of the liver.

Lady Flora's remains were removed from the palace, at an early hour in the morning, to be conveyed, by steamboat, to Scotland. Even as early as two o'clock, a considerable number of spectators were assembled, which increased in every street through which the procession passed. Four Royal carriages, including those of the Queen and the Queen Dowager, and many belonging to the nobility, accompanied the hearse. Lady Flora's body was interred, on the 15th of July, in the family vault at Loudon, Ayrshire.

There were many books and pamphlets published with regard to this affair, among which were her mother's letters to the Queen : " The Lady Flora Hastings, a Brief Sketch "— " A Warning to the Baroness Lehzen,* etc."—" The Palace Martyr, a Satire "—" The Dangers of Evil Council, etc."—" A Dirge on the Death of Lady Flora Hastings "—" The late Lady Flora Hastings : Statements of the Marquis of Hastings, etc."—" The Victim of Scandal."

At the time of which I write, climbing boys were still employed to sweep chimneys, and as a sample of the manner

---

* The Queen's most intimate companion from her childhood.

in which they were treated by their masters, I give the following police case.   25 Jan. :

MARLBOROUGH STREET.—Henry Riddle, foreman to Robert Towser, a chimney sweep, appeared before the magistrates on a summons charging him under the 4 & 5 Wil. IV., c. 35, with the following act of cruelty towards James Arnold, a boy about 12 years of age, and who, for some time past, had been in Towser's employ.

Mr. Rice, a baker, of 31, Up. Seymour St., Portman Sq., deposed that, on the afternoon of the 18th instant, his kitchen chimney, by some accident, caught fire; and, in consequence of information thereof being communicated to the defendant Riddle, he, soon afterwards, came to the house, bringing with him the boy Arnold, whom he, at once, desired to ascend, notwithstanding that the lighted soot was, at the time, coming down into the grate in large flakes.

Mr. Rawlinson: Did you remonstrate with Riddle upon the inhumanity of his conduct?

Complainant: I did, and begged of him not to send the boy up, as he would, inevitably, be suffocated; to which he replied, "Oh, d——n it, I've many a time been up a chimney ten times worse than that, myself, and why can't he do it?" At this period, I had occasion to go upstairs, and made my way on to the roof, just as a friend of mine was about to pour down a quantity of water, when I begged of him not to do so, as I fancied I heard the voice of someone within a short distance of the top of the chimney; we both listened, and heard someone faintly say, "For God's sake, take the chimney pot off, or I shall be suffocated." With some difficulty we tore away the mortar, and, having removed the pot, we beheld the poor boy Arnold, who kept crying out, "Oh! pull me up, pull me up!" My friend then thrust down his arm, and, laying hold of the little sufferer, succeeded in extricating him from his perilous situation.

Mr. Rawlinson: Was the chimney, at the time, still on fire?

Complainant: It was, Sir.

Mr. Rawlinson: In what condition did the boy seem when lifted out of the chimney?

Complainant: He seemed almost in a lifeless state, and when carrying him in my arms downstairs, I was fearful he would not recover. After the lapse of a little time, I gave him a small quantity of brandy, and he, in a great measure, revived; Riddle then took hold of him, and leading him to the roof of the house, insisted upon his descending from the top to the bottom of the chimney, which he did, and he and Riddle then left the place.

Mr. Rawlinson (to Riddle): What answer have you to make for ill-treating this poor boy in so shameful a manner?

Riddle: The boy is not an apprentice, and he was not sent up the chimney until a quantity of water had been thrown down.

Mr. Rawlinson, after remarking upon the atrocious nature of the offence, ordered Riddle to find bail to answer the charge at the Sessions; at the same time expressing a hope that a severe example would be made of him.

From 1838 to 1841, there was exhibiting in London a famous lion tamer named Van Amburgh, and, in January, 1839, the Queen went to Drury Lane Theatre to witness his performance, with which she was so pleased, that she commissioned Sir Edwin Landseer to paint a picture of Van Amburgh and his lions, which was exhibited in 1839, and is now in the Royal Collection at Osborne. If I am not very much mistaken there is another, by the same artist, of the same subject, in the Duke of Wellington's town mansion, at Apsley House.

We can see how long it takes to carry out well-known and wanted improvements—take the Thames Embankment for example. Originally suggested by Wren after the great fire of London in 1666, and afterwards by William Paterson, the founder of the Bank of England, about 1694, the matter slumbered until 1767, when the Corporation of the City of London embanked one mile of the river. The question arose spasmodically until 1838, when the Corporation consulted with the Government as to the advisability of embanking the Thames all the way between London and Vauxhall Bridges, and, in Jan., 1839, the Government sanctioned surveys being made and estimates prepared ; the whole correspondence concerning which may be found in the *Times* of 2 Feb., 1839. But no practical steps were taken in the matter until 1860, when the Metropolitan Board of Works memorialised the House of Commons, and a Committee was appointed which sat for the first time on 30 Ap., 1861. An Act for carrying cut the scheme was passed on 7 Aug., 1862, and the work was commenced in Nov. of the same year. The northern (Victoria) embankment, which terminated at Whitehall Stairs, was opened (as far as the footway went) to the public on 30 July, 1868.

Victoria Park took a shorter time to mature. The first mention of it, that I can find, is in the *Times* of March, 1839 : "The inhabitants of St. Mary, Whitechapel, are bestirring themselves to obtain the formation of a Royal Park in their neighbourhood, and the Vestry of the parish are about to bring the matter before the public." And they did so with such good effect that an Act was passed on 21 June, 1841 (4 & 5 Vic., c. 27), "To enable Her Majesty's Commissioners of Works to complete the Contract for the Sale of York House, and to purchase certain lands for a Royal Park." York House was sold to the Duke of Sutherland, and with the whole, or part, of the purchase money, the Commissioners were to purchase certain lands or hereditaments containing about 290 acres, which "shall for ever, thereafter, be taken and be a Royal Park, by the name of 'Victoria Park.'" The Park was completed, and opened to the public, in 1845.

On Monday, 25 March, occurred a most daring robbery of gold dust valued at £4,600, which, at the time, created a great sensation. It seems that two boxes of gold dust were brought to this country from Mexico, in the Sea Gull Packet, consigned to the Brazilian Mining Co., and were landed at Falmouth. They were, subsequently, transshipped on board the City of Limerick steamer, which arrived at Dublin on Sunday afternoon. The boxes were not landed at the wharf until Monday morning, and, at noon on that day, the stranger who obtained possession of them drove up to the wharf in a cab which he had hired in the city. The letter which he presented to the wharfinger for the delivery of the boxes was in the same handwriting as one which the wharfinger had received from Falmouth, and which bore the postmark of that place, in the morning. It gave particular directions respecting the boxes, and that they were only to be delivered to a gentleman who would call in the course of the day, and present a letter in the same handwriting for their delivery. The person who obtained the boxes accurately described their contents, the marks on them, and the time they were landed at Falmouth. The wharfinger, as might be expected, was completely put off his guard by the ingenuity and cunning of the thief, and delivered them over to him.

On 3 April, two Jews, Ellis and Lewis Caspar, father and son, were brought up at Lambeth Street Police Station for being concerned in the robbery; afterwards, two other prisoners, Emanuel Moses and his daughter, Alice Abrahams, were arrested, and all were committed for trial, the Caspars for stealing the gold, the other two for feloniously receiving the same, well knowing it to be stolen. They were tried at the Central Criminal Court on 24 June, the trial lasting eight days. The jury found them all guilty, but recommended Alice Abrahams to mercy, believing that she acted under the advice and influence of her father. Judgment was not pronounced on them until 3 Feb., 1840, when the three male prisoners were sentenced to fourteen years' transportation, and the female to four months' hard labour. The Jewish community tried all their influence to get these sentences modified, but the convicts sailed for Sydney in the following October. The expenses of the prosecutor in connection with the trial amounted to £2,900!

CHAPTER IX.

Times, 25 Ap.—" The workmen engaged some time since in taking down an old public house adjoining St. Dunstan's Church, in Fleet St., discovered in one of the cellars the ancient stone statue of Queen Elizabeth, which formerly stood in the nave of the old church. The parochial authorities have resolved to place it on the east end of the church, fronting Fleet Street." An unfortunate position, for many raw, un-lettered Irishmen, or women, have mistaken it, owing to its environment, to be a statue of the Virgin Mary, and have devoutly crossed themselves, and said their " Aves."

About this time occurred a political complication which afforded great scope for gossip, and which showed that it was about time that the Queen was freed from her female *entourage*, and had the protective advice of a husband. On the 7th May, Lord Melbourne, having been beaten, by a small majority, on the Bill concerning the Suspension of the Con-stitution in Jamaica, resigned, and Sir Robert Peel was commissioned by the Queen to form a new Ministry. He did so, but, for valid reasons, he required the resignation, as was, and is, usual, of the ladies of the household. In order that there shall be no bias on this divergence of opinion between the Sovereign and her Minister, I quote a portion of Sir Robert Peel's speech in the House of Commons, on 13 May, taking it from the authorised version of *Hansard*. Sir Robert said that there was but one subject of disunion between himself and Her Majesty.

" The difficulty arose with respect to certain portions of
that part of the establishment which is filled by the Ladies
of the household. Sir, I think it infinitely better, on this
point—the one on which the difficulty arose—I think it infinitely better, after mature consideration—that I should not
enter—in the first instance, at least, nor unless invited by
the noble Lord (John Russell)—into any statement whatever
of impressions on my own mind with respect to what took
place—but that I should refer exclusively to the letters which
passed on the subject; because if I were to state, here, impressions of my own, I must detail verbal communications
that passed, where two parties only were present; and myself
one of the party, being alone in this House to offer explanations of what occurred. I approach, then, that point with
respect to which the difficulty, on this occasion, arose; and,
for the purpose of enabling the House to form a judgment
with respect to the nature of that difficulty, I shall confine
myself, altogether, to the written documents which passed on
the occasion, in which are conveyed the impressions on the
mind of Her Majesty, and the impressions on my own mind,
with regard to the purport and effect of the communications
which passed between Her Majesty and myself, in respect
to certain appointments in the household, which are held by
Ladies. Now, whatever blame may attach on account of
imperfect explanations, I am content to bear it; whatever
consequences may result from misconception, let them be
visited on me ; but, as to my intentions in regard to the Ladies
of the household, I must not only state them, but I must prove
them by most unequivocable testimony.

" On the Wednesday evening—that is, the day before I
saw Her Majesty on this particular point—I had an opportunity of conferring with all those whom I proposed to submit
to Her Majesty as Ministers. I saw them on Wednesday
night, at my own house, about ten o'clock. I then stated to
them—and there are four of them now present, who heard
the communication, and can give their evidence upon it—
I stated to them, and to the peers whom I have before named,
the course which I meant to pursue with respect to the house-

hold, and had very little considered the matter (I am speaking of the female part of it); I, really, scarcely knew of whom it consisted. I took the ' Red Book' into my hand, and saw there the different appointments of the household. I said to those who were intended to be my future colleagues, that, with respect to all the subordinate appointments—meaning every appointment, without exception, below the rank of a Lady of the Bedchamber—I should propose to Her Majesty no change whatever with respect to those. With respect to the superior classes, I stated, that those Ladies who held offices of that class, and who were immediate relatives of our political opponents, would, I took it for granted, relieve us from any difficulty by, at once, relinquishing their offices. But, I stated, at the same time, that I did think it of great importance, as conveying an indication of Her Majesty's entire support and confidence, that certain offices in the household, of the higher rank, if not voluntarily relinquished by the Ladies holding them, should be submitted to some change. Even with respect to the higher offices, namely, the Ladies of the Bedchamber, I did state, however, that there were some instances, in which, from the absence of any strong party, or political, connection, I thought it would be wholly unnecessary to propose a change. My noble and Right Hon. friends will confirm what I assert. This passed on the evening of Wednesday; and I mention it only in complete proof of my intentions, being perfectly willing, as I have before observed, to have transferred, exclusively to me, whatever blame may be attached to the imperfect explanation of my views.

" I saw Her Majesty on Thursday, and verbal communications took place on this subject. As I stated before, into the nature of those communications I shall not now enter in the slightest degree. I shall merely read the two letters which passed; one conveying the impressions of Her Majesty, and the other my own. The letter which I had the honour of receiving from Her Majesty is dated May the 10th, 1839. I received it at an early hour on Friday morning, and it is as follows :

" ' Buckingham Palace.—May 10, 1839.

" ' The Queen, having considered the proposal made
to her, yesterday, by Sir Robert Peel, to remove the Ladies
of her Bedchamber, cannot consent to adopt a course which
she conceives to be contrary to usage, and which is repugnant
to her feelings.'

" Immediately—that is, in two or three hours after having
received the letter from Her Majesty, I addressed to Her
Majesty a letter, of which this is a copy:

" ' Whitehall.—May 10, 1839.

" ' Sir Robert Peel presents his humble duty to your
Majesty, and has had the honour of receiving your Majesty's
note of this morning.

" ' In respectfully submitting to your Majesty's pleasure,
and humbly returning into your Majesty's hands the important
trust which your Majesty had graciously pleased to commit
to him, Sir Robert Peel trusts that your Majesty will permit
him to state to your Majesty his impression with respect to
the circumstances which have led to the termination of his
attempt to form an Administration for the conduct of your
Majesty's service.

" ' In the interview with which your Majesty honoured Sir
Robert Peel, yesterday morning, after he had submitted to
your Majesty the names of those whom he proposed to recommend to your Majesty for the principal executive appointments, he mentioned to your Majesty his earnest wish to be
enabled, with your Majesty's sanction, so to constitute your
Majesty's household, that your Majesty's confidential servants
might have the advantage of a public demonstration of your
Majesty's full support and confidence; and that, at the same
time, as far as possible, consistently with that demonstration,
each individual appointment in the household should be
entirely acceptable to your Majesty's personal feelings.

" ' On your Majesty's expressing a desire that the Earl
of Liverpool should hold an office in the household, Sir Robert
Peel requested your Majesty's permission at once to offer

to Lord Liverpool the office of Lord Steward, or any other which he might prefer.

"'Sir Robert Peel then observed, that he should have every wish to apply a similar principle to the chief appointments which are filled by the Ladies of your Majesty's household; upon which your Majesty was pleased to remark, that you must reserve the whole of those appointments, and that it was your Majesty's pleasure, that the whole should continue as at present, without any change.

"The Duke of Wellington, in the interview to which your Majesty subsequently admitted him, understood, also, that this was your Majesty's determination, and concurred with Sir Robert Peel in opinion that, considering the great difficulties of the present crisis, and the expediency of making every effort, in the first instance, to conduct the public business of the country with the aid of the present Parliament, it was essential to the success of the commission with which your Majesty had honoured Sir Robert Peel, that he should have that public proof of your Majesty's entire support and confidence, which would be afforded by the permission to make some changes in that part of your Majesty's household, which your Majesty resolved on maintaining entirely without change.

"Having had the opportunity, through your Majesty's gracious consideration, of reflecting upon this point, he humbly submits to your Majesty that he is reluctantly compelled, by a sense of public duty, and in interest of your Majesty's service, to adhere to the opinion which he ventured to express to your Majesty."

*   *   *   *   *

In a later portion of his speech, Sir Robert remarks:

"I, upon that very question of Ireland, should have begun in a minority of upwards of twenty members. A majority of twenty-two had decided in favour of the policy of the Irish Government. The chief members of the Irish Government, whose policy was so approved of, were the Marquis of Normanby and Lord Morpeth. By whom are the two chief offices in the household at this moment held? By the sister of Lord Morpeth, and the wife of Lord Normanby. Let me not, for a moment, be supposed to say a word not fraught with respect towards those two ladies, who cast a lustre on the society in which they move, less by their rank than their accomplishments and virtues ; but still, they stand in the situation of the nearest relatives of the two Members of the Government, whose policy was approved by this House, and disapproved by me. Now, I ask any man in the House, whether it is possible that I could, with propriety and honour, undertake the conduct of an Administration, and the manage- ment of Irish affairs in this House, consenting previously, as an express preliminary stipulation, that the two ladies I have named, together with all others, should be retained in their appointments about the court and person of the Sovereign? Sir, the policy of these things depends not upon precedent— not upon what has been done in former times ; it mainly depends upon a consideration of the present. The household has been allowed to assume a completely political character, and that on account of the nature of the appointments which have been made by Her Majesty's present Government. I do not complain of it—it may have been a wise policy to place in the chief offices of the household, ladies closely connected with the Members of the Administration ; but, re- member that this policy does seriously to the public em- barrassment of their successors, if ladies, being the nearest relatives of the retired Ministers, are to continue in their offices about the person of the Sovereign."

So Lord Melbourne returned to power.

The genial Caricaturist John Doyle, as there were no illus- trated comic papers in those days, illustrated this incident in his H. B. Sketches. No. 591 is " A Scene from the farce of *The Invincibles*, as lately performed in the Queen's Theatre " —in which the Duke of Wellington and Sir Robert Peel are being expelled at the point of the bayonet, by ladies clad as soldiers. Sir Robert says : " These Household Troops charge

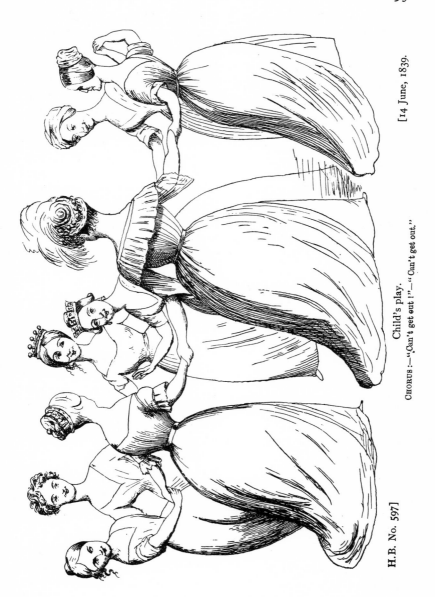

[14 June, 1839.

Child's play.

CHORUS:—"Can't get out!"—"Can't get out."

H.B. No. 597]

in a most disorderly manner, but they are too many for us."
While the Duke observes: "Our position is no longer ten-
able; draw off in good order, while I cover the retreat." No.
592 is "The Balance of Power. The figure proposed to
displace the old one of Justice at the top of Constitution Hill."
It shows a statue of the Queen, as Justice, holding a pair
of scales, in which "Private Friendship," typified by two
ladies of the household, weighs down "Public Service" full
of Ministers. I have here reproduced No. 597, "Child's Play,"
in which figure the Queen, the Duchess of Sutherland, the
Marchioness of Normanby, and other ladies of the household.
No. 599 is a "Curious instance of (Ministerial) 'Resuscitation,'
effected by distinguished members of the *Royal* Humane
Society." Lord Melbourne is lying on a couch, attended by
the Queen and ladies of the household. The Queen holds a
smelling bottle to his nose, and says: "Ah, there's a dear,
now do revive."

Whether it was owing to this affair, or not, I know not, but
at Ascot races this year the Queen was absolutely hissed at
by some one, or more persons—and the *Times* of 25 June
quotes from the *Morning Post* thus:

"At the last Ascot races, we have reason to believe that
the Duchess of Montrose and Lady Sarah Ingestre received
an intimation that Her Majesty was impressed with the
idea that they were among the persons who had hissed at
a moment when no sounds but those of applause, gratulation
and loyalty ought to have been heard. It was, we believe,
further intimated to the noble ladies we have mentioned, that
the Royal ear had been abused, to the effect already stated,
by Lady Lichfield. The ladies, who had reason to think
that they had been thus unjustly and ridiculously accused,
applied immediately to their supposed accuser, who denied
that she had made any such communication. On being urged
to give this denial in writing, she declined to do so without
first consulting her lord. But, on the application being renewed at a subsequent period, her ladyship, as we understand,
explicitly, and in writing, denied that she had given utterance

to the calumny in question. Here the matter stood, until, from some incidents connected with the late ball at Buckingham Palace, the two ladies, thus impeached, saw reason to believe that the erroneous impression communicated to Her Majesty at Ascot had not been entirely removed. It was an impression, however, which they could not permit to remain without employing every means of removing it ; and, accordingly, the Duchess of Montrose went to Buckingham Palace, and requested an audience of Her Majesty. After waiting for a considerable period (two hours, as we have been informed), her Grace was informed by the Earl of Uxbridge, that she could not be admitted to an audience, as none but Peers and Peeresses in their own right could demand that privilege. Her Grace then insisted upon Lord Uxbridge taking down in writing what she had to say, and promising her that the communication should immediately be laid before Her Majesty. In this state, we believe, the matter remains, substantially, at the present moment, although it has taken a new form, the Duke of Montrose having, we understand, thought it necessary to open a correspondence upon the subject with Lord Melbourne."

There was only a partial denial given to the above, which appeared in the *Times* of 5 July. "We are authorised to give the most positive denial to a report which has been inserted in most of the public papers, that the Countess of Lichfield informed the Queen that the Duchess of Montrose and Lady Sarah Ingestre hissed Her Majesty on the racecourse at Ascot. Lady Lichfield never insinuated, or countenanced any such report, and there could have been no foundation for so unjust an accusation."

Melbourne, in Australia (named, of course, after the Premier), was founded 1 June, 1837, and I mention the fact to shew the prosperity of the infant city—for in two years' time, on this its second anniversary, certain lots of land had advanced in price from £7 to £600, and from £27 to £930.

I cannot help chronicling an amusing story anent Sunday trading. For some time the parish authorities of Islington had been rigidly prosecuting shopkeepers for keeping open their shops on Sunday, for the sale of their goods, such not being "a work of necessity, or mercy," and numerous convictions were recorded. Most of the persons convicted were poor, and with large families, who sold tobacco, fruit, cakes and sweets, in a very humble way of business, and considerable discontent and indignation was manifested in the parish in consequence of such prosecutions; the outcry was raised that there was one law for the rich and another for the poor, and a party that strongly opposed the proceedings on the part of the parish, resolved to try the legality and justice of the question, by instituting proceedings against the vicar's coachman, for "exercising his worldly calling on the Sabbath day," by driving his reverend master to church, that not being a work of necessity, or mercy, as the reverend gentleman was able both to walk and preach on the same day. For this purpose a party proceeded to the neighbourhood of the vicar's stables one Sunday, and watched the proceedings of the coachman, whom they saw harness his horses, put them to the carriage, go to the vicar's house, take him up, and drive him to church, where he entered the pulpit, and preached his sermon. One day, the following week, they attended Hatton Garden Police Office and applied to Mr. Benett for a summons against the coachman. The magistrate, on hearing the nature of the application, told them it was a doubtful case, and the clerk suggested that if they laid their information the magistrate might receive it, and decide on the legal merits of the case. This was done, the summons was granted, and a day appointed for hearing the case.

This took place on June 14, when John Wells, coachman to the vicar of Islington, appeared to answer the complaint of Frederick Hill, a tobacconist, for exercising his worldly calling on the Sabbath day.

John Hanbury, grocer, of 3, Pulteney Street, being sworn, stated that, on Sunday, the 9th inst., about 1 o'clock, he saw the defendant, who is coachman to the vicar of Islington, drive his coach to the Church of St. Mary, Islington, where he took up the vicar and his lady, and drove them to their residence in Barnsbury Park.

Mr. Benett: Are you sure it was the vicar?

Witness: I heard him preach.

John Jones, of Felix Terrace, Islington, corroborated this evidence.

Mr. Benett said, that the Act of Parliament laid down that no tradesman, labourer, or other person shall exercise his worldly calling on the Lord's day, it not being a work of necessity or charity. He would ask whether it was not a work of necessity for the vicar to proceed to church to preach. A dissenter might say it was not a work of necessity. The coachman was not an artificer who was paid by the hour or the day, but he was engaged by the year, or the quarter, and was not to be viewed in the light of a grocer, or tradesman, who opened his shop for the sale of his goods on the Sabbath day. After explaining the law upon the subject, he said that he was of opinion that the defendant driving the vicar to church on Sundays, to perform his religious duties, was an act of necessity, and did not come within the meaning of the law, and he dismissed the case.

The clergy did not seem to be much in favour with their flocks, for I read in the *Annual Register*, 1 Aug., of "A NEW WAY OF PAYING CHURCH RATES.—Mr. Osborne, a dissenter, of Tewkesbury, having declined to pay Church Rates, declaring that he could not conscientiously do so, a sergeant and two officers of the police went to his house for the purpose of levying under a distress warrant to the amount due from him. The officers were asked to sit down, which they did, and Mr. Osborne went into his garden, procured a hive of bees, and threw it into the middle of the chamber. The officers were, of course, obliged to retreat, but they secured enough of the property to pay the rate, and the costs of the levy, besides which, they obtained a warrant against Mr. Osborne, who would, most likely, pay dearly for his new and *conscientious* method of settling Church Rate accounts."

7*

CHAPTER X.

The Eglinton Tournament—Sale of Armour, &c.—The Queen of Beauty and her Cook—Newspapers and their Sales.

THE Earl of Eglinton had a " bee in his bonnet," which was none other than reviving the tournaments of the Age of Chivalry, with real armour, horses and properties; and he inoculated with his craze most of the young aristocracy, and induced them to join him in carrying it out. The preliminary rehearsals took place in the grounds of the Eyre Arms Tavern, Kilburn. The last of these came off on 13 July, in the presence of some 6,000 spectators, mostly composed of the aristocracy. The following is a portion of the account which appeared in the *Times* of 15 July :

· " At 4 o'clock the business of the day commenced. There might be seen men in complete steel, riding with light lances at the ring, attacking the ' quintain,' and manœuvering their steeds in every variety of capricole. Indeed, the show of horses was one of the best parts of the sight. Trumpeters were calling the jousters to horse, and the wooden figure, encased in iron panoply, was prepared for the attack. A succession of chevaliers, *sans peur et sans reproche*, rode at their hardy and unflinching antagonist, who was propelled to the combat by the strength of several stout serving-men, in the costume of the olden time, and made his helmet and breastplate rattle beneath their strokes, but the wooden

> . . . . . . Knight
> Was mickle of might,
> And stiff in Stower did stand,

grinning defiance through the barred aventaile of his head-piece. It was a sight that might have roused the spirit of old Froissart, or the ghost of Hotspur. The Knight had, certainly, no easy task to perform ; the weight of armour was rather heavier than the usual trappings of a modern dandy, and the heat of the sun appeared to be baking the bones of some of the competitors. Be this as it may, there was no flinching. The last part of the tournament consisted of the Knights tilting at each other. The Earl of Eglinton, in a splendid suit of brass armour, with *garde de reins* of plated chain mail, and bearing on his casque a plume of ostrich feathers, was assailed by Lord Cranstoun, in a suit of polished steel, which covered him from top to toe, the steel shoes, or sollarets, being of the immense square-toed fashion of the time of Henry VIII. The lances of these two champions were repeatedly shivered in the attack, but neither was unhorsed ; fresh lances were supplied by the esquires, and the sport grew ' fast and furious.' Lord Glenlyon and another knight, whose armour prevented him from being recognized, next tilted at each other, but their horses were not sufficiently trained to render the combat as it ought to have been, and swerved continually from the barrier. It was nearly eight o'clock before the whole of the sports were concluded and the company withdrawn. We believe no accident happened, though several gentlemen who essayed to ' witch the world with noble horsemanship ' were thrown, amidst the laughter of the spectators. Captain Maynard proved himself a superior rider, by the splendid style at which he leaped his horse, at speed, repeatedly over the barrier, and the admirable manner in which he performed the modern lance exercise, and made a very beautiful charger curvet round and round his lance placed upright on the ground. The whole of the arrangements were under the direction of Mr. Pratt, to whose discretion the ordering of the tilting, the armour and arming, and all the appliances for the tournament have been entrusted.

" Considering that the business of Saturday was but a rehearsal, and, putting entirely out of the question the folly, or wisdom, of the whole thing, it must be acknowledged that

it has been well got up.   Some of the heralds' and pursuivants'
costumes are very splendid.   There is an immense store of
armour of all sorts, pennons, lances, trappings, and all the
details of the wars of the middle ages.   The display in Scotland will, certainly, be a gorgeous pageant, and a most extraordinary, if not most rational, piece of pastime."

The three days' jousting and hospitality at Eglinton Castle,
Ayrshire, which commenced on the 28th, and ended on the
30th, August, are said to have cost the Earl of Eglinton the
sum of £40,000.   He invited the flower of the aristocracy to
attend—all the armour was choice and old, and the costumes
were splendid.   Every accessory was perfect in its way ; and
so it should have been, for it was two years in preparation.
The Marquis of Londonderry was King of the Tourney, and
Lady Seymour, a grand-daughter of *the* Sheridan, was the
" Queen of Love and Beauty."

By the evening of the 27th, Eglinton Castle was not only
filled from cellar to garret, but the surrounding towns and
villages were crammed full, and people had to rough it.
Accommodation for man, or beast, rose from 500 to 1,000
per cent. ; houses in the neighbourhood, according to their
dimensions, were let from £10 to £30 for the time ; and
single beds, in the second best apartments of a weaver's cabin,
fetched from 10/- to 20/- a night, while the master and mistress
of the household, with their little ones, coiled themselves up in
any out of the way corner, as best they might.   Stables, byres,
and sheds were in requisition for the horses, and, with every
available atom of space of this description, it was found all
too little, as people flocked from all parts of the country.

The invitation given by the Earl was universal.   Those
who applied for tickets of admission to the stands were requested to appear in ancient costume, fancy dresses, or
uniforms, and farmers and others were asked to appear in
bonnets and kilts, and many—very many—did so ;   but
although all the bonnet makers in Kilmarnock, and all the
plaid manufacturers in Scotland, had been employed from the
time of the announcement, onwards, they could not provide

for the wants of the immense crowd, and many had to go in their ordinary dress.

Unfortunately, on the opening day, the weather utterly spoilt the show. Before one o'clock, the rain commenced, and continued, with very little intermission, until the evening. This, necessarily, made it very uncomfortable for all, especially the spectators. Many thousands left the field, and the enjoyment of those who remained was, in a great measure, destroyed. The Grand Stand, alone, was covered in, and neither plaid, umbrella, nor great-coat could prevail against a deluge so heavy and unintermitting; thousands were thoroughly drenched to the skin; but the mass only squeezed the closer together, and the excitement of the moment overcame all external annoyances, although the men became sodden, and the finery of the ladies sadly bedraggled.

It had been arranged that the procession should start from the Castle at one o'clock, but the state of the weather was so unfavourable, that it did not issue forth till about half-past two, and the weather compelled some modifications; for instance, the Queen of Beauty should have shown herself " in a rich costume, on a horse richly caparisoned, a silk canopy borne over her by attendants in costume," but both she, and her attendant ladies, who were also to have been on horseback, did not so appear, but were in closed carriages, whilst their beautifully caparisoned palfreys—riderless—were led by their pages.

There were 15 Knights, besides the " Lord of the Tournament," the Earl of Eglinton, and much as I should like to give their description and following, I must refrain, merely giving two as a sample :—

" Retainers of the Lord of the Tournament.
Halberdiers of the Lord, in Liveries of his Colours.

Man at Arms in half armour.	The GONFALON, Borne by a Man at Arms.	Man at Arms in half armour.

THE LORD OF THE TOURNAMENT.
EARL OF EGLINGTON.

Groom.	In a suit of Gilt Armour, richly chased, on a barded Charger—caparisons, &c., of blue and gold.	Groom.

THE BANNER.

Borne by LORD A. SEYMOUR

Esquire.	Esquire.	Esquire.
G. DUNDAS.	F. CAVENDISH, Esq.	G. M'DONAL, Esq.

Retainers of the Lord, as before.

Halberdiers of the Knight of the Griffin,
in Liveries of his Colours.

Man at Arms	THE GONFALON,	Man at Arms
in half armour.	Borne by a man at Arms.	in half armour.

The Knight of the Griffin.

THE EARL OF CRAVEN,

Groom.	In a suit of engraved Milanese Armour	Groom.
	inlaid with gold, on a barded charger.	
	Caparisons, &c., of Scarlet, White and Gold.	

Esquire.	THE BANNER,	Esquire.
The HON. F. CRAVEN.	Borne by a man at Arms in	The HON. F. MACDONALD.
	Half Armour.	
	Retainers——"	

The other Knights were:—*The Knight of the Dragon,* MARQUIS OF WATERFORD; *Knight of the Black Lion,* VISCOUNT ALFORD; *Knight of Gael,* VISCOUNT GLEN-LYON; *Knight of the Dolphin,* EARL OF CASSILIS; *Knight of the Crane,* LORD CRANSTOUN; *Knight of the Ram,* HON. CAPT. GAGE; *The Black Knight,* JOHN CAMPBELL, ESQ., of Saddell; *Knight of the Swan,* HON. MR. JERNINGHAM; *Knight of the Golden Lion,* CAPT. J. O. FAIRLIE; *Knight of the White Rose,* CHARLES LAMB, ESQ.; *Knight of the Stag's Head,* CAPT. BERESFORD; *The Knight of the Border,* SIR F. JOHNSTONE; *Knight of the Burning Tower,* SIR F. HOPKINS; *The Knight of the Red Rose,* R. J. LECHMERE, ESQ.; *Knight of the Lion's Paw,* CECIL BOOTHBY, ESQ.

There were, besides, Knights Visitors, Swordsmen, Bowmen, the Seneschal of the Castle, Marshals and Deputy Marshals, Chamberlains of the household, servitors of the Castle, a Herald and two Pursuivants, a Judge of Peace, and a Jester—besides a horde of small fry.

The first tilt was between the Knights of the Swan and the Red Rose, but it was uninteresting, the Knights passing each other twice, without touching, and, on the third course, the Knight of the Swan lost his lance.

Then came the tilt of the day, when the Earl of Eglinton met the Marquis of Waterford.   The latter was particularly remarked, as the splendour of his brazen armour, the beauty of his charger, and his superior skill in the management of the animal, as well as in the bearing of his lance, attracted general observation.   But, alas! victory was not to be his, for, in the first tilt, the Earl of Eglinton shivered his lance on his opponent's shield, and was duly cheered by all.   In the second, both Knights missed; but, in the third, the Earl again broke his lance on his opponent's armour; at which there was renewed applause from the multitude ; and, amidst the cheering and music, the noble Earl rode up to the Grand Stand, and bowed to the Queen of Beauty.

There were three more tilts, and a combat of two-handed swords, which finished the outdoor amusements of the day, and, when the deluged guests found their way to the Banqueting Hall, they found that, and its sister tent, the Ballroom, utterly untenantable through the rain ; so they had to improvise a meal within the Castle, and the Ball was postponed.

Next day was wild with wind and rain, and nothing could be attempted out of doors, as the armour was all wet and rusty, and every article of dress that had been worn the preceding day completely soaked through, and the Dining Hall and the Great Pavilion required a thorough drying. The former was given up to the cleansing of armour, etc., and, in the latter, there were various tilting matches on foot, the combatants being clothed in armour.   There was also fencing, both with sticks and broadsword, among the performers being Prince Louis Bonaparte, afterwards Napoleon III.   His opponent with the singlesticks was a very young gentleman, Mr. Charteris, and the Prince came off second best in the encounter, as he did, afterwards, in some bouts with broadswords with Mr. Charles Lamb.   Luckily, in this latter contest, both fought in complete mail, with visors down, for had it not been so, and had the combat been for life or death, the Prince would have had no chance with his opponent.

On the third day the weather was fine, and the procession

was a success. There was tilting between eight couples of Knights, and tilting at the ring, and the tourney wound up with the Knights being halved, and started from either end of the lists, striking at each other with their swords in passing. Only one or two cuts were given, but the Marquis of Waterford and Lord Alford fought seriously, and in right good earnest, until stopped by the Knight Marshal, Sir Charles Lamb.

In the evening, a banquet was given to 300 guests; and, afterwards, a ball, in which 1,000 participated. As the weather, next day, was so especially stormy, the party broke up, and the experimental revival has never again been attempted, except a Tourney on a much smaller scale, which was held on 31 Oct., 1839, at Irvine, by a party from Eglinton Castle; but this only lasted one day.

I regret that I have been unable to find any authentic engravings of this celebrated tournament, but I reproduce a semi-comic contemporaneous etching from the *Satirical Prints, Brit. Mus.*

The armour and arms used in this tournament were shown in Feb., 1840, at the Gallery of Ancient Armour in Grosvenor Street, and they were subsequently sold by Auction on July 17 and 18 of that year. They fetched ridiculously low prices, as the following example will show :

A suit of polished steel *cap à pied* armour, richly engraved and gilt, being the armour prepared for the Knight of the Lion's Paw, with tilting shield, lance, plume and crest *en suite*, 32 guineas.

The emblazoned banner and shield of the Knight of the Burning Tower, with the suit of polished steel, *cap-à-pied* armour, with skirt of chain mail, 35 guineas.

The splendid suit of armour worn by the Knight of the Ram, with crest and plume, 24 guineas.

The magnificent suit of polished steel armour, worn by the Knight of the Swan, with the emblazoned tilting apparel, horse armour, and caparison, tilting saddle, lances to correspond, and a splendid modelled horse of life size, carved and painted after nature, £36.

The Eglinton Tournament.

The armour worn as a Knight Visitor by Prince Louis Napoleon, with an elaborate visored headpiece, and other appurtenances complete, 9 guineas.

The two beautifully-fashioned *mêlée* swords, used in the combat between Prince Louis and the Knight of the White Rose, seven shillings.

On the second day's sale some of the suits fetched better prices. The splendid suit of fluted mail, worn by the Marquis of Waterford, was the gem of the collection. It was in the finest preservation, elaborately worked, and beautifully bright. It was considered one of the most perfect and complete suits in existence, and was bought at 240 guineas for the Tower of London. Lord Alford's and Mr. Lechmere's suits both went for 100 guineas each.

The spirit of the Tournament seems even to have affected the ladies, for we read of a passage of arms between Lady Seymour, the Queen of Beauty, and Lady Shuckburgh. It originally appeared in the *Observer* of 8 Feb., 1840, but was copied into the *Times* and other papers.

(Copy 1). "Lady Seymour presents her compliments to Lady Shuckburgh, and would be obliged to her for the character of Mary Stedman, who states that she has lived twelve months, and still is, in Lady Shuckburgh's establish- ment. Can Mary Stedman cook plain dishes well? make bread? and is she honest, good tempered, sober, willing and cleanly? Lady Seymour would also like to know the reason why she leaves Lady Shuckburgh's service. Direct, under cover, to Lord Seymour, Maiden Bradley."

(Copy 2.) "Lady Shuckburgh presents her compliments to Lady Seymour. Her Ladyship's note, dated Oct. 28, only reached her yesterday, Nov. 3. Lady Shuckburgh was un- acquainted with the name of the kitchenmaid, until mentioned by Lady Seymour, as it is her custom neither to apply for, or give characters to any of the under servants, this being always done by the housekeeper, Mrs. Couch, and this was well known to the young woman ; therefore Lady Shuck-

burgh is surprised at her referring any lady to her for a character. Lady Shuckburgh having a professed cook, as well as a
housekeeper, in her establishment, it is not very likely she, herself, should know anything about the ability or merits of the
under-servants; therefore she is unable to answer Lady
Seymour's note. Lady Shuckburgh cannot imagine Mary
Stedman to be capable of cooking for any, except the servants'
hall table. Nov. 4, Pavilion, Hans Place."

(Copy 3.) "Lady Seymour presents her compliments to
Lady Shuckburgh, and begs she will order her housekeeper,
Mrs. Pouch, to send the girl's character without delay; otherwise, another young woman will be sought for elsewhere, as
Lady Seymour's children cannot remain without their dinners,
because Lady Shuckburgh, keeping 'a proffessed cook and a
housekeeper,' thinks a knowledge of the details of her establishment beneath her notice. Lady Seymour understood from
Stedman that, in addition to her other talents, she was actually
capable of dressing food for the little Shuckburghs to partake
of, when hungry."

[To this note was appended a clever pen-and-ink vignette,
by the Queen of Beauty, representing the three little Shuckburghs, with large, turnip-looking heads and cauliflower wigs,
sitting at a round table, and voraciously scrambling for mutton
chops, dressed by Mary Stedman, who is seen looking on with
supreme satisfaction, while Lady Shuckburgh appears in the
distance, in evident dismay.]

(Copy 4.) "MADAM,—Lady Shuckburgh has directed me
to acquaint you that she declines answering your note, the
vulgarity of which is beneath contempt; and, although it
may be the characteristic of the Sheridans to be vulgar, coarse
and witty, it is not that of 'a lady,' unless she happens to
be born in a garret and bred in a kitchen. Mary Stedman
informs me that your Ladyship does not keep either a cook,
or a housekeeper, and that you only require a girl who can
cook a mutton chop. If so, I apprehend that Mary Stedman,

or any other scullion, will be found fully equal to cook for, or manage the establishment of, the Queen of Beauty.

"I am, your Ladyship's etc.—ELIZABETH COUCH (not Pouch.)"

Even in those days, Newspapers were somewhat given to vaunt themselves as to their circulation, but they had no need to call in the aid of the chartered accountant, as they could get their facts from the number of stamps supplied— the stamp then being of the value of three halfpence per newspaper, an impost which was not removed until 15 June, 1855, by the Act 18 and 19 Vict., c. 27.   The *Times* of 5 Aug., 1839, gives us

"A return of the number of Newspaper Stamps issued to the several Newspapers in London, from 1 Ap. to 29 June, 1839, inclusive ; specifying each Newspaper by name, and the number of Stamps issued each month during that period to each Newspaper."

	April.	May.	June.
Morning Chronicle	180,000	210,000	140,000
Morning Post	85,000	90,000	80,000
Morning Herald	140,000	175,000	140,000
Times	330,000	330,000	430,000
Courier	29,000	33,000	27,000
Globe	72,000	90,000	72,000
Standard	83,000	80,000	101,000
Sun	111,000	105,000	105,000
Evening Chronicle	30,000	20,000	10,000
Evening Mail	25,000	50,000	35,000
St. James's Chronicle	52,000	58,000	66,000

CHAPTER XI.

The Chartists—Their going to church—Dissolution of the Convention—Approaching marriage of the Queen—The Queen and lunatics—Raid on a Gaming House—Act of Penance.

THIS year Chartism was rampant and very militant. On 1 April there were riots at Devizes, on 3 May, seven men were arrested at Manchester for drilling, and, on the 25th of that month a great meeting was held on Kersall Moor, four miles from Manchester. On 4th July there were very serious riots at Birmingham, and again on the 15th. On the same date between 3,000 and 4,000 Chartists met on Clerkenwell Green to condemn the action of the authorities at Birmingham, and, towards the end of the month, numerous meetings were held in the North of England, and there were riots at Newcastle and Stockport. In August there was great unrest in the North, and some trials took place at Birmingham and Manchester for rioting and sedition.

A new, and somewhat unexpected method of agitation, was, about this time, adopted by the Chartists. They betook themselves, suddenly, to attendance in a body at public worship, taking early possession on the Sundays of the various cathedrals and parish churches, to the exclusion of the more regular attendants. On the afternoon of Sunday, 11 Aug., a party of them, about 500 in number, met together in West Smithfield, and walked in procession to St. Paul's Cathedral. On arriving there, many of them refused to take off their hats; but, after some remonstrance from the Vergers, they submitted. The majority of them wore a little piece of red ribbon in their button holes, and conducted themselves quite peaceably. On the Sunday following, their brethren at Nor-

wich pursued a similar course at the Cathedral of that city,
which was crowded almost to suffocation.   The Bishop, who
preached, took the opportunity to deliver an impressive remonstrance on the folly and danger of their proceedings.   The
Chartists behaved well in the Cathedral ; but, at St. Stephen's
Church in the evening, they made a disturbance.   The Chartists at Manchester, following the advice of Feargus O'Connor,
attended the Old Church (now the Cathedral) in great numbers.   The authorities, having been previously advised of their
intention, had the military in readiness to act, should the
Chartists behave in a disorderly manner : but they conducted
themselves with great decorum.   It is said that, previous to
Divine Service, they handed the clergyman a Chartist text
to preach from, but he selected as his text, " My house is
the house of prayer, but ye have made it a den of thieves " ;
on announcing which, the Chartists rose, and quitted the
church.   The same tactics were followed in the principal
towns all over the country, but, either from the success of
them not being very apparent, or from the distastefulness of
the method employed, the practice was not followed up for
long—nor with any great regularity.

On the 14th Sep. the Chartist National Convention was
dissolved ; and, on the 20th Feargus O'Connor was arrested
for sedition, on a Judge's Warrant, at Manchester, and things
were fairly quiet during the remainder of the year, with the
exception of a serious Chartist riot, on 4 Nov., at Newport, in
Monmouthshire, where many rioters were killed.

We have seen how, in the beginning of the year, the *Sun*
had prophesied the marriage of the Queen and Prince Albert,
for which it was duly pooh-poohed by the *Times*—but on
22 Aug., the *Morning Post* had the dreadful temerity to announce the same—and the *Court Circular* of 11 Oct. tells
us, that " The Hereditary Prince (Ernest) and Prince Albert
of Saxe-Coburg-Gotha, landed at the Tower, at 4 o'clock
yesterday afternoon, from the Continent.   Their Serene High-
nesses were conveyed in two of the Royal landaus to the
Royal Mews at Pimlico, and, shortly afterwards, left town

with their suite in two carriages and four, for Windsor Castle, on a visit to the Queen."

On the 14th Oct., the Queen informed Lord Melbourne of her intention to marry Prince Albert, which met with the Premier's warm approbation. Next day she told the Prince that she wished to marry him. He had been out early, with his brother, hunting, but returned at twelve, and half-an-hour afterwards, the Queen sent for him, and he found her alone in her room. That it was a love match on both sides is well known, and, until the untimely death of the Prince Consort, they were models of conjugal love and felicity.

On 14 Nov. the Prince and his brother left Windsor—and departed for the Continent, via Dover; and, at a Privy Council held at Buckingham Palace on 23rd of that month, the Queen communicated her intention of marriage. The declaration was as follows:

" I have caused you to be summoned at the present time, in order that I may acquaint you with my resolution in a matter which deeply concerns the welfare of my people, and the happiness of my future life.

" It is my intention to ally myself in marriage with the Prince Albert of Saxe-Coburg and Gotha. Deeply impressed with the solemnity of the engagement which I am about to contract, I have not come to this decision without mature consideration, nor without feeling a strong assurance that, with the blessing of Almighty God, it will at once secure my domestic felicity, and serve the interests of my country.

" I have thought fit to make this resolution known to you, at the earliest period, in order that you may be fully apprised of a matter so highly important to me and to my Kingdom, and which, I persuade myself, will be most acceptable to all my loving subjects."

Upon this announcement, all the Privy Councillors present made it their humble request that Her Majesty's most gracious declaration to them might be made public; which Her Majesty was pleased to order accordingly.

The Queen suffered severely from lunatics. In June a man got into the gardens of Buckingham Palace; and, when arrested, declared he had come there for the sole purpose of killing Her Majesty, and was duly committed to Tothill Bridewell. Within a day or two of his release, in the middle of October, he went to Windsor and broke three or four panes of glass in the Castle. He was afterwards apprehended, but what became of him, I do not know; in all probability he was sent to a lunatic asylum.

In the paper which gives the account of the above, I read, " James Bryan, the Queen's Scotch suitor, was in Windsor the whole of yesterday (Sunday, 13 Oct.). In the morning, he was waiting, for a considerable period, at the door of St. George's Chapel, leading to the Cloisters, to have a view of the Queen, as Her Majesty and the two Princes of Saxe-Coburg, and the Duchess of Kent left the Chapel. In the afternoon, he walked on the Terrace, and conducted himself in his usual manner, very respectfully bowing to the Queen, as Her Majesty passed him on the New Terrace."—By the above, he must have been well known.

On 29 Nov., a respectably-dressed man got over the high iron gates leading to the Castle, a place at which there were no sentries, and walked across the Park, to the grand entrance to the Castle. Upon seeing the porter in attendance at the lodge, he said : " I demand entrance into the Castle as King of England "; to which the porter replied : " Very well, your Majesty, but be pleased to wait until I get my hat," and then taking him to the Castle, handed him over to the police. He turned out to be a man named Stockledge, who was partner in an extensive wholesale business in Manchester. He had been in two lunatic asylums, and when questioned by the Mayor of Windsor, as to the object of his visit, said that : " he was like all other men who wanted wives—he was looking after one," evidently alluding to Her Majesty. On being further questioned, he said " he was the King of England, and was impelled by the Spirit." He afterwards said that " an unknown power had done it," and that " it was the Spirit which helped him over the gates." Of course he *was* mad.

There was yet another fool this year, but, this time, he was not a maniac—only a Post Office Clerk, who wanted to have an interview with Her Majesty.   On the afternoon of the 8th Dec., a carriage and four drove up to Windsor Castle, and, from it, alighted a personage wearing a foraging cap, a fur boa round his neck, and fur gloves, who announced himself as the bearer of important despatches which he must deliver into the Queen's own hands.   This, of course, was not complied with, and as he would not part with the documents, he was handed over to the police, and taken to the station, where he made a sturdy resistance when they were taken from him.   He turned out to be a junior clerk in the Foreign Post Office, named William Saunders, who, being on duty when the Foreign Mails arrived, found some letters and papers addressed to the Queen, and put them into his pocket with the intention of delivering them himself.   He was suspended from his duties, but I do not know his ultimate fate.

Gambling houses were still in existence, although the Police Act of this year (2 & 3 Vict., c. 47, s. 48) gave the police great and additional power towards suppressing them.   Here is a sample raid as reported in the *Observer* of 15 Dec.:

"Superintendent Baker, C, succeeded on Saturday night week, in breaking his way into a gambling house, 60 Jermyn Street (commonly called the Cottage), and some persons, therein found, were fined, on Monday, at Marlborough Street Office.   In all, seven persons were captured, of whom, two were connected with the management of the gambling house; the others were gentlemen players.   They were taken to the Station house in Vine Street; and, as we know it to be the anxious desire of the police authorities to suppress the nuisance of gaming houses, we feel that we are but lending our humble aid towards effecting that object in now publishing the real names of those gentlemen who were captured, and who passed themselves off to the police and the magistrate as being 'Jones,' 'Smith,' and other conventional misnomers. (Here follow the names.)   Our Correspondent has told us of a certain noble lord, who was running here and there, on the

8*

night of the capture of his friends, striving, in the first instance, to get them bailed out, and, failing in that, to provide for them creature comforts in their cells. We cannot avoid mentioning one or two little incidents connected with this affair. The admission of spirits to prisoners in a station house is strictly forbidden, but, on this occasion, their friends outside succeeded in introducing eight soda water bottles filled with excellent pale brandy, so regularly corked and wired, as to deceive even the sharp eyes of the Inspector.

"Next day (Sunday), at 12 o'clock, they were bailed out, but, on the following morning at Marlborough Street Office, a sad mishap had all but blown up the misnomers ; for, when the name of 'Jones' was called from the police sheet, the gentleman who had honoured that name by assuming it, quite forgot his condescension, until one of his companions in trouble nudged him in the side, saying, 'D——n it, that's you.' By the way, the croupier escaped through the skylight, with the bank, amounting, it is supposed, to, at least, £500. He, and a boy who escaped with him, had but a minute or two the start of the police. As it was, the croupier met with a most severe accident, having cut his thigh so deeply as to cause a most serious hemorrhage. The gutter was flooded with his blood."

I wind up the year by chronicling an event which, I fancy, will never occur again, one of the most singular circumstances connected with it being, that the penitent was a Jewess. It occurs in a letter in the *Times* of 19 Dec. :

"ACT OF PENANCE, ST. JOHN'S, CLERKENWELL.

"Sir.—Understanding that many stories are afloat concerning the above act, performed on Sunday last (15 Dec.) by a young woman of the Jewish persuasion, named Deborah Cohen, I thought the particulars might be acceptable. This affair appears to have arisen from some family quarrel, the action in the Ecclesiastical Court, having been brought against her by her brother, for having made use to her sister-in-law, Rosetta Cohen, of a term contrary as well to this part of our

laws, as to the usages of society. To avoid expenses she
had no means to meet, and the consequences thereof, her
solicitor advised her to admit her fault, and abide the award
of the Court. This having got wind, the unpretending church
of St. John's was beset, early on Sunday last, by great crowds,
amongst whom it required great exertion of the parish officers
and the police to preserve a proper decorum. The crowds
were, however, disappointed in seeing this young woman
exposed in the open church, with the covering of a white
sheet, etc., the order from the Ecclesiastical Court only having
enjoined her to appear in the vestry room of this church, on
Sunday morning last, after service and a sermon, and before
the minister, churchwardens, and five or six of the plaintiff's
friends (some of whom attended), to recite, after the minister,
her regret, etc., in the words laid down in the order. This
was carried into effect, accordingly, the crowds in the church
and St. John's Square remaining long after the ceremony
had been performed, and the parties had left the vestry.

" W."

CHAPTER XII.

THE most important event in the beginning of this year was
the inauguration of the Penny Post on Jan. 10. At the end
of 1839, an uniform postage rate of 4d. per letter was tried
on Dec. 5, which was so successful that the present penny
postage was established, one feature of which, the prepayment
of letters, was much appreciated by the public. The number
of letters despatched by the Mails from the Metropolis, on
the 10th, was much greater than was expected, amounting to
112,000, the daily average for January, 1839, having been
about 30,000 only. Out of the 112,000 letters there were
only 13,000 or 14,000 unpaid, and this was probably owing
to the fact that people could not get out of their old habits
all at once.

The Postage Stamps, however, were not ready, for we read
in the *Times* of 17 Jan.: "The construction of the stamps
is advancing with all speed, the several artists to whom they
are intrusted being actively engaged upon them. In the
stamp for letter paper and the adhesive stamp, a profile of
the Queen is the principal ornament. The letter paper stamp
is being engraved by Mr. Wyon, R.A., medallist to the Mint.
Charles Heath is engraving the drawing taken from Wyon's
City medal, by H. Corbould, intended for the adhesive stamp.
W. Mulready, R.A., has furnished the design for the cover
and envelope, which is in the hands of John Thompson for
engraving."

And, now, until the Queen was married, all the talk was of that event. First of all Prince Albert must be made a naturalised Englishman, and a bill to that effect was read for the third time in the House of Lords on 21 Jan., in the Commons on the 22nd, and received the Royal Assent on the 24th.* On the 23rd he was invested with the Order of the Garter at Gotha. The second reading of the Act for his naturalization was heard in the House of Lords on the 27th, but owing to some dispute as to the question of his precedence, it was adjourned until the 31st, when it was read, and on 3 Feb. it was read a third time, and it received the Royal Assent on 7 Feb. But there was another thing yet to be done, which was to supply His Serene Highness with Funds, and on Jan. 22 Lord John Russell proposed the sum of £50,000 per annum. The discussion thereon was adjourned until the 24th, and re-adjourned until the 27th, when Mr. Hume moved a reduction to £21,000, which was lost by a majority of 267. Col. Sibthorp then proposed a sum of £30,000, which was agreed to, and the Act received the Royal Assent on 7 Feb.

The feeling of the country on the subject of the Royal Marriage is, to my thinking, very fairly summarised in a leading article in the *Times* of 10 Feb., portions of which I transcribe : " It has followed from this policy,† that an English monarch should, *cœteris paribus*, rather avoid than court an alliance with one of the first-rate powers of Europe, but should prefer security to aggrandizement, satisfied with a consort selected from a less prominent, and, therefore, less exposed, position. If there be safety, therefore, in comparative weakness and insignificance, we know not that, on such a ground, any other princely house throughout Europe, could offer inducements preferable to those possessed by those of Saxe-Coburg. Objections against this individual member of

---

* This was preliminary, and was entitled "An Act for Exhibiting a Bill in this present Parliament for naturalising His Serene Highness Prince Albert of Saxe-Coburg and Gotha."

† That of intermarriage with Protestants only.

the family might, perhaps, present themselves to reflecting minds, on the score of his close consanguinity to Queen Victoria, a circumstance not usually looked upon as propitious to the hope of a flourishing offspring.

" Another argument might be urged against the match, from the undoubted fact that the name of Saxe-Coburg is not popular in this country, a misfortune for which we do not undertake to account ; nor shall we longer dwell upon either of the above considerations, which we have hinted at, merely to shew that they have not wholly escaped our notice.   .   .   .

" Prince Albert has now become one of us.   He is, actually, now an English subject.   He is tied to us by law and self-interest.   Let us bind him to us by gratitude and affection. The happiness of our youthful Queen is now in his hands. He has the means of so directing and assisting her future footsteps, as to retrieve for Her Majesty (we speak with frankness, but with all respect) all she has forfeited in the hearts of the most loyal, enlightened and virtuous of her subjects, through her unhappy bias towards persons and principles which are hourly undermining the deep foundations of her Throne.

" We have said that it devolves upon Prince Albert to counteract a host of ' evil influences,' and to aid his Royal Consort in repairing ' many very grievous errors ' into which selfish and treacherous counsellors have betrayed her, and which her constant separation (contrived by them) from all but one section, or coterie of her subjects, has served to render extremely difficult of correction.

" Queen Victoria has scarcely been permitted to see the general aspect of the British aristocracy, or to become acquainted with their sentiments, their characters, or their manners.   The petty, artificial world framed and got up for her deception, is no more capable of suggesting to her mind the vast moral and social creation beyond its narrow boundaries, than one or two leaves of a *hortus siccus* exemplify the productions of a noble forest, or a varied and inimitable landscape.   .   .   .   .   .   .

" Are the heads of the nation to be discovered at the Queen

of England's Court ?   Has the worth, or wisdom, or eminence
of the nation any access to the society of the Sovereign ? Have
the clergy of England, or any of them—have their representatives—bishops, priests, or deacons, the opportunity of com-
municating personally with the temporal head of the Church
of England ?   Are they, or any of them, ever seated at the
Royal table, or received into the Royal presence, or favoured
with the Royal smile?   No ;   such associations comport not
with the policy of her ministers ; the ear of the Sovereign
is whispered from the choicest of her subjects—the palace
doors are locked inexorably against all but a certain clique."

Let us turn from this little lecture to the Queen, honest
and faithful though it be, to the all-absorbing subject of
Gossip, the Royal Marriage—and first, and foremost, comes
the Royal Wedding Cake, which weighed nearly 300lbs.   It
was three yards in circumference and about 14 inches deep.
This was the cake itself, which, according to a contemporary
account, " is covered with sugar of the purest white ; on the
top is seen the figure of Britannia in the act of blessing the
illustrious bride and bridegroom, who are dressed, somewhat
incongruously, in the costume of ancient Rome.   These figures
are not quite a foot in height ; at the feet of His Serene
Highness is the effigy of a dog, said to denote fidelity ; and,
at the feet of the Queen is a pair of turtle doves, denoting
the felicities of the marriage state.   A Cupid is writing in a
volume expanded on his knees, the date of the marriage, and
various other Cupids are sporting and enjoying themselves
as such interesting little individuals generally do.   These little
figures are well modelled.   On the top of the cake are
numerous bouquets of white flowers tied with true lover's knots
of white satin ribbon, intended for presents to the guests at
the nuptial breakfast."

On 6 Feb. the Prince landed at Dover from Ostend, and
on the 7th went to Canterbury ; on the 8th he reached London
and Buckingham Palace ; and, on the 10th they were married
at the Chapel Royal, St. James' ; spent the honeymoon at
Windsor, and made their *rentrée* into society on 26 Feb.,
when they went, in State, to Drury Lane Theatre.

Duelling, although on the wane, was far from dead. I could have given numerous instances of duels in the earlier part of this reign, but have refrained, as they were of no particular interest ; but the following is an exception, as it relates to one who, in after years, was to make a great name in history for himself.

Times, 4 March :

BOW STREET.—Shortly after the opening of the court yesterday morning, and before any of the night charges had been disposed of, Prince Louis Napoleon and Le Comte Leon, who is said to be the son of Bonaparte, to whom he bears a striking resemblance, were brought before Mr. Jardine, charged by Nicholas Pearce, inspector of the A division, with having met at Wimbledon Common, and attempted to commit a breach of the peace, by fighting a duel with swords and pistols.

Lieut.-Col. Jeremiah Ratcliffe, 6th Dragoons, as second to the last defendant, and Col. Charles Parquin, second to the Prince, together with Count D'Orsay, and a servant, named Mertial Kien, with aiding and assisting the principals in the intended combat.

Previous to the evidence being taken, two brace of pistols, with powder flasks, and a pair of rapiers, were laid on the table for the inspection of the magistrate.

Inspector Pearce, being sworn, said, about 2 o'clock this morning he received information from Superintendent Baker, that certain parties had an intention of meeting in a hostile manner on Wimbledon Common, some of whom were to start from Fenton's Hotel and the others from Carlton Gardens ; in consequence of which I went into St. James's Street, where I saw a post-chaise drive up to the door of the hotel, about 7 o'clock, but I could not ascertain if any person had got into it. After delaying a short time, it moved slowly on in the direction of Piccadilly, followed by Col. Ratcliffe, and stopped again at Tattersall's, where another person followed towards Hyde Park Corner.   The chaise was then driven westward, and I followed it on horseback ; but, previous to arriving at Hyde Park Corner, the defendant Ratcliffe passed, on horseback, in Piccadilly.

Mr. Jardine : What hour might it be then ?

Witness : It was then nearly 7 o'clock.   On arriving at the Common, I saw the entire party collected near to the Windmill, and the post-chaise proceeding in that direction. Having dismounted, and left the horse in the care of a countryman, I proceeded to where the chaises were standing, and then I saw the defendants walking away, from them, some yards down, to a hollow part of the ground, each party apparently making arrangements about the duel.   They then stopped, and as I approached Col. Parquin, seeing two letters in one hand, and the two swords produced, in the other, I took them from him.   At that time, the pistols produced, in a case, were lying on the ground, near to another brace, which were wrapped up in paper.   Some conversation passed between Count D'Orsay and Col. Parquin, which appeared to be whether the combat was to be fought with pistols or with swords, and the Count asked me what I wanted ; my authority for interfering ; and who it was that gave me information of the circumstance.   At that moment, Inspector Partridge, accompanied by Sergt. Otway and other constables, came up, and, on Col. Ratcliffe taking the pistols from the case, he was taken into custody.   I instantly went to him, and, shewing him my staff, told him I was an officer, and that I was, in duty, bound to take him into custody, for attempting to commit a breach of the peace.   Count D'Orsay requested to be told who it was who had given the information, and, on being refused, the entire party were quietly conveyed to the station house.

Mr. Jardine : Have you since ascertained that the pistols contained powder and balls?

Witness : Yes, Sir ; there are balls in them, and caps upon them.

Colonel Ratcliffe declared there was no powder in the pistols, which belonged to him, as could be seen ; for it had been arranged that the duel was to be fought with swords.

Mr. Jardine inquired if any of the defendants, who were

foreigners, and not sufficiently conversant with the English language, would wish to hear the evidence read over to them in French?

Le Comte Leon replied in French, that he could not sufficiently understand the evidence that had been given, but he was quite satisfied that all the proceedings were perfectly legal and correct.

Prince Louis said, he was prepared, if required, to enter into an explanation of the circumstances which gave rise to the offence with which he was charged.

Mr. Jardine did not wish to hear any statement on either side, as his duty was only to prevent a breach of the peace, and he hoped the defendants were prepared with the sureties he would require, to prevent further inconvenience.

Count D'Orsay said, he had come prepared with bail, which he thought there could be no objection to.

Prince Louis requested that the two letters, which had been taken from his friend, should be delivered up to him.

Mr. Jardine immediately delivered up the letters, saying he should require the principals to enter into bail, themselves in £500 each, and two sureties in £250 each, to keep the peace with all Her Majesty's subjects, and particularly with each other, for the next 12 months.

Count D'Orsay : One surety in £500, would, perhaps, answer as well as two in £250 each, if it meets with your approbation.

Mr. Jardine said he had no objection to such a course, and, if the other defendants were prepared with bail, it might be taken.

Col. Ratcliffe said his surety was present.

Mr. Jardine : The bail I shall require is, that each of the other defendants enter into his own recognizance in £100, and two sureties in £50 each, to keep the peace for the same period, with the exception of the defendant Kien, who may put in his own recognizances in £100.

Mr. Joshua Bates, of Portland Place, having offered himself as surety for Prince Louis Napoleon and Col. Parquin, was accepted.

Mr. Fenton was accepted as bail for Le Comte Leon, and

the Hon. Francis Baring, M.P., became surety for Col. Ratcliffe and Count D'Orsay.

The Chief Clerk having conducted the parties into the Magistrate's private room, where they were furnished with the requisite notices, returned to the Court to take directions respecting the disposal of the weapons and other articles which were found upon the defendants on their being taken into custody.

Mr. Jardine said he could make no order about them, but he thought that, as the defendants had put in bail, there could be very little apprehension of their committing a similar offence, if they were restored to their proper owners.

It appeared that the two letters had been written by the Comte Leon to his cousin, as he was styled, demanding that he would retract certain expressions respecting their relationship, which he was alleged to have made use of ; and, his not complying, gave rise to the quarrel.

On the 10th of April the offer of Messrs. Grissell and Peto was accepted, to erect the Nelson Column in Trafalgar Square, within two years, for a sum of £17,860.

There is a curious police case as to the habits and customs of Noblemen's servants, which may be interesting to my readers. It was brought before the Magistrate at Queen Square on 14 April, when the House Steward of the Earl of Galloway applied for summonses against the footmen attending the carriages of Viscount Melbourne, the Marquis of Normanby, the Marquis of Lansdowne and Lord Tankerville, for assault and damage.

It appeared from the statement of the applicant, that the servants attending the carriages of peers, to the House of Lords, have a waiting room, which they call their Club room, and that they have formed themselves into a society, governed by one of their body, whom they call their "Constable." They have a set of rules, dated as far back as 1759, obedience to which is strictly enforced under pain of certain fines.

On Friday evening, the coachman of the Earl of Galloway set his lordship down at the House of Lords, with orders to wait. The footman, who was, it appears, a new comer, was, on entering the club room, called upon to pay a fine, or " footing " of two shillings, to be spent in beer, but he replied that he had no money about him ; and, on their insisting on its being paid, he left the room, and got on the carriage box, with the coachman, but the "members," headed by their Constable, with his staff of office, pursued him, insisted upon his coming down, and were about to pull him off the box, when the coachman told them that his fellow servant had no money with him, but, if they would go, he would be answerable that it should be paid. They, however, insisted that it should be spent in their Club, and that the new servant should be present.

Mr. Burrell: How many were there of them?

Applicant said there were, he understood, 10 or 12, but it was only intended to proceed against the four ringleaders. The coachman, finding that they were determined to have his fellow servant off the box, drove on a little way, and, on returning to his place, Lord Normanby's carriage ran against his, and seriously damaged it. The footman was, at length, dragged from the box, and very roughly handled: his foot was hurt. The coachman was also struck with the long " staff " carried by the " constable."

Samuel Linturn, the footman, corroborated this statement.

The summonses were granted.

It was stated that Lord Normanby, at once, offered to make good the damage done, but this the Earl of Galloway declined, having determined that the whole matter should be publicly investigated by a magistrate.

Two days afterwards, four footmen in the employ of Lords Melbourne, Lansdowne, Normanby and Tankerville appeared to answer the summonses.

The complainant, in the course of his evidence, said that he had been to the House of Lords on several previous occasions, but had never been asked for anything, nor did he even know of the existence of such a room. Turk asked him whose servant he was, but he refused to tell him. Turk, at the time, had, in his hand, a pointed stick, which he called a staff; he made no demand for money then, but went away, and the complainant got on the box with the coachman, who took the coach to the stand. Turk, accompanied by several others, then came up. The Marquis of Bute's footman said he would pay the fine, or footing, and placed two shillings on the footboard of the carriage for that purpose. This did not satisfy them. Several persons, amongst whom were the defendants, got upon the coach, and swore that if he did not come down, they would pull him down. There were several police about, and, although he called upon them for assistance, they would not come.

Both he and the coachman told them that he had no money, and the coachman said he would secure them payment, if they would go and drink the beer, but they insisted upon the complainant's presence in the "club." He still refused, and then they brought a long pole, which they called a "horse." The coachman drove up Abingdon Street to avoid them, but several of the carriages drew out of the rank, and followed them, and, as the coachman turned to regain his station, Lord Normanby's carriage was driven against him, and the Earl of Galloway's carriage sustained considerable damage; it was forced on the footway, and was obliged to stop, upon which, several of the footmen ran, and seized the horses by their heads. The defendants dragged the complainant off the box; one had hold of his foot, and another, who seized upon his greatcoat, tore the buttons from it, and from his gaiters and breeches. They then placed him upon the pole, which they called "putting him on horseback."

They then rode him into the room mentioned, where Lord Holland's footman sat as chairman, and decided that he should pay two shillings. He borrowed the money from Lord Lansdowne's servant, and was about to leave the room, but he was forced to resume his seat, as he was told he could, from the room, easily hear when the carriage was called, and that "he must sit and drink his beer." He was also told that he was now sworn in, and had only to kiss the staff, which was presented to him, but he refused to do it. He was detained three-quarters of an hour, against his will. His foot was hurt, and the coachman was injured by a blow from the " staff."

The coachman corroborated the evidence, and the defendants were fined ten shillings each.

On the 29th April, there was an uproar in the Italian Opera House, which might have expanded into another O.P. riot of 1809. The Impresario, M. Laporte, had not engaged Tamburini, because his terms were too high, and the singer's friends were highly indignant. On this evening, at the conclusion of the opera of *I Puritani*, several voices began calling for M. Laporte, with shouts of " Tamburini ! " Poor M. Laporte appeared and began a speech in which he sought to excuse himself, but it was drowned by a torrent of groans and hisses, which came, principally, from the occupants of the " omnibus " box.* M. Laporte so clearly perceived this, that, in a few minutes, his speech to the audience merged into a private conversation with its occupants. The noise increased, and M. Laporte declared that he was not to be " intimidated," a word which roused the " omnibus " party to perfect fury He retired, and the curtain rose for the ballet, in which a new dancer was to have made her appearance. The noise, now, became terrible ; yells, hisses, and all sorts of uncouth sounds were blended in frightful discord. The dancers, perceiving all attempts at a performance were in vain, and, at the same time, being afraid to quit the stage, sat quietly, all round.

Again and again Laporte came forward, and tried to bring matters to a settlement, and once he ventured to say, that, as manager, he had a right to engage performers at his own discretion, and that he was not to be responsible to an audience—which, it is needless to say, added fuel to fire. Then he told them his engagements would not allow him to employ Tamburini, which meant ruin to him, but it only provoked more noise. Then he appealed to their better feelings by telling them of the many years he had catered for their amusement, and this did bring him some support, for cries of

* A private box, on the level of the stage, with which it communicated.

"Shame," "No Tamburini," and "No Intimidation," were heard, but this only had the effect of dividing the audience, and increasing the hubbub.

Once again poor Laporte came forward, and talked of engaging Tamburini on "Conditions." This word upset all, and the Tamburinists asked : "Will you engage him ? Yes, or No ?" Laporte said he would make proposals, and, if those proposals, etc. This would not do ; "Yes, or No ?" said his persevering interrogators. "Say 'No,'" said his supporters. He began talking about terms. "Same terms as last year," shouted all the "Omnibus" party, upon which he retired, without proposing anything satisfactory. Everyone was getting tired, when, at last, a gentleman, in a box opposite the "Omnibus," stepped over the front of his box on to the stage, and was followed by a party ; the "Omnibus" party entered the stage from the opposite side, and, at one o'clock, the Tamburinists had taken possession, and waved their hats triumphantly, on the stage, as the curtain fell.

It was this episode that the Rev. R. H. Barham has immortalized in his *Ingoldsby Legends*, under the title of "A Row in an Omnibus (box)," beginning :

Doldrum the Manager sits in his chair,
With a gloomy brow and dissatisfied air,
    And he says, as he slaps his hand on his knee,
    'I'll have nothing to do with Fiddle-de-dee !

' —But Fiddle-de-dee sings clear and loud,
And his trills and his quavers astonish the crowd.
        Such a singer as he,
        You'll nowhere see,
They'll all be screaming for Fiddle-de-dee !

' —Though Fiddle-de-dee sings loud and clear,
And his tones are sweet, yet his terms are dear !
        The glove won't fit !
        The deuce a bit.
I shall give an engagement to Fal-de-ral-tit ! ' "

CHAPTER XIII.

The Mulready Envelope—Plans of Royal Exchange decided on—Fire at York Minster—Queen shot at by Oxford—Oxford in Bedlam—Scientific Agriculture—Electro-metallurgy—Embossed envelope—Sale of Louis Napoleon's effects.

ON the 1st of May, the Post Office issued the long expected postal envelope designed by W. Mulready, R.A., and the opinion of *The Times* may be taken as the expression of most people's feelings about it.

Times, 2 May.—" We have been favoured with a sight of one of the new stamp covers, and we must say we never beheld anything more ludicrous than the figures or allegorical device by which it is marked with its official character—why not add embellished ? Cruickshank could scarcely produce anything so laughable. It is, apparently, a spirited attempt to imitate the hieroglyphic which formed one of the ornaments to *Moore's Almanack;* Britannia is seated in the centre, with the lion couchant (Whiggish) at her feet ; her arms are extended, scattering little flying children to some elephants on the left ; and, on the right, to a group of gentlemen, some of whom, at all events, are not enclosed in *envelopes*, writing on their knees, evidently on account of a paucity of tables. There are, besides, sundry figures, who, if they were to appear in the streets of London, or any of our highways, would be liable to the penalties of the Vagrant Act for indecent exposure. Under the tableland by which these figures are supported, some evidence of a laudable curiosity is depicted, by three or four ladies, who are represented reading a billet doux, or valentine, and some little boys, evidently learning to spell, by the mental exertion which their anxious faces disclose. One serious omission we must notice. Why have those Mercuries in red jackets, who traverse London and its environs on lame ponies, been omitted? We must admit that,

as they have been, recently, better mounted, that is one reason why they should not appear in this Government picture."

But the reader can judge how far this description is borne out.

As a matter of fact, it was so universally disapproved of by the public, and was the object of so much ridicule, as to

9*

necessitate the destruction of nearly all the vast number prepared for issue.   To do this, a machine had to be specially
constructed; the attempt to do the work by fire, in close
stoves (fear of robbery forbade the use of open ones), having
absolutely failed.   They are now somewhat scarce, but are
extensively forged.   It was satirized and laughed at by all,
and a contemporary criticism, which has been reproduced in
The Philatelist, vol. vii., p. 145, is very amusing :

> " Britannia is sending her messengers forth
> To the East, to the West, to the South, to the North :
> At her feet is a lion wot's taking a nap,
> And a dish-cover rests on her legs and her lap.
> To the left is a Mussulman writing a letter,
> His knees form a desk, for the want of a better ;
> Another believer's apparently trying
> To help him in telling the truth, or in lying.
> Two slaves 'neath their burden seem ready to sink,
> But a sly-looking elephant ' tips us the wink ' ;
> His brother behind, a most corpulent beast,
> Just exhibits his face, like the moon in a mist.
> On each is a gentleman riding astraddle,
> With neat Turkey carpets in lieu of a saddle ;
> The camels, behind, seem disposed for a lark,
> The taller's a well-whisker'd, fierce-looking shark.
> An Arab, arrayed with a coal-heaver's hat,
> With a friend from the desert is holding a chat ;
> The picture's completed by well-tailed Chinese
> A-purchasing opium, and selling of teas.
> The minister's navy is seen in the rear—
> They long turned their backs on the service—'tis clear
> That they now would declare, in their typical way,
> That Britannia it is who has done it, not they.
> A reindeer and Laplander cutting through snow,
> The rate of their progress (down hill) seems to show.
> To the right, is the King of the Cannibal Islands,
> In the same pantaloons that they wear in the Highlands
> Some squaws by his side, with their infantile varments,
> And a friend, in the front, who's forgotten his garments.
> Frost, Williams and Jones* have this moment been hook
> And are fixing the day they would choose to be cook'd.

---

* Three Chartist leaders, who were condemned to death on 16 Jan., 1840,
but were never executed, and subsequently pardoned.

Left—Lord Monteagle and Mr. Baring, Britannia, Lord Palmerston. Right — O'Connell and the Duke of Wellington.

> There a planter is giving and watching the tasks
> Of two worthy niggers, at work on two casks.
>   Below, to the left, as designed by Mulready,
>   Is sorrow's effect on a very fat lady ;
> While joy at good news may be plainly descried,
> In the trio engaged on the opposite side."

There were very many pictorial satires on this unfortunate wrapper, but none bore so near a resemblance to it as the accompanying illustration by John Doyle (H.B. Sketches, 26 May, 1840, No. 639). Lord Palmerston, as Britannia, is dispatching Mercuries with fire and sword, to the east, typical of the wars in Egypt and China. On the other hand, he sends a flight of Cupids to Father Mathew, the apostle of Temperance, who was then doing such good work in Ireland, whilst a man is knocking the bung out of a whisky barrel. Beneath this group is O'Connell, who is roaring out " Hurrah for Repeal ! " to the horror of the Duke of Wellington, who is behind him. On the left is Lord Monteagle, late Chancellor of the Exchequer, ill in bed ; whilst his successor, Mr. Baring, reads to him the result of his policy : " Post Office deliveries in the quarter, £272,000 ! Total deficiency in the year, to be made up by new taxation, £2,000,000 ! "

On 7 May, the Gresham Committee met to decide on the two plans for the New Royal Exchange, one prepared by Mr. Cockerell, R.A., and the other by Mr. Tite, President of the Architectural Society, which was in favour of the latter by 13 votes to 7. The works were immediately proceeded with.

Talking of one fire seems to lead on to another, for on 20 May, York Minster was for the second time visited with a conflagration—this time, however, it was caused accidentally, and not the work of an incendiary.

The following extract from a letter dated York, 21 May, gives a graphic account of the fire, and is of especial interest, as being from the pen of a spectator.

" You may hear the rumour of the alarming and truly awful calamity that has occurred in this city, before you receive this.

I have witnessed it, and shall hold the recollection as long as my memory exists. About 20 minutes to 9 last evening, I was told the Minster was on fire. I ran out, immediately, towards it, and stood by it, just as the flames had issued from the top part of the south-west tower, at a height that an engine could not have played upon. The fire continued to rage until it had entire possession of the upper part; flames issuing from every window, and piercing the roof. To describe the feelings under which I witnessed the devouring flames preying upon a national monument, which every man must look upon with admiration, requires a pen more descriptive than mine. Grief, awe, wonder and admiration were the emotions with which I regarded the destruction of this venerable church. I soon obtained admission into the nave of the Cathedral, and observed the first falling down of the burnt embers. The flames illumined the interior with more than mid-day brightness; the light, pouring through the crevices, threw a brilliancy over the scene which imagination cannot paint. The fire, at this time, was wholly confined to the tower.

"After the space of half an hour, the flooring of the belfry in the tower began to be forced by the falling bells and lighted beams. At this period, my nerves were strung to the highest excitement. The noise was extraordinary. The shouting of the firemen, the roaring of the flames rushing up the tower with the rapidity of a furnace draught, sounded in the high and arched space, awful and terrific. The falling masses of wood, and bells, sounded like the near discharge of artillery, and were echoed back from the dark passages, whose glomy shade, and hollow responses seemed mourning at the funeral pile that burned so fiercely. In one hour, the tower was completely gutted, and masses of burning timber lay piled against the south-west door. The upper and under roof, composed principally of fir timber, covering the nave, as far as the centre tower, had, by this time, become fired, and burned with extraordinary rapidity. The firemen, by a well-managed direction of the water, prevented the flames passing through the west windows of the centre tower, and continued their exertions at that spot, until the whole of the roof had fallen in, and lay, in the centre of the aisle, a sea of fire.

" The west doors had, now, become nearly burnt through, and planks were brought to barricade them, and prevent the rushing of air to fan the embers to flame, which might have communicated to the organ, and thence, throughout the whole pile of buildings.

" At 1 o'clock, this morning, I again entered the Cathedral, and then concluded there was no further danger of destruction. The tower is standing, also the walls and pillars of the nave ; and, beyond that, the building, I am happy to state, is saved.

" The fire is supposed to have originated from a clock maker, who has been, for some time past, occupied in repairing the clock in that tower, who might accidentally, have dropped a spark from a candle."

The repairs in 1829, when the Cathedral was fired by the fanatic, John Martin, cost £65,000, which was raised by subscription, and it was estimated that the cost of the present repairs would amount to about £20,000.

I know of no other general topic of conversation in May, but, in June, there was one which set every one in the United Kingdom, and the whole civilized world, a talking.—THE QUEEN HAD BEEN SHOT AT!!! A little after 6 p.m. the Queen and Prince Albert left Buckingham Palace for their before-dinner drive, and had barely got one-third up Constitution Hill, when a young man, who had been walking backwards and forwards, as the carriage came near, and was nearly opposite him, turned round, and, drawing a pistol from his breast, fired at the carriage, which, however, went on its way. The man then looked back, to see whether any person was standing near enough to prevent him, and drew another pistol, which he discharged at the carriage. Prince Albert ordered the postillions to drive on, and they went as far as Hyde Park Corner, and thence to the Duchess of Kent's mansion in Belgrave Square, and, after staying there some little time, drove to Buckingham Palace, where the Queen was received by crowds of her subjects, cheering vociferously. To say that she was not affected by the incident would not be true, but she soon recovered from its effects.

The person who shot at her was a little undersized boy (5ft. 4in.), about 18, named Edward Oxford, a publican's barman, out of work, and as "Satan finds work for idle hands to do," this boy must needs buy two pistols, bullets, powder and caps, and begin practising shooting. Whatever made it enter into his wicked little head to shoot at the Queen, no one knew, but he did, and was speedily in the hands of the police. He was examined and re-examined, and finally tried at the Central Criminal Court on 9 July, the trial lasting two days. The defence was the plea of insanity, and, as no bullets could be found, the jury brought in a verdict of "Guilty, he being, at the time, insane"; and, in accordance with such verdict, the judge sentenced him to be imprisoned during Her Majesty's pleasure.

On the day after being shot at, the Queen and Prince Albert took their wonted drive in the Park, amidst the shouts of crowded thousands, and the next day, she, in State, received the congratulations of the Houses of Lords and Commons, the latter having the first audience. At two o'clock, the state carriage of the Speaker entered the court, followed by 109 carriages filled with members of the House of Commons; never before, it was said, was the Speaker followed by so numerous a *cortège*, on the occasion of presenting an address. As soon as the carriages of the Commons had left the court, the procession of the Lords began to enter, the barons first, then the other peers, rising in rank to the royal dukes. They wore all their stars and garters, and made a brave show.

We get a glimpse of Oxford in prison in a paragraph of the *Times*, 28 Feb., 1843, copied from a Sunday paper.

"As numberless strange and conflicting rumours have been propagated, relative to the treatment experienced by Edward Oxford, in his place of incarceration, the curiosity of the visitor on this head was, naturally, great, especially as it is generally understood that those who are favoured with permission to visit Bethlehem, are not allowed to see Oxford. This is not, however, the fact. In a compartment of the establishment, principally allotted to those who are supposed to have committed heinous crimes in moments of madness, Edward Oxford is confined. He is not separated from the other unfortunate persons who reside in that division of the building, but is allowed free intercourse with them. Among his comrades are Mr. Pierce, surgeon, who shot his wife whilst labouring under a paroxysm of madness produced by jealousy ; and Captain Good, whose favourite phantasy is the assumption of the attribute of Majesty. There is, in the same division of the establishment, a very diminutive man, who imagines himself to be Lord John Russell. He amuses himself, nearly all day long, with knitting. Captain Good is fond of smoking, and Pierce hovers over the fireplace (a stove) all day. Oxford diverts himself with drawing and reading. He told the visitor, who furnished us with this account, that he had taught himself to read French with ease, during his incarceration, but that he was unable to speak the language, for want of an opportunity of studying the pronunciation. He said that he was terribly tired of his sojourn at Bethlehem, and that he wished he could obtain his liberty, even though he should be placed under *surveillance* during the remainder of his life. The visitor remarked that there was no such thing as *surveillance de police* in England. To which Oxford replied that he was perfectly acquainted with that fact ; and that the condition upon which he thus desired his liberty, was rather an imaginary one, than a strictly legal and feasible one. Upon another question being put to him, he said he knew he had been placed in Bethlehem under an impression that he was mad, but that he was, really, very far from being mad. He exhibited some of his drawings, which were uncommonly well executed, and evinced a natural talent for the art. There were a view of Abbotsford, a horse's head, a portrait of the Virgin Mary, and one or two other designs, which were, really, most tastefully sketched and shaded. He appeared pleased when complimented on his proficiency in the art of drawing, and observed that he was self-taught. In manners, he is modest, civil and unassuming, and certainly exhibits not the slightest symptom of insanity. We know that medical jurisprudence admits that it is very difficult to determine the exact line of demarcation where sound sense stops, and insanity commences; but he, who has visited a receptacle for the insane, will speedily observe the strange state and appearance of the eyes of those whose intellects are unhinged. This appearance cannot be mistaken either in lucid or rabid intervals; it is still perceptible, although, of course, in a greater or lesser degree. Now, the visitor to Bethlehem, on the occasion here refered to, particularly observed the eyes of all the inmates; and those of one only showed not the least—not the most remote symptoms of insanity. This one individual was Edward Oxford. He appears in his conversation, his manners, his countenance and his pursuits, as sane, collected, and intelligent as possible. Of course, the deed for which he is now in durance was not touched upon; nor was any information relative to that subject sought of the turnkeys, or keepers. With respect to food, Oxford is not treated one atom better than his fellow sufferers; the diet of the inmates of the hospital is plentiful and good, but no favour is shown to any particular individual, with regard either to quality, or quantity. Oxford appears to enjoy very excellent health; and he is remarkably clean and neat in his person."

He was, afterwards, removed to Broadmoor, and I have been told, although I cannot vouch for the fact, that he was liberated some years ago, and sent to Australia.

Early in July, we begin to hear of a higher style of farming than that previously in use, as we find the *Dumfries Courier* advocating the use of nitrate of soda as a manure, but, yet, are cautious on the subject.—"An extensive trial of it will be necessary before any proper judgment can be pronounced. It is, as yet, unknown whether its effects are lasting, and until this is ascertained, caution must be used."

Another thing, too, was just beginning to attract attention—Electro-metallurgy. True it is that Wollaston applied the principle of the Voltaic pile to the deposition of one metal upon another in 1801, and it was further developed by Bessemer (1834), Jacobi and the Elkingtons in 1838, and Spencer in 1839, but for practical utility it was still in its infancy, and we can see how far it had advanced, in the following extract from a German Paper : " Munich, 22 July, 1840.— Much is at present said in the public papers respecting the imitations of medals, reliefs, etc., by means of a galvanic deposition of copper. This art, called Galvano plastic, first discovered by Professor Jacobi of St. Petersburg, and brought to greater perfection by Mr. Spencer, of Liverpool, and by Professor Von Kebel, of Munich, may justly be classed as one of the most useful of modern inventions ; and, from its great importance, its employment in technical operations must soon become general. Indeed, some persons in England, perceiving the great influence which this invention is destined to have on manufacturing industry, are already applying it to the production of buttons, arabesques, and various ornaments in Copper. Herr G. A. Muller, mechanician of Leipsic, has recently called attention to the application of Galvano plastic to typography. He has, however, been, in some measure, anticipated by the experiments made in 1839, in Rosel's printing office, in Munich ; where, by following the methods of Jacobi and Spencer, the lines of copperplate were produced in relief. Wood cuts were, also, converted into metallic plates, which, to say nothing of the advantage of the solidity of the metal, far exceeded the effect of the most perfect casting. The experiments for making stereotype plates in copper have, also, been successful. In short, the invention has now reached that stage which must secure for it the attention of all practical men."

Mulready's postal wrapper having been killed by universal derision : in July was produced an envelope with an embossed head of the Queen thereon, and these could be bought until the close of her reign.

Prince Louis Napoleon, previously to his ill-starred expedition to Boulogne, had left instructions for his furniture and jewellery to be sold ; and sold they accordingly were by

Christie and Manson on 21 Aug., and Mr. Bernal and other *virtuosi* went to the sale to see what Napoleonic relics they could pick up. Among these were two silver cups, with the eagle and initial of Queen Hortense, £5 10/- and a casket of camei, formerly the property of the Empress Josephine, was divided into 22 lots, one of which was a pair of earrings, the gift of Pius VI. to Josephine during the first campaign in Italy, in 1796, sold for £46 4/-, and the original marble bust of Napoleon, when Consul, dated 1804, by Canova, fetched £232 11/-.

On 28 Aug. Prince Albert received the freedom of the City of London; and, on 11 Sep., he was made a Privy Councillor.

CHAPTER XIV.

Lord Cardigan and the " Black bottle " case—Lord Cardigan's duel with Lieut. Tuckett—Steam to India—Nelson Column—Mormonism—" The Boy Jones ' —Napoleon's body transferred to France.

ABOUT this time the Earl of Cardigan made himself particularly conspicuous before the public, and the commencement of it was the famous " black bottle " question, and I well remember that that useful utensil was, for many years, called a " Cardigan." My Lord was Colonel of the 11th Hussars, " Prince Albert's Own," and it so happened that, on the 18th May, 1840, when the Inspecting Officer dined with the mess, Captain Reynolds of " Ours " ordered, at mess, a bottle of Moselle, which, instead of being decanted, was served in its original envelope, a proceeding which gave offence to the aristocratic taste of the Colonel, and, according to a statement which was published in many newspapers :

" The following morning Capt. Jones delivered the following message to Capt. Reynolds : ' The Colonel has desired me, as president of the mess committee, to tell you that you were wrong in having a black bottle placed on the table, at a great dinner like last night, as the mess should be conducted like a gentleman's table, and not like a tavern, or pothouse,' or words to that effect. Capt. Reynolds received the message with astonishment, but without remark, and, subsequently, waited on the Earl of Cardigan, and complained of it, but received no satisfactory answer.

" A short time afterwards, Capt. Reynolds met Capt. Jones in the mess-room, and, in the presence of two officers, said to him : ' Captain Jones, I wish to speak to you about the message you brought me this morning. In the first place, I do not think you were justified in giving it at all; as a brother captain, having no possible control over me, it would have been better taste if you had declined to deliver it.' He replied: 'I received it from the Commanding Officer, and, as such, I gave it; and, if you refuse to receive it from me, I shall report it.' Capt. Reynolds replied: 'Do not misunderstand me, Captain Jones; I have received, and do receive it; but the message was an offensive one; and I tell you, once for all, that, in future, I will not allow you, or any man, to bring me offensive messages.' Capt. Jones said: 'If I am ordered to give a message, I shall give it.' Capt. Reynolds said: 'Well, you may do as you please; but if you bring me improper messages, you must take the consequences.' Capt. Jones replied, 'he should certainly do so,' and left the room.

"The two captains who were present (one not an officer of the regiment) proved that Capt. Reynolds' manner was quiet and inoffensive. Capt. Jones reported the conversation; and, soon afterwards, Capt. Reynolds was summoned to the orderly room; where, in presence of Major Jenkins, the adjutant, and Capt. Jones, Lord Cardigan thus addressed Capt. Reynolds, in no very agreeable tone, or manner: 'If you cannot behave quietly, Sir, why don't you leave the regiment? This is just the way with you Indian officers; you think you know everything; but I tell you, Sir, that you neither know your duty, nor discipline. Oh, yes, you do know your duty, I believe, but you have no idea whatever of discipline, and do not, at all, justify my recommendation.' Capt. Reynolds remained silent; when Lord Cardigan added, 'Well, I put you in arrest.'

"Capt. Jones then offered Capt. Reynolds his hand, upon which, Capt. Reynolds, turning towards him, said, 'No, Capt. Jones, I will not shake hands with you; nothing has passed which renders it necessary. I have no quarrel with you, and I deny having insulted you, and see no reason why I should shake hands with you, or the contrary.'

"Lord Cardigan said, 'But I say you have insulted Capt. Jones.' Capt. Reynolds quietly replied, 'I have not, my

Lord'; upon which Lord Cardigan said, 'Well, I put you under arrest, and shall report the matter to the Horse Guards.' Capt. Reynolds said, 'I am sorry for it;' and retired.

"The matter was reported to the Horse Guards, after Capt. Reynolds had been in close arrest three days. Lord Hill sent a memorandum, recommending Capt. Reynolds to acknowledge the impropriety of his conduct towards Lord Cardigan, and to declare his readiness to resume friendly intercourse with Capt. Jones. This recommendation Capt. Reynolds obeyed; but he still refused to shake hands with Capt. Jones, which would seem to imply a previous quarrel, or to drink wine with him within any specified time.

*   *   *   *   *

"On the 9th of June, Gen. Sleigh went to Canterbury; had all the officers of the regiment brought before him, and, without any investigation, read to them a letter from Headquarters, condemning Capt. Reynolds's conduct in very strong language; approving of that of Lord Cardigan, throughout, in every particular, stigmatizing Capt. Reynolds's motives as pernicious and vindictive, and refusing a court-martial, because many things would be brought to light which would not be for the good of the Service.

"Capt. Reynolds then requested that he might be brought to a court-martial for the offences for which he had now been charged. This was also refused, as it was stated Lord Hill had determined it should be considered as settled. And, as if this was not enough, Gen. Sleigh told Capt. Reynolds that he had forfeited the sympathy of every officer of rank in the Service.

"Capt. Reynolds applied for copies of all letters referred to in this statement, which are not given at length, and was refused them."

He still kept in the regiment, which, perhaps, was unwise on his part, as the sequel shows. Early in September, an evening party was given by the Earl of Cardigan, to which, as usual, several officers of the regiment were invited. In the course of the evening, a young lady casually observed, aloud, that she "did not see Capt. Reynolds there." The Earl of Cardigan, who happened to be near, heard the remark, and replied, "Oh, no; he is not one of my visitors." The words were uttered without any marked expression, and did not, at the time, attract particular attention. They were, however, carried to Capt. Reynolds, who, conceiving that the expression was calculated to affect him as a gentleman, wrote a letter to the Earl of Cardigan, to know if the expression had been used, and in what sense. This letter remained unanswered, and the consequence was, that Capt. Reynolds, stung with this apparently further slight, was induced to send a second and a stronger letter, couched in terms which could bear no other interpretation than that of a challenge.

On receiving this letter, the Earl of Cardigan consulted with his friends; and, after fairly considering the matter, it was determined to submit the letters with the whole of the circumstances connected with the case, to the consideration of the Colonel of the regiment, Prince Albert. The Prince, on receiving the papers, laid them before the Commander-in-Chief, Lord Hill, for his opinion thereon, when it was resolved, by the latter, to let the matter come fairly before the public, in the shape of a court-martial, which was, shortly afterwards, held at Brighton. This court confined itself chiefly to the consideration of the second letter written by Capt. Reynolds, which they conceived to be couched in a spirit so insubordinate, ungentlemanly, and insolent, as to afford the writer no sort of excuse, or palliation for his conduct, on the alleged grounds of previous provocation on the part of his commanding officer, and they adjudged that Capt. Reynolds should be cashiered (Oct. 20).

It certainly was not from a wish not to fight a duel that Lord Cardigan thus acted with regard to Capt. Reynolds (and no one who remembers his heading the charge of the Light Brigade at Balaclava, can question his courage), for he challenged and fought with Lieut. Tuckett, on 12th Sep.; a duel which was thus reported in the papers:

10

In consequence of the Earl of Cardigan having ascertained that certain letters published recently in the *Morning Chronicle*, reflecting, as his lordship supposed, on his character as an officer and a gentleman, were written by Lieut. Tuckett, late of the same regiment (11th Hussars), the noble lord sent him, through Captain Douglas, of the 11th, a challenge, which was at once accepted, and Capt. Wainwright (half-pay) was the friend selected by Mr. Tuckett to arrange the pre-liminaries. An apology was demanded by the noble lord, to which the reply was, that if he would deny the allegations contained in the letters referred to, it should be given. Lord Cardigan declared that certain portions of those letters were true, but that the greater part were calumnies. On this, the apology was refused, and a meeting was the consequence. It took place on the afternoon of the 12th Sep., on Wimbledon Common. The first shot was ineffectual, on both sides; but, on the second fire, Mr. Tuckett received his adversary's ball in the back part of the lower ribs, which traversed round to the spine. The ball was extracted, and Mr. Tuckett, after a time, recovered

Subsequently, warrants were issued, and Lord Cardigan and his second were brought before the Bench of Surrey Magistrates, at Wandsworth; and after several examinations, Lord Cardigan was committed for trial on the charge of "Shooting at Capt. H. Tuckett with a pistol, with intent to murder, or do him some bodily harm"; and his second, for aiding and abetting him. The charge was laid under "An Act to amend the Laws relating to Offences against the Person" (1 Vic., c. 85, s. 3), which makes the offence set forth in the charge, a felony, punishable, at the discretion of the Court, with transportation beyond the seas, for the term of his, or her, natural life, or for any term not less than fifteen years, or to be imprisoned for any term not exceeding three years.

He was tried in the House of Lords, on 16 Feb., 1841, by his peers, and the case against him broke down through a technicality. His counsel, Sir William Follett, pointed out that the prosecution had failed in proving a material part of their case, inasmuch as no evidence had been given that Captain Harvey Garnett Phipps Tuckett was the person alleged to have been on Wimbledon Common on the 12th September last, and whose card only bore the name of Captain Harvey Tuckett. The peers present returned a verdict of " Not guilty," with the exception of the Duke of Cleveland, who added " Not guilty, legally."

The use of steam at sea was beginning to assert itself. It was only two years since, that I had to chronicle the voyages of the *Sirius* and the *Great Western* across the Atlantic—now we have the first steamship to India, sailing on 25 Sep. She was called *The India*, and was 1,200 tons and nearly 400 horse-power. She sailed for Calcutta, calling at the Cape of Good Hope, where she was to stop five days. It was expected that she would complete her voyage, including stoppages, within 75 days.

On 30 Sep. the foundation stone of the Nelson Column in Trafalgar Square was laid, without ceremony. It was a large block of Dartmoor granite, weighing 14 tons; and, on 16 Oct. the tenders for building the new Royal Exchange were settled. They varied very considerably, and the contract was given to the lowest, that of Messrs. Webb, of Clerkenwell, whose tender was £2,000 under the architect's estimate.

About this time we begin to hear of Mormonism in England; not that it was absolutely new, for, on 20 July, 1837, Heber C. Kimball, Orson Hyde, Willard Richards, Joseph Fielding and others, landed at Liverpool, on the first mission sent out by the Mormons. Three days after landing they began preaching at Preston, and met with such remarkable success that, within the next eight months, at the expiration of which time, Kimball and Hyde returned to America, they had converted and baptised about 2,000 people. But the sect was uncommon, as we may see from the following extract from the *Leeds Times*, copied into the *Times* of 31 Oct. :

" A NEW SECT.—One of the most recent developments
10*

of fanaticism is the appearance of a new sect, in different parts of England, entitled *Latter Day Saints*. We believe that it made its first appearance in Hertfordshire and Leicestershire, from which counties great numbers of its members have lately emigrated to the United States. The sect has extended to Lancashire and Yorkshire ; and, by the labours of its preachers, is now travelling northward into Durham and Northumberland. The *Latter Day Saints* assume to do many extraordinary things. Among other accomplishments peculiar to those who believe in the new doctrines, they are declared to possess the power of casting out devils, or curing the sick by laying hands on them, of resisting the operation of the deadliest poisons, of speaking with new tongues, and of working miracles of various kinds. They state that no ministers, now on earth, preach the Gospel, but themselves, and that, only to them have the supernatural gifts of the Church been vouchsafed. The Kingdom of God, they say, is only open to those who have been baptised by immersion. In addition to the Bible, they state they are in possession of another work, of equal authority, entitled *The Book of Mormon*, the original of which was found engraved on brass plates, in the central land of America. Finally, they consider this is the last generation of mankind, and that they have been sent into the world, expressly to prepare the way for the Son of Man ! ''

Has my reader forgotten THE BOY JONES? He turns up again in this chronicle, for, on Wednesday, the 2nd of December, the inmates of Buckingham Palace were, shortly after midnight, aroused by an alarm being given that a stranger had been discovered under the sofa in Her Majesty's dressing-room, and the officers of the household were quickly on the alert. It was soon ascertained that the alarm was not without foundation, and the daring intruder was immediately secured, and safely handed over to the tender mercies of the police. The report of the occurrence spread very rapidly, and created the most lively interest in London, as it was feared that the consequent alarm might be attended with the most dangerous effects to the health of the Queen, who had been confined only eleven days previously. Happily, neither mother, nor child suffered in any way.

The facts, as far as can be gathered—the examination being a private one, conducted by the Privy Council—seem to have been as follows: Shortly after midnight, one of Her Majesty's pages, accompanied by other domestics of the Royal household, was summoned into Her Majesty's dressing-room, which adjoined the bed chamber in which Her Majesty's accouchement had taken place, by Mrs. Lilly, the nurse, who thought she heard a noise. A strict search was made; and, under the sofa on which Her Majesty had been sitting, only about two hours' previously, they discovered a dirty, ill-looking fellow, who was immediately dragged from his hiding place, and given into custody. The prisoner was searched, but nothing of a dangerous nature was found upon him, and the police, at once, recognised their captive as the Edward Jones, who had, two years previously, entered the palace in such a mysterious way. He is described as being very short for his age, seventeen, and of a most repulsive appearance; but he was, apparently, unconscious of this defect, as he affected an air of great consequence, and repeatedly requested the police to address him in a becoming manner; also behaving with the greatest nonchalance at his examination before the Privy Council, the next day.

His first version of the matter was this: On Monday night, the 30th of November, he scaled the wall of Buckingham Palace, about half-way up Constitution Hill; he then proceeded to the Palace, and gained an entry through one of the windows. He had not, however, been long there, when he considered it unsafe for him to stay, as so many people were moving about; and he left by the same manner as he entered. The next day, Tuesday, about nine o'clock in the evening, he again effected an entrance by the same means as before. He then went on to state that he remained in the Palace the whole of Tuesday night, all Wednesday, and up to one o'clock on Thursday morning, when the inquisitive youth was captured. He was not satisfied with this dull and prosaic account of his entry; but, on the following day, he tried to invent something marvellous, and alleged that he ascended the roof of the Palace, and got down the chimney; but there were no marks of soot on his person, and his first story was, doubtless, the correct one.

The greatest mystery attending the affair was, how he could have found his way to the room adjoining that in which Her Majesty slept, without being observed. The delinquent stated that, during the day, he secreted himself under different beds, and in cupboards, until, at length, he gained an entrance into the dressing room; he, moreover, alleged that he sat upon the throne, that he saw the Queen, and heard the Princess Royal cry, but his story was such a romance, that no reliance could be placed upon it. He was extremely reticent as to the cause of his intrusion into the Palace, the only explanation which he vouchsafed, on being arrested, was, that he wanted to see what was going on in the Palace, that he might write about it, and, if discovered, he should be as well off as Oxford, who fared better in Bedlam, than he, Jones, did out of it. Even the stern discipline of the treadmill, to which he was promptly consigned, failed to extract anything more out of him; his only remark, when interrogated, being that he had got into the scrape, and must do the best he could.

His father stated that, in his belief, his unfortunate son was not of sound mind; but the medical evidence went to show that, though his head was of a most peculiar formation, he was not insane. The Council, therefore, came to the decision that it would be better to inflict summary punishment, and he was committed to the House of Correction for three months, as a rogue and vagabond.

If he is to be believed, he fared remarkably well whilst in his royal residence, as he said he helped himself to soup and other eatables from a room, which he called the " Cook's Kitchen," but no dependence whatever could be placed on his word.

Prince Albert was taking leave of Her Majesty for the night, when the miscreant was discovered; and the Prince, hearing a noise proceeding from the adjoining apartment, opened the door, and ascertained the cause; but it was not made known to the Queen till the following day, so as to prevent any undue alarm on her part.

It is needless to say that this event excited the greatest interest, and engrossed public attention, nothing else being talked of. The punishment was considered far too light to deter a repetition of the offence, which opinion was subsequently justified. Such an occurrence, of course, was considered fair material for the humourists of the day to exercise their wit upon, and there are many allusions to it in the *Age* and *Satirist* of the period; but, as their remarks are not always conceived in the best taste, they are better left in the obscurity in which they now dwell. Perhaps, however, this little couplet from the *Satirist* may be excepted:

> " Now he in chains and in the prison garb is
> Mourning the crime that couples Jones with darbies."*

It was Jones's extraordinary powers of finding an entrance into the Palace that caused Samuel Rogers to declare that he must be a descendant of the illustrious In—i—go.

On the 15 Dec. the remains of the Emperor Napoleon, which had been removed from St. Helena, were laid, with great pomp, into the tomb prepared for them at the Invalides, Paris; and, contrary to all expectation, there was no disturbance on the occasion.

* Handcuffs.

CHAPTER XV.

Dæath of Scott, "the American Diver"—Prince Albert's ducking—Monster
cheese—"The Boy Jones"—"Tracts for the Times," Tract XC—Earl of
Cardigan flogs a soldier on Sunday—Dispute as to the discovery of Electric
Telegraph—Sale of Shakspere autograph—The Census—Astley's burnt—
Behaviour of "gentlemen."

THE first bit of gossip of this year was the tragic death of
Sam Scott, "the American diver," who was born at Phila-
delphia, and, at an early age, entered the American navy.
His extraordinary courage and prowess as a diver rendered
him very popular, and, after quitting the naval service, he
travelled about the Union exhibiting. He, subsequently,
visited Canada, and made some tremendous leaps from the
banks of the St. Lawrence, and the lakes which intersect that
country; but his *chef d'œuvre* was leaping from a precipice
below the Falls of Niagara, where, according to his own statement, he jumped the amazing distance of 595 feet, into the
water, which he accomplished without injury or inconvenience!

He was performing in England in 1838, and came to
London in the latter part of 1840; and we now hear of him
as issuing a "Challenge to the World for 100 Guineas!
Monday next, Jan. 11, 1841, and during the week, Samuel
Scott, the American diver, will run from Godfrey's White
Lion, Drury Lane, to Waterloo Bridge, and leap into the
water, forty feet high from the bridge, and return back within
the hour, every day during the week, between one and two
o'clock." There were about 8,000 or 10,000 people assembled
to see the feat, which was to be performed from a scaffolding
overhanging the river. Here he swung by a rope noose round
his chin, and afterwards, with his head downwards and one

of his feet in the noose. He then again hung suspended by his chin, but the noose slipped, and he was hanged in sight of all that huge crowd. This fatal accident created a great impression at the time.

I do not know the Evening paper from which the following "small beer" chronicle is copied into the *Times* of 12 Feb., but it purports to be an "authentic account" of an accident to Prince Albert : " It appears that His Royal Highness was walking in the Royal gardens, in company of Her Majesty, the only attendant present being the Hon. Miss Murray, one of the Maids of Honour in waiting upon the Queen. It not being understood by Col. Bouverie and Lieut. Seymour that His Royal Highness intended to skate, they were not, as usual, in attendance on the Prince, who had left the Palace, with Her Majesty, without their knowledge. After walking for a short time with the Queen, on the margin of the lake, His Royal Highness put on his skates, and left Her Majesty, who remained watching the movements of the Prince from the gardens. He had not been on the ice more than two or three minutes, when, as he was proceeding at a rapid rate towards the spot where the Queen was standing, and had reached between three or four feet of the water's edge, the ice suddenly broke, and, instantaneously he was immersed, head over ears, in the water. His Royal Highness imme-diately rose to the surface, when Her Majesty, with great presence of mind, joined her hand to that of the Hon. Miss Murray (telling her to stand firm, and to betray no fear), and, extending her right hand to the Prince, dragged him to the shore. Her Majesty manifested the greatest courage upon the occasion, and acted with the most intrepid coolness As soon as the Prince was safe on dry land, the Queen gave way to the natural emotions of joy and thankfulness at his providential escape.

" The Prince then lost no time in proceeding to the Palace, where a warm bath was immediately prepared, and His Royal Highness, within an hour afterwards, was sufficiently well to receive the King of the Belgians, upon His Majesty's arrival from Claremont. The ice in the centre of the lake being nearly a foot in thickness, some surprise has been created that the accident should have occurred ; but it appears that the keepers appointed to attend on the numerous and various aquatic birds which are preserved in the gardens of the palace, had broken the ice along the sides of the lake to enable them to take the water during the frost. These portions had again become slightly frozen over, since they were broken at an early part of the morning. This was unknown to the Prince, or the Queen, and, hence, the accident occurred. There was no person present, at the time, connected with the gardens, to point out his danger to His Royal Highness. Yesterday morning, the Prince was suffering from the effects of a slight cold ; but, beyond this, His Royal Highness has sustained no inconvenience."

On the 10th Feb. the Princess Royal was christened.

On 19 Feb. the Queen had a monster cheese presented to her, " on which occasion, she was pleased to express her satisfaction." It was made from the morning's milking of 737 cows, prepared by the labour of 50 dairy women, at West Pennard, Somersetshire, and it weighed 11 cwt. It was octagon in shape, and its upper surface was decorated with the Royal Arms, surmounted with a wreath of roses, thistles and shamrocks. Unfortunately, although it had been made over two years, it was not considered to be fit to eat for another eighteen months.

Ecce iterum the irrepressible BOY JONES! Prison evidently had no terrors for him ; for, no sooner was he liberated from Tothill Fields, on 2 Mar., than he, almost immediately, set to work to repeat his former escapades. On the day previous to his liberation, he was visited by Mr. Hall, a magistrate, who tried to persuade him to go to sea ; but Jones made certain conditions which could not be acceded to, and he did not go. This gave an opportunity for the *Satirist* to come out with the following appropriate lines :

> " The impudent urchin, whom sure the devil owns,
>   And Government wants to send into the Navy ;
> Will not go to sea—and 'tis cunning of Jones,
>   Who, thus, may avoid his relation, Old Davey."

He was then delivered into the care of his parents, with strict injunctions to them to watch his actions ; and, for some days, his conduct was unexceptionable ; he frequently attended a Methodist chapel, and expressed his intention of joining a teetotal society. But the charms of notoriety were too strong for him ; and, again, he was drawn, as it were by a magnet, to Buckingham Palace. Indeed, it possessed such attractions for him, that, when required to pledge himself, before leaving prison, not to visit the Palace again, he said he would not promise, as his curiosity was so great.

On 15 March, shortly after 1 a.m., the sergeant of police on duty at the Palace imagined, as he was going along the Grand Hall, that he saw someone peeping through the glass door, and this turned out to be the case ; for, on his approach, Jones ran up against him, and was, of course, immediately secured. In consequence of his previous visits, two extra policemen had been appointed, whose duty it was, on alternate nights, to watch all the staircases and interior of the building, and it was owing to this arrangement that Master Jones was stopped early in his career, on this last occasion.

Like most boys, Jones had a keen appreciation of a feast, all the more enjoyable because irregularly come by ; and, when he was arrested, he was found to have been sitting at his ease in one of the royal apartments, regaling himself with some cold meat and potatoes, which he had conveyed upstairs in his handkerchief. On being questioned how he obtained an entrance, his reply was, " the same way as before " ; and he boasted, moreover, that he could, at any time he pleased, get into the palace ; but he was extremely taciturn, and refused to satisfy curiosity, more particularly on this point.

What he confessed at his examination by the Privy Council is not known, as the proceedings were in private, reporters being excluded, and the public were left in possession of only the above bare facts. He persisted that the only motive for his intrusion was to hear the conversation at Court, and to write an account of it ; but this plea of simplicity did not save him from a repetition of his old sentence of three months' imprisonment in the House of Correction, with the uncomfortable addition, this time, of hard labour. Perhaps the best punishment for this juvenile addition of Paul Pry would have been that suggested by the *Satirist*, in the following paragraph : " As the urchin Jones, in a letter to his father, stated that his reason for entering the Queen's house was to ' seek for noose, in order to rite a book,' it is a matter of general regret that, instead of magnifying the affair into Home Office importance, the young rogue was not accommodated with a rope's end." His visit, however, necessitated the appointment of three additional sentries at the palace.

What became of him afterwards, nobody knows and nobody cares, but, one thing is certain, he was *persuaded* to go to sea, and *Punch* (born 17 July) devotes a page (vol. i., p. 46) to " The Boy Jones's Log," a portion of which is as follows :

" This mellancholly reflexion threw me into a poeticle fitte, and though I was werry uneasy in my *stommik*, and had nothing to rite on but my *chest*, I threw off as follows in a few 2nds, and arterards sung it to the well-none hair of ' Willy Reilly ' : —

> " Oakum to me,* ye sailors bold,
>   Wot plows upon the sea ;
> To you I mean for to unfold
>   My mournful historie.
> So pay attention to my song,
>   And quick-el-ly shall appear,
> How innocently, all along,
>   I was in-weigle-ed here.
>
> " One night, returnin home to bed,
>   I walk'd through Pim-li-co,
> And, twigging of the Palass, sed,
>   ' I'm *Jones* and In-i-go.'
> But afore I could get out, my boys,
>   Pollise-man 20A,
> He caught me by the corderoys,
>   And lugged me right a-way.

* The nautical way of writing " Oh, come to me."

Printer's Devil.

> " My cuss upon Lord Melbun, and
>   On Jonny Russ-all-so,
> That forc'd me from my native land,
>   Across the waves to go-o-oh !
> But all their spiteful arts is wain,
>   My spirit down to keep ;
> I hopes I'll soon git back again,
>   To take another peep."

To follow Chronology compels me to turn suddenly from gay to grave topics. In September, 1833, Newman commenced the *Tracts for the Times*, which, according to its advertisement, had the object of " contributing something towards the practical revival of doctrines (such as the Apostolic Succession, and the Holy Catholic Church) which, although held by the great divines of our Church, have become practically obsolete with the majority of her members." Keble and others joined him at once, as did Pusey as soon as the state of his health permitted, together with nearly all the advanced thinkers at Oxford. These Tracts, issued from time to time, caused a mighty upheaval in the Church of England, which was known as the " Tractarian movement," the effects of which have lasted to this day, as may be witnessed in the vast extension of Church building, the larger attendance and more devout behaviour of congregations, the brighter and more ornate services, which are so great a contrast to the general sleepiness both of pastor and flock which then existed.

Some of these Tracts went farther than people were, as yet, able to follow, they were " strong meat for babes," and the publication of Tract XC., by Newman, on the Thirty-nine Articles, brought things to a climax, and on 15 March, the Vice-Chancellor and the Heads of Houses met to censure the publication ; they came to the resolution : " That modes of interpretation, such as are suggested in the said Tract, evading rather than explaining the sense of the Thirty-nine Articles, and reconciling subscription to them, with the adoption of errors which they were designed to counteract, defeat the object, and are inconsistent with the due observance of

the Statutes of the University." They only expressed their
opinion which was all they could do, but Newman avowed
the authorship of the Tract, and whilst he was still uncon-
vinced of his error, he wrote, "I am sincerely sorry for the
trouble and anxiety I have given to the members of the Board,
and I beg to return my thanks to them, for an act which, even
though founded on misapprehension, may be made as pro-
fitable to myself, as it is religiously and charitably intended."

At this time, neither the writers of the Tracts, nor their
readers, had any intention of severing themselves from the
Church of England, their sole endeavours were to wake it
from the torpor into which it had fallen ; and, had there been
any tolerance on the other side, such men as Newman,
Manning, and others, would have been kept to the Church,
for they merely enunciated doctrine and practices which are
now almost universal.

The old flint-lock Brown Bess was still in use in the Army,
although percussion arms were introduced in 1840 ; but we
read (13 Ap.) that "the exchange of flint for percussion cap
guns to the Army, will cost, this year, £130,000."

That amiable gentleman, the Earl of Cardigan, was still
making himself notorious. This time it was flogging a soldier
on Easter Sunday, after Church ; and the very first question
asked in the House of Commons, when it met after the Easter
recess, was by Mr. Hume, relating to it. Mr. Macauly replied
that : "Whatever other imputations there might be cast on
Lord Cardigan, a disposition for the infliction of corporal
punishment was not one which could justly be thrown on
him. From inquiries which he had made, he had found that,
since 1839, up to the recent case, there was not an instance
of the infliction of corporal punishment in this regiment. The
charge, however, for which he was justly liable to public
censure, was the immediate infliction of punishment, on a
Sunday, after Divine Service. Such a proceeding was clearly
contrary to the religious feelings and habits of the people of
this country, and could not be reconciled with either good
sense, or good feeling." Lord Hill, the Commander-in-Chief,
only felt " surprised " at Lord Cardigan's conduct ; but the

Times of 24 Apl. had a most scathing leading article on the subject, winding up with "we trust some independent member of the House of Commons will take an early opportunity of cutting the Gordian knot, and move an address to the Crown for the removal of the Earl of Cardigan from the Lieut.-Colonelcy of the 11th Hussars."*

The Electric Telegraph being now a *fait accompli*, the honour of the discovery was disputed between Cooke and Wheatstone—both claiming it. It was settled by arbitration, the referees being Marc Isimbard Brunel, the eminent civil engineer, and Professor Daniell, the inventor of the Galvanic battery which bears his name, and their Solomonian judgment was as follows: "While Mr. Cooke is entitled to stand alone, as the gentleman to whom this country is indebted for having practically introduced and carried out the Electric Telegraph as a useful undertaking, promising to be a work of national importance; and Professor Wheatstone is acknowledged as the scientific man, whose profound and scientific researches had, already, prepared the public to receive it as a project capable of practical application; it is to the united labours of two gentlemen so well qualified for mutual assistance, that we must attribute the rapid progress which this important invention has made during the five years since they have been associated."

On 24 May was sold by auction an undoubtedly authentic signature of Shakspere, attached to a deed, thus described in the catalogue:- "Shakspere's autograph affixed to a deed of bargain and sale of a house purchased by him, in Blackfriars, from Henry Walker, dated March 10, 1612, with the seals attached." The poet is described as "Wm. Shakspeare, of Stratforde upon Avon, in the countie of Warwick, gentleman"; and the premises thus: "All that dwelling house, or tenement, with the appurtenance, situate and being within the precinct, circuit and compasse of the late black ffryers, London, sometymes in the tenure of James Gardiner, Esqre., and

---

* He put up for election at the Senior United Service Club, was balloted for on 6 June, 1840, when out of 194 balls, 166 were black

since that time, in the tenure of John Ffortescue, gent, and now, or late being in the tenure or occupacon of one William Ireland, or of his assignee or assignees; abutting upon a streete leading down to Pudle Wharffe on the east part, right against the King's Majesties Wardrobe; part of wch said tenement is erected over a great gate leading to a capitall messuage, wch sometyme was in the tenure or occupacon of the Right Honourable Henry now Earle of Northumberland." The deed, at the commencement is stated to be " betweene Henry Walker, Citizen and Minstrell, of London, of thone partie, and William Shakspeare, of Stratforde upon Avon, in the countie of Warwick, gentleman; William Johnson, Citizen and Vintner, of London; John Jackson and John Hemyng, of London, of thother partie "; and that the property was absolutely sold to all four, " theire heires and assigns for ever." The deed is regularly entered in the Rolls' Court. Sir F. Madden (continues the catalogue) states in his " Observations on the autograph of Shakspere, in Florio's translation of *Montaigne's Essays*, which was sold in 1838 : " There are five acknowledged genuine signatures in existence, exclusive of the one which forms the subject of this communication. Of these, three are attached to his will in the Prerogative Court, executed the 25th March, 1615-16; the fourth is written on a mortgage deed, dated 11 March, 1612-13; of a small estate purchased by Shakspere, of Henry Walker, in Blackfriars; and the fifth, on the counterpart of the deed of bargain and sale of the said property, dated 10 March, 1612-13; and, speaking of the last, Sir F. Madden says, at p. 14: ' What has become of this document?' a query which the auctioneers say is answered. Of these six signatures, three to the will are in Doctors' Commons (two of them much injured by the hands of the lovers of Shakspere): the one in *Montaigne's Essays* is now in the British Museum; what has become of the mortgage deed is quite unknown: this, then, is the only autograph of Shakspere ever likely to be offered for sale." After many and very animated biddings it was eventually knocked down to Mr. Elkins for £165 15s. These two deeds are now in safe keeping, one being in the

British Museum, the other belonging to the Corporation of the City of London. The authenticity of the signature in *Montaigne's Essays* is open to discussion. At the same sale was sold "the Shakspere Cup," made from the mulberry tree said to have been planted by Shakspere, carved on the sides with a medallion of Shakspere, and his Coat of Arms. This was for nearly 30 years in the possession of Munden, the actor, and it realised £21. In the British Museum is a beautifully-carved casket, made of the same wood, which, together with the freedom of Stratford-on-Avon, was given to Garrick by the Corporation of the town in 1769.

The decennial Census, which began in 1801, was, according to the Act 3 and 4 Vic., c. 29, taken of the number of individuals who slept in the respective houses in each parish, throughout England and Wales, on the night of Sunday, 6 June. Scotland, the Channel Islands, and the Isle of Man were also taken, but Ireland was not; and the following return includes only such part of the Army, Navy, and Merchant Seamen, as were, at the time of the Census, within the Kingdom on shore :

	Males.	Females.	Total.
England	7,321,875	7,673,633	14,995,508
Wales	447,533	463,788	911,321
Persons ascertained to have been travelling by railroads and canals on night of 6 June	4,003	893	4,896
Scotland	1,241,276	1,379,334	2,620,610
Islands in the British Seas	57,598	66,481	124,079
		Total	18,656,414

On 8 June, Astley's Amphitheatre was burnt down, one life being sacrificed, and causing a monetary loss of over £30,000. This calamity so affected the proprietor, Mr. Ducrow, that he lost his reason, and died soon after, on 28 Jan., 1842.

Here is another little story of the behaviour of gentlemen in those days, copied from the *Times*, 11 June :

"WINDSOR, 10 June. Yesterday evening there was a large party consisting of the officers of the 60th Rifles, and several of the 1st Life Guards, at the mess of the infantry barracks, in Sheet Street, in consequence of several promotions which have recently taken place in the Rifles, occasioned by vacancies caused by the decease of the Hon. Col. Molyneux. The festivities of the evening were kept up till past 12 o'clock, when a large party sallied forth for 'a spree.' They first proceeded to the extensive canvas amphitheatre of Mr. Van Amburgh, in the Bachelor's Acre, but, there, they were, fortunately, kept at bay by several of Mr. Van Amburgh's men, before they had committed any excesses. The knockers, bell handles and brass plates from several doors in the neighbourhood were then wrenched off, and the whole party then made for a well-known gambling house (which has been tolerated in this town for upwards of twelve months), at No. 4, Augusta Place, where they were immediately admitted. What took place there before the row commenced, or what was the occasion of the havoc and destruction which almost immediately afterwards ensued, I have not been able to ascertain. However, they had not been there more than half an hour before there was a scene of the greatest confusion throughout the whole house, causing alarm and terror, from the noise which was created, around the entire neighbourhood. The police were sent for soon after 1 o'clock, previously to which a portion of the 60th Rifles, who were on guard at the Castle, had been despatched to the scene of action, and whom the police met on their return to the guard room. Upon the Superintendent, Sergeant and several policemen entering the house (which they found empty, with the exception of one of the gamblers, who, it appeared, had secreted himself) they found scarcely one piece of furniture left whole. The green baize was torn from the billiard and other tables, the doors of the different rooms broken down, the windows, with the sashes and frames, broken to pieces ; all the lamps smashed, chairs and tables dislocated, the fanlight over the front door gone, and the balustrades upon the stairs torn away. At this time, the whole of the party had gone off ; and, as for the proprietors of the gaming house, they were glad to effect their escape, across the garden, into a large piece of waste land, called the Lammas. It was expected that some complaint would have been lodged before the borough magistrates, to-day, at the Town Hall ; but no application was made to the Bench on the subject during the hours of business. A large brass plate, which had been wrenched from a garden gate, was found, this morning, by the police, in the infantry barracks, where there are sundry knockers and bell handles awaiting to be identified and returned to their respective owners."*

The following incident is very little known, and is copied from the *Salopian Journal* of 3 July : " It is known to many of our readers that the Whig-Radical faction in Shrewsbury, despairing (as the event has proved) of winning the election by fair and honest means, have resorted to the infamous trick of publishing anonymous slanders against Mr. Disraeli, one of the Tory Candidates. He rebutted the slanders so promptly and effectually, that, at last, the opposite party resolved to try the desperate expedient of publishing them with a name attached, as a sort of guarantee. Accordingly, a letter, repeating these slanders, " with additions," appeared in the *Shrewsbury Chronicle* on Friday, signed by a barrister, who had been employed by the Radical candidates to manage their part of the contest. Mr. Disraeli, without any loss of time, issued a handbill commenting on conduct which appears to us at once ungentlemanly and unprofessional, and plainly designated the barrister's statements as ' utterly false.' This handbill appeared early in the forenoon of Friday, and, at an advanced hour of the afternoon, a gentleman waited upon Mr. Disraeli with a hostile message from his calumniator. He found Mr. Disraeli in company with his lady, and communicated that he had business of

---

* An action was brought against them at Reading, and on 24 Feb., 1843, the jury found for the plaintiff against all the defendants, and gave 1*s*. damages for the assault, and £55 for the injury done to the house and furniture.

importance to settle with him. A challenge from the barrister was then handed to Mr. Disraeli. About an hour afterwards, Mr. Jonathan Sheppard having learnt that such a transaction had taken place—and it is certain that the information had not come from the challenged party—waited upon the Mayor, and, upon his information, our worthy Chief Magistrate called upon both parties to enter into recognizances to keep the peace. How far Mr. Disraeli would have been justified in meeting a person who had acted as the barrister had acted, is a question which need not be discussed here."

CHAPTER XVI.

WE have known something about Irish crime, but the following true tale takes a lot of beating. On the last day of the Clonmel Assizes, in July, Judge Torrens heard a case of arson, in which the prisoners, who were four in number, were all acquitted, after a trial which lasted eight hours.

The principal witness for the prosecution was an approver, named Lysaght; and, in all the annals of informers, it would be extremely difficult to find a parallel to this same Lysaght. Indeed, the admission by the Crown of the testimony of such a miscreant, in the matter of life or death, appears to be highly reprehensible, as the following abstract of his evidence will plainly evince:

John Lysaght examined: I remember the time when Walsh's house was burnt. Anthony Ryan came to me before the house was burned to borrow a gun. I brought it to him on a Monday night, and he told me to come with him to McCarthy's house, who wanted to see me. I went to McCarthy's, and near his place was an old house, in which some of our party were assembled. McCarthy brought some bread and spirits, and we took share of it. McCarthy asked me if I would go with the men to frighten Walsh, and burn the house. I promised to do so, and he then furnished us with powder and ball; we went down to the river side, and McCarthy gave his pistols and 7/6 in money to Anthony

Ryan. He gave me some powder, flax, and something like saltpetre, and showed me, by putting some powder into the pan, and snapping it, how the flax was to be lighted. McCarthy then parted with us, and we, after eating the bread and meat, went to Walsh's. I lighted the tow, and Paddy Ryan put the fire into the roof. I and two of the party then went and stood sentry near the road. After a time, I heard a noise, and ran back to give an alarm. We then left, and went by Toom homewards, and separated near Marshall's gate; this was about three or four in the morning. I and Paddy Ryan had shot guns, Ned Ryan had a long one, Darby Ryan a bayonet on a pole, and the two Ryans had McCarthy's pistols. We left the house after it was in flames. I knew a man named Bryan Noonan; he is dead.

Judge Torrens: Was it you murdered Noonan?

Witness: No. I joined in it.

Mr. Hatchell: How many men did you murder before this?

Witness: None.

You say it was Anthony Ryan went to you to get the gun?—It was.

He has, since, been transported?—Yes.

You went with the party to the burning for the love of amusement?—They induced me to go with them, but did not force me; I was not very unwilling to go after getting the liquor; but, when I brought the gun, had no such intention.

Did you load the gun before you went out?—I did.

Had you liberty to carry a gun?—Yes, from a magistrate, Mr. Coates, who is since dead.

Were you ever tried before you committed the murder on Noonan?—Indeed I was; I was tried before, for posting a threatening notice, but it was no such thing.

Were you not sentenced to be transported?—I was.

Did you not fire shots at the same time?—Yes.

Judge Torrens: And the reward you gave the Government for bringing you back was murdering Noonan.

Mr. Hatchell: Was not your brother Caravat tried?—Yes.

You say you were only present at the murder of Noonan; now, was it not you who knocked down the unfortunate man with the butt-end of a blunderbuss?—Yes, the very first. (Sensation.)

And you don't call that murdering the man?—We were all murdering him.

Were you not one of the men who carried him into the ditch to hide the body?—I was.

Where is your brother, the Caravat?—I don't know.

Was he at the burning of Walsh's house?—No.

Did you know Leonard, the smith?—I did.

Did you see him killed?—I saw him struck, but was not looking on at his killing.

Did you give him a blow then?—I did not strike a blow at the man.

Did you give a blow that day?—Yes, when myself was struck.

Do you remember Wat Hayes?—Yes.

You attacked him, but he shot you off?—No, he did not.

Was not one of your companions shot by Mr. Hayes?—No, but a man near me.

Now, tell me, did he not kill one of your friends?—Oh, he had a party against us, and waylaid us.

Did you remember Jemmy Hughes, who was killed with a hatchet?—I did.

Were you not looking at his murder?—Oh, no; he was married to my first cousin.

Were you not taxed with the murder?—The whole country knew who was in that affair.

You recollect David Hickey, who was killed at Bilboa?—I was in the fair.

You were of the party?—I was looking at him.

That was your third murder.

A Juror: His fifth murder.

Did you rob Michael Rogers?—No, but I got the course of law, and was acquitted.

You knew Mick Griffin, Lord Stradbroke's herd?—I heard he was shot.

Was your brother Caravat accused of this business?—No, I never heard of it.

Did you not say you would put a rope about McCarthy's neck ?—I did not. I remember when Kennedy was put out of possession. McCarthy's cattle and premises were burned after this, but the country say it was himself did it. I never asked a farm of Lord Stradbroke, but my father or brothers might. I never heard that McCarthy prevented us getting the farm, on the ground of our being so bad.

Do you remember you and your uncle carrying away a woman ?—I do.

Your uncle was transported ?—He was.

So you have been guilty of one abduction, five murders, and one burning ; what else did you do ? Would you suggest any other crime in the catalogue, of which you were not guilty ?

Judge Torrens : Did you commit a rape ?—No.

Mr. Hatchell : Were any of your brothers convicted of a rape ?—Yes.

Were you not charged with holding the unfortunate woman while your brother committed the rape ?—No, but another brother was.

Judge Torrens : Did you steal cattle ?—No.

Mr. Hatchell : That would be too shabby an offence. When you came to Walsh's house, you lifted one of the Ryans up in the roof ?—Yes.

And you lit the fire ?—I did.

Did you know there were women in the house ?—I partly guessed there were.

Did you mind how many innocent people might have been burned ?—I did not care.   (Great sensation.)

Judge and Counsel, with great disgust, ordered the wretch off the table.

In these days of Motor Cars, any gossip about their pro-genitors must be of interest. On 7 Aug., a steam carriage, carrying 16 persons, belonging to the General Steam Company, was tried between the York and Albany, Regent's Park, and the Manor House at Tottenham—i.e., along the Camden Road to Finsbury Park—doing the distance in rather

less than half-an-hour.   Another ran on 13 Sep. from Deptford to Sevenoaks, about 21 miles, in 2 hours 37 minutes,
but there were small accidents by the way.   Later on in
the month the first-named carriage performed about Windsor,
Frogmore and Dachet, and frequently reached a speed of
18 to 20 miles an hour; and on Oct. 1 it was shown to the
Queen and Prince Albert, the latter expressing himself highly
pleased with it.   It then only did 16 miles an hour.

On 9 Sep. Vauxhall Gardens, which had been a place of
amusement since the time of Charles I., were sold for £20,000.
In *Punch* of 14 Aug. we find a sad account of a last visit:

"Impelled by a sense of duty, we wended our way to the
'Royal property,' * to take a last look at the long expiring
gardens.   It was a wet night—the lamps burnt dimly—the
military band played in the minor key—the waiters stalked
about with so silent, melancholy a tread, that we took their
towels for pocket handkerchiefs; the concert in the open
rain went off tamely—dirge-like, in spite of the 'Siege of
Acre,' which was described in a set of quadrilles, embellished
with blue fire and maroons, and adorned with a dozen double
drums, thumped at intervals, like death notes, in various parts
of the doomed gardens.   The *divertissement* was anything
but diverting, when we reflected upon the impending fate of
the 'Rotunda,' in which it was performed.

"No such damp was, however, thrown over the evolutions of
'Ducrow's beautiful horses and equestrian *artistes*,' including
the 'new grand *entrée* and calvacade of Amazons.'   They
had no sympathy with the decline and fall of the *Simpsonian* †
empire.   They were strangers, interlopers, called in, like mutes
and feathers, to grace the 'funeral show,' to give a more
graceful flourish to the final exit.   The horses pawed the
sawdust, evidently unconscious that the earth it covered would
soon be 'let on lease for building ground'; the riders seemed
in the hey-day of their equestrian triumph.   Let them, how-

* It was held copyhold of the Queen, as Lord of the Manor.

† Mr. Simpson had been a famous Master of the Ceremonies.

ever, derive from the fate of Vauxhall a deep, a fearful lesson!
—though we shudder as we write, it shall not be said that
destruction came upon them unawares—that no warning voice
had been raised—that even the squeak of *Punch* was silent!
Let them not sneer, and call us superstitious—we do *not* give
credence to supernatural agency as a fixed and general principle; but we did believe in Simpson, and stake our
professional reputation upon Widdicomb!*

"That Vauxhall Gardens were under the special protection
of, that they drew the very breath of their attractiveness from,
the ceremonial Simpson, who can deny? When he flitted
from walk to walk, from box to box, and welcomed everybody
to the 'Royal property,' right royally did things go on! Who
would *then* have dreamt that the illustrious George†—he of
the Piazza—would ever be 'honoured with instructions to
sell'? that his eulogistic pen would be employed in giving
the puff superlative to the Elysian haunts of quondam fashion
—in other words—painting the lily-gilding refined gold?
But, alas! Simpson, the tutelar deity, departed ('died,' some
say, but we don't believe it), and, at the moment he made
his last bow, Vauxhall ought to have been closed; it was
madness—the madness which will call us, peradventure, superstitious—which kept the gates open when Simpson's career
closed—it was an anomaly, for, like Love and Heaven,
Simpson was Vauxhall, and Vauxhall was Simpson!

"Let Ducrow reflect upon these things—we dare not
speak out—but a tutelar being watches over, and giveth
vitality to his arena—his ring is, he may rely upon it, a fairy
one—while *that* mysterious being dances and prances in it,
all will go well; his horses will not stumble, never will his
clowns forget a syllable of their antiquated jokes. Oh! let
him, then, whilst seriously reflecting upon Simpson and the
fate of Vauxhall, give good heed unto the Methuselah, who
hath already passed his second centenary in the circle!

"These were our awful reflections while viewing the

---

* Ring Master at Astley's.

† George Robins, a famous auctioneer.

scenes in the circle, very properly constructed in the Rotunda. They overpowered us—we dared not stay to see the fire-works, ' in the midst of which Signora Rossini was to make her terrific ascent and descent on a rope three hundred feet high.' She *might* have been the sprite of Madame Saqui ;* in fact, the ' Vauxhall Papers,' published in the gardens, put forth a legend which favours such a dreadful supposition. We refer our readers to them—they are only sixpence apiece.

" Of course, the gardens were full, in spite of the weather ; for what must be the callousness of that man who could let *the* Gardens pass under the hammer of George Robins, with-out bidding them an affectionate farewell? Good gracious! we can hardly believe such insensibility does exist. Hasten then, dear readers, as you would fly to catch the expiring sigh of a fine old boon companion—hasten to take your parting slice of ham, your last bowl of arrack—even now, while the great auctioneer says 'going.'"

On 24 August Sir J. L. Goldsmid was made a Baronet, and was the first Jewish gentleman who ever received that title. Perhaps it is not generally known that an honour, not much inferior, had, once, very nearly fallen to the lot of a brother Israelite. At one of those festive meetings at Carlton House, in which George IV. sometimes allowed a few of his most favoured subjects to participate, Mr. Braham was introduced to sing his then newly-composed song, " A Bumper of Burgundy," when the gratified monarch, rising from his chair, was, with difficulty, restrained from conferring imme-diate knighthood on the flattered musician.

Three well-known railways were opened this year ; the Great Western, from London to Bristol, on 30 June ; the London and Blackwall, on 2 Aug. ; and the London and Brighton, on 21 Sep.

On 18 Oct. was a remarkably high tide in the Thames, which did an immense amount of damage. This, and another event were celebrated in a contemporary ballad, beginning :

* A famous Rope dancer.

" There's lately been a great high tide,
   Nor can it be surprising,
When everything is getting dear,
   That water should be rising,"

and after dealing with that event in a very witty manner, it
went on :

" The Tower of London, envying
   Father Thames's notoriety,
Resolved to have a ' flare up '
   And be talked of in society ;
Ten thousand guns were fired at once,
   With very few escapers,
But, though no one heard the great report,
   There was one in the papers."

This terrible conflagration was first noticed about half-past
ten, on the night of 31 Oct., by a sentinel on duty on the
terrace near the Jewel Office, whose attention was attracted to
a glimmering light under the cupola of the Round, or Bowyer
Tower—which was close to the Armoury, in which was deposited an immense amount of stores, such as muskets, etc.,
and many priceless trophies of war.   When the sentinel found
the light increased, he gave the alarm by firing his musket, and
the whole of the garrison, officers and men, turned out ; but the
fire had got so great a hold that, before a sufficient supply
of water could be obtained, the entire roof of the Armoury
was in flames.

Unfortunately, it was low tide in the Thames, and, although
the fire-engines soon arrived, and there were the Garrison
and 250 policemen to render assistance, the flames spread
rapidly ; so fast, indeed, that the only things then got out and
saved, were the Duke of York's sword and belt, and a beautiful Maltese gun.

The grand staircase of this Armoury was considered one
of the finest in Europe, and the following is a contemporary
description of it.   " In a recess on the landing was a platform
supported on eight brass six-pounder guns, taken at Waterloo,
and which served as pillars.   On this was a splendid trophy,

consisting of arms and weapons, ancient and modern, comprising nearly 200 varieties, and nearly all differing in form or pattern. In the centre was a marble bust of William IV. Upon the walls, at the sides, were two large stars, formed of swords, and their brass scabbards, bayonets and pistols, one representing the Star of the Garter, and the other of the Bath. Also two figures in gilt suits of armour on ornamented pedestals. The rails of the stairs and the cornice of the ceiling were ornamented with architectural figures, curiously formed with arms. Below, upon pedestals, were two very striking groups, one representing a knight in gilt armour, preparing for action, attended by his esquire, who was in the act of buckling on his spurs, and a pikeman, with his 18 feet pike. The other group was a knight in a handsome suit of bright armour, of the time of Elizabeth, in action, having seized a banner from the enemy, waving his followers on. On each side of the entrance door was a knight in a suit of gilt armour, and two others, similarly clad, stood on brackets. The whole of these were destroyed, with the exception of the Waterloo cannon."

The fire was soon perilously near to the Jewel Office, which was scorching hot—yet Mr. Swifte, the keeper of the jewels, saved the whole of the Regalia, down to the minutest article, and was earnestly begged to retire and leave the last thing, a huge silver wine fountain, to its fate, but he would not, and this, also, was salved.

> " Then Mr. Swifte was nothing slow
>   The Crown and Jewels saving ;
> And to get the great Wine Cooler out,
>   Great danger he was braving.
> Now, Mr. Swifte, of all the wine,
>   Should now be made the ruler,
> For while the fire was getting hotter,
>   He was getting *the Wine Cooler.*"

There was an awful scare as to the chance of the store of gunpowder catching alight—but 400 barrels of powder, and 200 boxes of grenades and ball cartridges, were removed to the magazine, and the remainder was thrown into the moat.

On the 8th Dec. the general public were allowed to inspect the ruins, and to purchase mementos of the fire; the prices were, 6d. for half-a-dozen gun-flints, and the same amount for a few burnt percussion caps; pieces of fused iron and arms went at prices varying from 1s. to 20s., the latter, the maximum price. For many years I had a fused cavalry pistol, and some calcined flints which were very pretty. The fused cannon were sold as old metal.

On the 9 Nov. His Majesty Edward VII. was born, and, on the 8th Dec. was created Prince of Wales. His patent is as follows:

"Victoria, by the grace of God, of the United Kingdom of Great Britain and Ireland, Queen, Defender of the Faith.

"To all Archbishops, Dukes, Earls, Viscounts, Bishops, Barons, Baronets, Knights, Justices, Provosts, Ministers, and all other our faithful subjects, greeting——

"Know ye, that we have made and created, and by these our letters patent, do make and create, our most dear Son, the Prince of the United Kingdom of Great Britain and Ireland (Duke of Saxony, Duke of Cornwall and Rothsay, Earl of Carrick, Baron Renfrew, Lord of the Isles, and Great Steward of Scotland), Prince of Wales and Earl of Chester; and to the same, our most dear Son, the Prince of the United Kingdom of Great Britain and Ireland, have given and granted, and· by this our present Charter do give, grant and confirm, the name, style, title, dignity and honour of the same Principality and Earldom, and him, our said most dear Son, the Prince of the United Kingdom of Great Britain and Ireland, as has been accustomed, we do ennoble and invest with the said Principality and Earldom, by girting him with a sword, by putting a coronet on his head, and a gold ring on his finger, and, also, by delivering a gold rod into his hand, that he may preside there, and may direct and defend those parts. To hold to him and his Heirs, Kings of the United Kingdom of Great Britain and Ireland, for ever,· wherefore we will, and strictly command for us, our heirs, and successors, that our said most dear Son, the Prince of the United

Kingdom of Great Britain and Ireland, may have the name, style, title, state, dignity, and honour of the Principality of Wales, and Earldom of Chester aforesaid, unto him and his heirs, Kings of the United Kingdom of Great Britain and Ireland, as is above mentioned.

"In witness whereof, we have caused these, our letters, to be made patent. Witness ourself at Westminster, this 8th day of December, 1841.

> "By the QUEEN herself.
> "Edmunds."

We read in the *Times* of 25 Nov., anent the Thames Tunnel, that "a thoroughfare was, yesterday, effected in this work, and made use of, for the first time, by the whole of the directors, and some of the original subscribers, who had assembled upon the occasion. The shield having been advanced to the shaft at Wapping, a considerable opening was cut in the brickwork, and it was through this the party, who had met at Rotherhithe, were enabled to pass, thus opening the first subterranean communication between the opposite shores of the river. Upon their arrival at the shaft, the party was greeted by the workmen with most hearty cheers. A curious and interesting incident was connected with the event; a few bottles of wine, preserved since the dinner given on the occasion when the foundation stone was laid, with the understanding that it was to be drunk only when it could be carried under the Thames, having been opened and enjoyed by the company, to the health of Her Majesty and the infant Prince. It was remarked, too, as a singular coincidence, that a seal on one of the corks bore the impress of the Prince of Wales's feathers, a circumstance that caused some merriment. The engineer, Sir I. Brunel, appeared highly gratified at the happy result of his past anxiety and arduous labour. The shield will continue its advance, until it has afforded space for the formation of the remainder of the tunnel, which is expected to be completed in about three weeks."

By the end of the year the foundations of the New Royal

Exchange were dug out and concreted, and, as it was always anticipated that some important discoveries might take place in the course of the excavation, proper arrangements were made on the commencement of the work, that any articles of interest which might be disinterred, should be secured for the Gresham Committee. In the Specification for the Works, issued in 1840, the Contractor and Excavator were required, in taking out the soil, to deliver up " any plate, coins, antiquities, or curiosities, whether in metal, or otherwise, or any carved stones, or carvings in marble, pottery, terra cotta, or tesserae, which may be found in the course of the excavations; it being understood that all such matters, or things, are to be taken up with all requisite care, and are to remain the property of the Gresham Committee."

They found a portion of a Roman building, but the greatest haul was in an old gravel pit, some 50ft. by 34, filled with hardened mud, in which were contained considerable quantities of animal and vegetable remains, apparently the discarded refuse of the inhabitants of the vicinity. In the same depository were also found very numerous fragments of the red Roman pottery, usually called "Samian Ware," pieces of glass vessels, broken terra-cotta lamps, parts of amphorae, mortaria, and other articles made of earth, and all the rubbish which might naturally become accumulated in a pond in the course of years. In this mass likewise occurred a number of Imperial Roman coins, several bronze and iron styles, parts of writing tablets, a bather's strigil, a large quantity of caliga soles, sandals and remains of leather, all of which can now be seen in the highly interesting Museum of the Corporation of the City of London, at the Guildhall.

CHAPTER XVII.

Foundation of Royal Exchange laid—Medal connected therewith—Father Mathew's miracle—Christening of the Prince of Wales—King Edward VII.—
Hard work of the King of Prussia—The Earthquake in London—The Queen
drinking "grog"—Photography-Talbotype—Sale at Strawberry Hill—
Presents to the King of Prussia.

THE first event of note in this year was the laying, by Prince
Albert, of the foundation stone of the Royal Exchange, on
17 Jan., with all the pomp at the command of the City
authorities. The usual coins, etc., were deposited in a cavity,
together with a Latin inscription, engraved on zinc, of which
the following is a translation : " Sir Thomas Gresham, Knight,
erected, at his own charge, a building and colonnade for the
convenience of those persons who, in this renowned Mart,
might carry on the commerce of the World, adding thereto,
for the relief of indigence, and for the advancement of literature and science, an Almshouse and College of Lecturers, the
City of London aiding him, Queen Elizabeth favouring the
design ; and, when the work was complete, opening it in
person with a solemn procession. Having been reduced to
ashes with almost the entire city, by a calamitous and wide
spreading conflagration, they were rebuilt in a more splendid
form by the City of London and the Ancient Company of
Mercers, King Charles II. commencing the building on 23
Oct., A.D. 1667 ; and, when they had been again destroyed
by fire, on the 10th Jan., A.D. 1838, the same Bodies, undertaking the work, determined to restore them at their own
cost, on an enlarged and more ornamental plan ; the munificence of Parliament providing the means of extending the
site, and of widening the approaches and crooked streets, in
every direction ; in order that there might, at length, arise,

under the auspices of Queen Victoria, built a third time from the ground, an Exchange, worthy of this great Nation and City, and suited to the vastness of a Commerce extending to the circumference of the habitable Globe. His Royal Highness of Saxe-Coburg and Gotha, Consort of Her Sacred Majesty, laid the first stone on 17 Jan., 1842, in the Mayoralty of the Rt. Hon. John Pirie. Architect, William Tite, F.R.S. May God, our Preserver, ward off destruction from this building, and from the whole City."

After the manner of the City of London, a medal was struck to commemorate the event, having on the obverse a profile portrait of Prince Albert, with the legend "Albertus ubique honoratus," the reverse having a view of the western portico of the Exchange. On 13 Jan. Mr. Roach Smith exhibited at the Society of Antiquaries a medalet, found on the site of the Exchange, evidently struck to commemorate Queen Elizabeth's patronage of the original building, as it bore the Tudor Arms surrounded with the inscription "Angliœ Regina ubique honorata"

Father Mathew was still doing his grand work in Ireland, but there is a story told about him in the *Limerick Chronicle*, copied into the *Times* of 17 Jan., that is too good to be omitted : "The Rev. Mr. Mathew arrived in this city, last evening, by the Cork mail, *en route* to Loughrea, and put up at Moore's hotel. Immediately after his arrival became known, hundreds of persons visited him at the hotel, where he administered the pledge. One circumstance which came within public observation, we may mention here, as illustrative of the effects of breaking the temperance pledge :—A man, named Moynehan, a teetotaller, who worked at the Butter Weigh-house, got drunk on Christmas Eve, and the next day, became paralysed, his left arm, side and thigh being perfectly inanimate. He was removed to Barrington's Hospital, and remained there under the care of the surgeons, without improvement, until last evening, when his friends, having heard of Father Mathew's arrival in town, went to the hospital, and brought him out of his bed, on a man's back, to where the Rev. Mr. Mathew was staying ; a crowd had collected round the door, when the unhappy invalid was carried into his presence, and the reverend gentleman administered to him the pledge again, in a kind and impressive manner, and the man instantly stood up, was assisted by his friends to dress; and, to the astonishment of all, walked up William Street to his home, followed by a crowd of people."

On 25 Jan., the Prince of Wales was christened in St. George's Chapel, Windsor, by the name of Albert Edward, and on 20 Jan. appeared a letter in the *Times* from " A Conservative " :

" Sir.—We learn from the *Times* of to-day, that the Prince will be called Albert Edward.

" It is natural, indeed, that the illustrious father, and still more, that the illustrious mother, should prefer Albert Edward to Edward Albert.

" But as I pray God that the boy may live to be King, to whatever period his mother's life may be graciously extended, so I trust that he may have every qualification for popularity as well as goodness, and, amongst others, an old, and beloved, and accustomed *English name.*

" And what so fit as Edward? Who more beloved, or glorious, than Edward the Confessor—Edward I.—Edward III.—Edward VI.? A Catholic Saint—a law-giver—a conqueror—a Protestant Reformer?

" The Princess Alexandrina Victoria was known by her second name before she ascended the throne. So, I trust, may the young Prince be known as Edward, Prince of Wales, to the people, hereafter, Edward VII."

We all know how this gentleman's aspirations have been verified.

The King of Prussia was one of the Sponsors, and spent a few days after the christening in England. Poor man! how they did make him work!

On the 26th he had to be at the presentation of new colours to the 72nd Highlanders, and, in the afternoon, he visited Eton College.

12*

27th.—Came to London by railway, and held a Court at Buckingham Palace, where he received the *Corps Diplomatique* and the Corporation of the City of London On his return to Windsor, he visited Hampton Court.

28th.—Again came to London, visited the Zoological Gardens, lunched with Sir Robert Peel, and, afterwards, went to the Chapel Royal, Whitehall, and the National Gallery—dining at Windsor.

29th.—Saw a review in the Home Park, then went to London, and dined with his Minister, Chevalier Bunsen, in Carlton Terrace.

The 30th was Sunday, so the poor man was trotted off to St. Paul's Cathedral to hear the Bishop of London preach. Lunched at the Mansion House, visited the King of Hanover's apartments in St. James's Palace, and Stafford House; attended afternoon service at the Royal German Chapel, St. James's; visited the Duchess of Gloucester, in Piccadilly, and returned to Windsor.

After this rest on the 30th, he visited Newgate Prison, when he was received by the Lady Mayoress, Mrs. Fry, the Quaker philanthropist, the Sheriffs, etc., and thence proceeded to lunch with Mrs. Fry, at Upton, near Barking; at six he went to Drury Lane Theatre, and saw *The Two Gentlemen of Verona;* dined with the Duke of Sutherland at Stafford House, and slept at Buckingham Palace.

Next day, 1 Feb., at 10 a.m., he visited the Royal Society, Society of Antiquaries and the Geological Society. Thence he went to the British Museum, taking Mr. Solly's collection of pictures *en route;* and after spending three hours at the Museum, he lunched with the Duke of Sussex at Kensington Palace. In the evening, he underwent a dinner and concert given by the Duke of Wellington at Apsley House.

Early in the morning of the 2nd, he sat to Mr. Hayter for his portrait in a picture of the Christening. At 8.30 he embarked at Hungerford Wharf, on a steamer, bound for the Thames Tunnel; after visiting which, he went to the Tower of London. At 12 he returned to Buckingham Palace, where he received addresses from the Bishop and Clergy of the

Diocese of London; the members of King's College, London; the Society for Promoting Christianity among the Jews; the Prussian subjects resident in London; and the German Lutheran clergy. He also received deputations from the Bible Society, the Church Missionary Society, the Imperial Continental Gas Company; and gave audience to the Prince of Capua, etc.; visited the Archbishop of Canterbury at Lambeth; dined with the Duke of Cambridge; saw the *Merry Wives of Windsor* played at Covent Garden, and afterwards attended an evening party at Cambridge House.

On the 3rd he was present at the Queen's Opening of Parliament, then received a deputation from the general body of Protestant Dissenters; and visited the Queen Dowager, Earl of Jersey, the Dowager Duchess of Richmond, the Duke of Cambridge and the Duke of Wellington; winding up with dining with the Queen.

On the 4th they let him go—he paid a visit to the Queen at 9.30, went to Woolwich and saw a review of Royal Artillery, lunched there, visited Plumstead Marshes and the Arsenal, took leave of Prince Albert, and everyone else, and went off to Ostend.

About this time was a curious craze, which took strange hold on the people, that London was to be destroyed on the 16th of March, a belief which seems to have been founded on two metrical prophecies, dated respectively A.D. 1203 and 1598, said to be in the British Museum, where, however, I have failed to find them; the former is:

> " In eighteen hundred and forty-two
> Four things the sun shall view;
> London's rich and famous town
> Hungry earth shall swallow down;
> Storm and rain in France shall be,
> Till every river runs a sea;
> Spain shall be rent in twain,
> And famine waste the land again;
> So say I, the Monk of Dree,
> In the twelve hundredth year and three."

The other is fathered on the famous astrologer, Dr. Dee :

"The Lord have mercy on you all,
Prepare yourselves for dreadful fall
Of house and land and human soul—
The measure of your sin is full.

"In the year One, Eight, and Forty-two,
Of the year that is so new,
In the third month, of that sixteen,
It may be a day or two between.

"Perhaps you'll soon be stiff and cold,
Dear Christian, be not stout and bold ;
The mighty Kingly proud will see
This comes to pass, as my name's Dee."

And people were found to believe in this doggerel—especially frightened were the Irish in London, and the lower classes generally. There was a great exodus of the former, some even listening to the entreaties of their friends, and returning to Ireland, and many of the latter moved eastward of the church of St. Dunstan's, Stepney, which they considered would be the last edifice to fall. Nor was belief in the earthquake confined to the east end of London, for I read of a man, formerly a police constable, living in Paddington, St. Marylebone, who sold a good business to provide the means of his leaving London ; and of a clerk, with a salary of £20c a year, residing in the same parish, resigning his post, so that he might escape the calamity.

The fateful day arrived and passed, and, of course, the dreaded event did not take place, but the belief in it is evidenced in a paragraph in the *Times* of 17 March :

" THE EARTHQUAKE.—The scene witnessed in the neighbourhoods of St. Giles's and Seven Dials during the whole of yesterday was, perhaps, the most singular that has presented itself for many years. Many of the Irish resident in those localities have left for the shores of the Emerald Isle, but by far the larger number, unblessed with this world's goods, have been compelled to remain where they are, and to anticipate the fearful event which was to engulf them in the bowels of the earth. The frantic cries, the incessant appeals to Heaven for deliverance, the invocations to the Virgin and the Saints for mediation, the heartrending supplications for assistance, heard on every side during the day, sufficiently evidenced the power with which this popular delusion had seized the mind of these superstitious people. Towards the end of the day, a large number of them determined not to remain in London during the night, and, with what few things they possessed, took their departure for what they considered more favoured spots. Some violent contests arose between the believers and the sceptics—contests, which in not a few cases, were productive of serious results.

" The poor Irish, however, are not the only persons who have been credulous in this matter ; many persons from whom better things might have been expected, were amongst the number who left London to avoid the threatened catastrophe. To the Gravesend steamboat companies the 'earthquake' proved a source of immense gain ; and the same may be said with regard to the different railways. Long before the hour appointed for the starting of steamboats from London Bridge Wharf, Hungerford Market, and other places, the shore was thronged by crowds of decently attired people of both sexes ; and, in many instances, whole families were to be seen with an amount of eatables and drinkables which would have led one to suppose that they were going a six-weeks' voyage. About 11 o'clock, the *Planet* came alongside the London Bridge Wharf, and the rush to get on board of her was tremendous, and, in a few minutes, there was scarcely standing room on board. The trains on the various railways were, during the whole of Tuesday and yesterday morning, unusually busy in conveying passengers without the proscribed limits of the Metropolitan disaster. To those who had not the means of taking trips to Gravesend, or by railway, other places which were supposed to be exempted from the influence of the 'rude commotion' about to take place, were resorted to. From an early hour in the morning, the humbler classes from the east end of the Metropolis sought refuge in the fields beyond the purlieus of Stepney. On the north, Hampstead

and Highgate were favoured with a visit from large bodies
of the respectable inhabitants of St. Giles's ; and Primrose
Hill, also, was selected as a famous spot for viewing the
demolition of the leviathan city.   The darkness of the day,
and the thickness of the atmosphere, however, prevented it
being seen."

Brighton, too, felt the advantage of the "earthquake," as
numbers of families of the middle and upper classes went
there to avoid its consequences.   It was noted that on the
night of the 15th nearly 20 carriages arrived there, a circumstance that had not occurred since the opening of the London
and Brighton Railway.

To "talk scandal about Queen Elizabeth" is a matter
serious enough, but to say that Queen Victoria drank grog
on board one of her own ships is rank treason, and must
be explained, as it was by the *John Bull*.   "The true version
of Her Majesty's tasting the grog on board of *The Queen*,
during her late visit to Portsmouth, is as follows : Strict orders
had been given to the men, that when Her Majesty came
down to the lower deck, to see them at mess, they should
not speak a word, but preserve as profound a silence as
possible.   Jack, of course, was too much taken up with
watching the Royal visitor, to think of talking, save, perhaps,
the desire of whispering to his messmate a comment or so
on the meteor passing before him.   All was still.   Her Majesty
tasted the cocoa, and approved of it—yet all was still.   Her
Majesty then inquired whether there was no stronger bever-
age allowed the men, and forthwith a tumbler of 'three-water
grog ' was handed her.   She raised it to her lips—when Jack
forgot his orders, and three distinct cheers ran round the
deck, with such 'a will,' that the ship's sides seemed to start
with the sudden explosion ; the honour done was more than
a sailor could bear without clearing his heart with an huzzah."

It was on 8 Feb., 1841, that Fox Talbot provisionally registered his patent "for improvements in obtaining pictures, or
representations of objects," which is now in vogue, his improvement being the printing of the photo on paper.   He,

himself, made no public practical use of his invention, and one of the first, if not the first photographer who adopted it was Mr. Beard, of Parliament and King William Streets. It was quite a new thing when Prince Albert went to his studio on 21 Mar., 1842, and sat for his portrait. This made the process fashionable, and henceforth photography was a practical success.

There is nothing much to gossip about, until the Strawberry Hill sale. It was all very well for the Earl of Bath to eulogise the place,

> " Some cry up Gunnersbury,
>   For Sion some declare,
> And some say that with Chiswick House
>   No villa can compare ;
> But, ask the beaux of Middlesex,
>   Who know the country well,
> If Strawberry Hill, if Strawberry Hill
>   Don't bear away the bell."

but I fancy no one can endorse the opinion, or see anything to admire in this heterogeneous pile of Carpenter's and Churchwarden's Gothic. If it had applied to the contents that would have been another thing ; for, although there was, as is the case in most large collections, an amount of rubbish, it was counterbalanced by the undoubted rarity of the greater portion, which are thus set forth by the perfervid auctioneer, George Robins, who, speaking of himself in the third person, says :

"When there pass before him, in review, the splendid gallery of paintings, teeming with the finest works of the greatest masters—matchless Enamels, of immortal bloom, by Petitot, Boit, Bordier, and Zincke ; Chasings, the work of Cellini and Jean de Bologna ; noble specimens of Faenza Ware, from the pencils of Robbia and Bernard Palizzi ; Glass, of the rarest hues and tints, executed by Jean Cousin and other masters of the 15th, 16th and 17th centuries ; Limoges enamels of the period of the Renaissance, by Leonard and Courtoise ; Roman and Greek antiquities in bronze and sculpture ; Oriental and European china, of the choicest forms and colours ; exquisite and matchless Missals, painted by Raphael and Julio Clovo ; magnificent specimens of Cinque-Cento Armour ; Miniatures, illustrative of the most interesting periods of history ; a valuable collection of Drawings and Manuscripts ; Engravings in countless numbers, and of infinite value ; a costly Library, extending to fifteen thousand volumes, abounding in splendid editions of the Classics, illustrated, scarce and unique works, with ten thousand other relics of the arts and history of bygone ages, he may well feel over-powered at the evident impossibility of rendering to each that lengthened notice which their merits and their value demand."

The first private view took place on 28 March, and the sale lasted 24 days, commencing on 25 April and ending 21 May. No one can hazard a guess as to what such a collection would fetch now, the sum then obtained, £33,450 11s. 9d., being utter-ly inadequate according to modern ideas. The sale took place in a temporary shed, erected in the grounds, and on the first day of the sale, which was confined to books, there were not 200 persons present, and among them, not more than a dozen bidders.

By way of recognition to the King of Prussia for his being sponsor of the Prince of Wales, the Queen sent him some presents, which, if the *Wurtzburg Gazette* is to be credited, were of somewhat mixed description. 1.—A cradle with the figure of nurse holding an infant, representing the Prince of Wales, in her arms, all of pure gold. 2.—A pistol, which, when the trigger is pulled, opens and exhibits a completely furnished dressing-case. 3.—A gold mosaic snuff-box, upon which are seen allegorical *souvenirs* relating to the baptism of the Prince of Wales. 4.—Four boxes containing snuff. 5.—A dozen knives and forks of gold, except the blades of the knives, which are of Damascus steel, and the handles ornamented with a crown set in brilliants. 6.—A stone vase, containing the rarest Indian fruits. 7.—Two extraordinarily large legs of mutton.

CHAPTER XVIII.

THERE was a great flutter of excitement over the Queen's Fancy Dress Ball, which took place in the Throne Room of Buckingham Palace on 12th May. Its leading feature was the assembling and meeting of the two Courts of Anne of Bretagne (the Duchess of Cambridge) and Edward III. and Queen Phillipa (The Queen and Prince Albert).

A separate entrance to the Palace was set apart for the Court of Brittany, the Duchess of Cambridge assembling her Court in one of the lower rooms of the Palace, while the Queen and Prince Albert, surrounded by a numerous and brilliant circle, prepared to receive her Royal Highness in the Throne Room, which was altered so far, as to be made as much as possible to harmonise with the period. The throne was removed and another erected, copied from an authentic source, of the time of Edward III. It was lined (as well as the whole alcove in which it was placed) with purple velvet, having worked on it, in gold, the Crown of England, the Cross of St. George, and emblazoned shields with the Arms of England and France. The state chairs were as near those of the period as the archæology of the time could compass, and the throne was surrounded with Gothic tracery. At the back of the throne were emblazoned the Royal Arms of England in silver. Seated on this throne, the Queen and Prince Albert awaited the arrival of Anne of Bretagne, which, ushered in by heralds, took place at half-past ten.

The various characters then formed a procession divided into Quadrilles, the French, German, Spanish, Italian, Highland, Russian, Waverley and Crusaders Quadrilles, and marched into the Ball Room, where dancing at once commenced, the Queen and Prince Albert watching the scene, seated on a *haut pas*. At one o'clock, the Earl of Liverpool, the Lord Steward, conducted the Queen and Prince Albert to supper; and when they had finished the guests were attended to. After supper, the Queen danced a quadrille with Prince George of Cambridge, their *vis-a-vis* being the Duchess of Buccleugh and the Duke of Beaufort; then some reels were danced, and the Queen retired at half-past two.

This account would be strangely incomplete without some account of two or three of the principal dresses, to give an idea of the splendour of the show. The Queen's petticoat was of red velvet, trimmed with ermine. The ground of the jacket was garter blue, with a large pattern of leaves woven in it, of gold, and ornamented with precious stones; hanging sleeves, lined with ermine. The mantle was of cloth of gold, worked in silver, and trimmed with gold lace and pearls, lined with ermine, and fastened in front with a broad gold band, worked in diamonds and other precious stones. Her shoes were red silk, worked with gold and diamonds.

The crown was a *fac-simile* of that worn by Queen Philippa, and was ornamented with diamonds and precious stones. Under the crown, descending to the sides of the face, was a network of red velvet and diamonds.

Prince Albert's under dress, of a garter-blue ground, was worked in large gold flowers, lined with red silk. The collar and cuffs were ornamented with diamonds and precious stones. The cloak was of red velvet, trimmed with gold lace and pearls, and was fastened in front with a band of diamonds and different coloured precious stones, and was lined with ermine. His hose were of red silk, and he wore shoes of red velvet, embroidered with gold and satin. His crown was that of Edward III, ornamented with diamonds and precious

stones.   The sword-belt was of red velvet, studded with
rosettes of gold and diamonds ; the sword was richly ornamented with the rose, thistle, oak, and shamrock, in diamonds
and precious stones, the cross, forming the handle, containing some very large emeralds.

The mantle of the Duchess of Cambridge, as Anne of
Bretagne, was of crimson velvet, bordered with ermine, looped
up at the sides, displaying the petticoat of cloth of silver,
worked in silver and gold, fastened with diamond ornaments ;
the top was edged with two rows of large pearls, having between them a variety of ornaments, formed of sapphires,
emeralds and diamonds ; the lower row of pearls had beneath
it a fringe of large diamonds, formed into drops.   The
stomacher had rows of large pearls, of very great value, mixed
with diamonds.   Extending from the stomacher to the bottom
of the mantle were rosettes and other ornaments of diamonds,
sapphires and emeralds, forming a broad band down the
mantle.   The *ceinture* was also composed of brilliants,
emeralds and sapphires.   The sleeves were fastened with
diamonds and sapphires, and the necklace was of emeralds and
brilliants.

The diadem was composed wholly of pearls and diamonds,
except the *fleur de lys* by which it was surmounted, which
was composed of emeralds and sapphires.   The head-dress
was decorated with two rows of large diamonds and one of
pearls.   The veil was of gold tulle.

The Duke of Beaufort having been selected by the Duchess
of Cambridge to personate Louis XII., in the French Quadrille, of which Her Royal Highness was the leader, His Grace
appeared in one of the most splendid dresses handed down
by Monfaucon, in his *Monarchie Francaise*.   The dress consisted of rich blue velvet, sumptuously embroidered in gold,
with which were intermixed rubies, emeralds, pearls and other
precious stones, with a large diamond star in the centre, and
an opal, of priceless value, set with diamonds.   The cloak
was of cloth of gold, lined with white satin, and trimmed
over with powdered ermine.   The belt worn by the Noble
Duke, on this occasion, was of crimson, richly studded with

precious stones, and fastened in the centre by a large diamond buckle. Sword, a valuable specimen of the art of that period, the hilt being of gold, exquisitely chased; a crimson velvet hat with feathers, confined in the front by a costly jewel.

Space prevents my giving any more of the dresses, and I only notice that the Earl of Cardigan appeared in the French Quadrille, clad in armour, as *Bayard, the "Chevalier sans reproche"*!!!

As almost everyone's dress was ablaze with diamonds and other jewels, it is pleasant to think that very few losses were sustained, and those were, generally, of trifling value. The only loss of any moment was that sustained by Prince Albert, from the girdle of whose gorgeous dress, is supposed to have dropped a valuable brilliant of great size.

On 30 May, about half-past six in the evening, as the Queen was returning from her usual drive, and was close to Buckingham Palace, she was fired at by a young miscreant named John Francis, aged 20, described as a carpenter. He was at once seized, and examined by the Privy Council. The simplest account of the event was given at the boy's trial by Col. Arbuthnot, one of the Queen's equerries, whose testimony was as follows: "My general position is about five yards in the rear of Her Majesty. Before we left the Palace, I had received an intimation which induced me to ride as close to Her Majesty as I could; and Colonel Wylde, Prince Albert's equerry, rode in the same position, on the other side. Between 6 and 7 o'clock, we were coming down Constitution Hill, when, about halfway down the Hill, I observed the prisoner; and, on the carriage reaching him, he took a pistol from his side, and fired it in the direction of the Queen. As quickly as I could, I pulled up my horse, and gave the prisoner into custody. The prisoner had, before this, caught my attention as appearing anxious to see Her Majesty. The Colonel went on to say that the utmost distance from the carriage, when Francis fired, was seven feet. The *cortége* had been going at the rate of eleven miles an hour; but the Colonel had given instructions at this spot, to go faster, and the postillions were driving at the rate of twelve or thirteen miles an hour. The Queen was sitting on the back seat of the carriage, on the side nearest to the prisoner. The pistol seemed to the witness to be pointed in the direct line of Her Majesty."

On the news being communicated to the Houses of Parliament, they adjourned in confusion, as it was found impossible to carry on the public business whilst in that state of excitement. Next day both Houses voted congratulatory addresses, and the same were sent by every corporate body throughout the Kingdom. The Queen, who could not fail to be affected by this attempt upon her life, nevertheless attended the Opera the same evening, and met with a most enthusiastic reception.

Francis was tried, on the charge of High Treason, at the Central Criminal Court, on 17 June, and found guilty; there being no reasonable doubt but that the pistol was loaded with something more than gunpowder. His sentence was: " That you, John Francis, be taken from hence to the place from whence you came, that you be drawn from thence on a hurdle to the place of execution, and that you be hanged by the neck until you be dead: that your head be, afterwards, severed from your body, and that your body be divided into four quarters, to be disposed of in such manner as Her Majesty shall deem fit. And the Lord have mercy on your soul!"

This sentence was commuted to transportation for life, and on 6 July he left Newgate for Gosport, and he was sent to Norfolk Island by the first transport sailing thither.

This mania for shooting at the Queen was infectious. If Oxford had not been treated so leniently, there would have been no Francis; and if there had been no Francis, there would have been no Bean. This was another young miscreant, aged 18, deformed, and very short. It was on Sunday, 3 July, when the Queen was going from Buckingham Palace to the Chapel Royal, St. James's, that, in the Mall, this boy was seen to present a pistol at the Queen. A young man named Dassett saw the act, and this is a resumé of his evidence at the trial on 25 Aug.: He said he saw the royal carriages coming along, and saw the prisoner come from the crowd, draw a pistol from his breast, and present it at the carriage, at arm's length, and breast high ; and then he heard the click of a pistol hammer upon the pan ; but there was no explosion. He seized him, and, assisted by his brother, took him across the Mall, and gave him to Police Constable Hearn, who said "it did not amount to a charge." Another policeman, likewise, refused to take the prisoner, who only asked to have his pistol back again. The pressure of the crowd was so great, that he was obliged to let Bean go ; and, afterwards, the people said that witness himself had been shooting at the Queen, and a policeman took the pistol away from him.

In his cross-examination, Dassett said that some person in the crowd laughed, and others called out that the pistol was not loaded. An Inspector of Police deposed to having received the pistol from witness, and he unloaded it ; the charge was not large, and consisted of coarse gunpowder, some short pieces of tobacco pipe, and four small pieces of gravel.

Bean got away for a time, but was, afterwards, captured and tried, found guilty, and sentenced to 18 months' imprisonment in Millbank Penitentiary.

The old Duke of Cambridge (the Queen's uncle) had a fright, on the 6 July, when he was at a fête at Jesus College, Cambridge, for he lost the diamond star from his breast, valued at £500. Everybody thought it had been stolen by an expert thief, but it was afterwards found by a Police Inspector, in the gardens, much trodden on, and with three diamonds missing ; so it was "All's well that ends well."

There was great distress in the manufacturing districts, and disturbances originating in a strike for higher wages, were inflamed by the Chartists, and other political agitators. Beginning in Lancashire, the riots spread through Cheshire, Staffordshire, Warwickshire and Yorkshire, and, finally, extended to the manufacturing towns of Scotland, and the collieries of Wales. There were conflicts with the military, and people were killed ; altogether, matters were very serious.

It was better in London. On 19 Aug. a Chartist meeting was to be held on Clerkenwell Green, but plenty of police were there to meet them. Most of the mob were discouraged, and went home, but the police were obliged to arrest some 50 of them, and some banners were captured. Then they went to Lincoln's Inn Fields, and in Long Acre, they came into collision with the police, and some damage was done. So serious was the outlook, that all the military in the Metropolis and the suburbs were kept under arms, and there were large reserves of police at every Station House; and, next day, the magistrate, at Bow Street, had a busy day, hearing cases arising from this outbreak. On the 22nd Aug. there were Chartist meetings at Clerkenwell Green and Paddington (the latter numbering upwards of 10,000), but the worst cases were managed by the police, and no very great harm came of them.

On 22 June, Sir Robt. Peel's Bill, imposing an Income Tax, received the Royal sanction. It is 5 and 6 Vic., c. 35 : " An Act for granting Her Majesty Duties on Profits arising from Property, Professions, Trades, and Offices, until the 6th day of April, 1845." We see that it was imposed only for three years, but the Old Man of the Sea, once on the popular back, has never come off; and, in all probability, never will. It began at 7d. in the pound, has been as high as 16d., and as low as 2d. There is in *Blackwood's Magazine* for Aug., 1842 :

" THE INCOME TAX.

An excellent New Song.

————————————

All you who rents, or profits draw,
Enough to come within the law,
Your button'd pockets now relax,
And quickly pay your Income Tax.

A pleasant medicine's sure to kill,
Your only cure's a bitter pill :
The drugs of base deluding quacks
Made Peel prescribe the Income Tax.

You can't enjoy your pint, or pot,
And then refuse to pay the shot ;

13

You can't pursue expensive tracks
With a toll, or Income Tax.

Ye Quakers, clad in sober suit,
And all ye Baptist tribes to boot,
'Twas right, perhaps, to free the blacks,
But, thence arose this Income Tax.

Ye bagmen bold, ye lovers fond,
Who daily like to correspond,
Remember, as you break the wax,
Cheap postage means an Income Tax.

Ye noisy fools, who made a rout
To try and keep the Tories out,
The blunders of your Whiggish hacks
Have brought us to this Income Tax.

Old Cupid's* wish to crush the Czar
Has cost us, in the Afghan war,
Both English lives and Indian lacs,
And hastened on the Income Tax.

Regardless of the price of teas,
They anger'd, too, the poor Chinese,
The Mandarins have shown their backs,
But war soon brings an Income Tax.

Yet now I hope the new tariff
Will something save in beer and beef ;
If that be so, you'll all go snacks,
And half escape your Income Tax.

At least, we poor folks fear no shock
At hearing the collector's knock ;
His jest, the poundless poet cracks
On him who calls for Income Tax."

The day of reckoning for the Rioters of August duly came, and both at York and Salford Assizes many were punished, and at the end of September Feargus O'Connor was arrested in London for sedition, as were other Chartist leaders at Manchester and Leeds. In October, more rioters were tried, and sentenced, at Stafford and Liverpool.

Even women meddled with Chartism, and on 17 Oct. a

---

* A well-known nick-name for Lord Palmerston.

meeting of female Chartists was held at the National Charter
Association in the Old Bailey, to form a female Chartist
Association to co-operate with the original society. A Mr.
Cohen created some dissatisfaction by speaking *against* the
interposition of women in political affairs; he "put it to the
mothers present, whether they did not find themselves more
happy in the peacefulness and usefulness of the domestic
hearth, than in coming forth in public, and aspiring after
political rights?" Miss Inge asked Mr. Cohen, did he not
consider women qualified to fill public offices? it did not
require much "physical force" to vote! Mr. Cohen replied
with an *argumentum ad fœminam:*—He would, with all
humility and respect, ask the young lady, what sort of office
she would aspire to fill? If she would fill one, she would
fill all? He was not going to treat the question with ridicule;
but he would ask her to suppose herself in the House of
Commons, as Member for a Parliamentary Borough, and that
a young gentleman, a lover, in that House, were to try to
influence her vote, through his sway over her affections; how
would she act? whether, in other words, she could resist, and
might not lose sight of the public interests? (Order!
Order!) He wished to be in order. He was for maintaining
the *social* rights of women; *political* rights, such as he understood that meeting to aspire to, she could never, in his opinion,
attain. This drew forth an energetic speech from Miss Mary
Anne Walker; she "repudiated, with indignation, the insinua-
tion that, if women were in Parliament, any man, be he
husband, or be he lover, would dare to be so base a scoundrel
as to attempt to sway her from the strict line of duty." Miss
Walker was much applauded; and, after the business of the
evening, she received the thanks of the meeting.

In the *Times* of Oct. 5, there is a paragraph about a gipsey
trial, and as that curious nomad race is fast disappearing, it
may prove of interest to my readers:

"A short time since, a very remarkable circumstance took
place in the New Forest, Hampshire, in the instance of a
gipsey, named Lee, being cast out of the fraternity. The

13*

spot where the scene took place was at Bolton's Bench, near Lyndhurst. Between 300 and 400 gipsies, belonging to different tribes, including the Lees, Stanleys, and Coopers, were assembled upon this unusual occasion. The concourse consisted of a great many females; and so secretly had the meeting been got up, that scarcely a person residing in the neighbourhood was aware that a circumstance of the sort was about to take place. The offender, a handsome-looking man, apparently between 38 and 40 years of age, was placed in the middle of a ring, composed of the King of the Gipsies, and the patriarchs of different tribes. This ring was followed by a second, made up of the male portion of the assembly; and an exterior circle was formed by the women. The King (one of the Lees), who was a venerable old man, and one who looked as though he had seen upwards of 90 summers, then addressed the culprit for nearly an hour, but in a tongue that was perfectly strange to the bystanders. The address was delivered in a most impressive manner, as might be conceived by the vehemence of the gesticulations which accompanied it. None but the gipsies themselves had the slightest knowledge of the crime which had been committed by the offender, but it must have been one evidently very obnoxious to the tribe, as the act of expulsion from among them is an exceedingly rare occurrence. As soon as the King had finished his speech to the condemned man, he turned round, and harangued the whole of the gipsies assembled; and, expressing himself in English, he informed them that Jacob Lee had been expelled from among them, that he was no longer one of their fraternity, and that he must leave the camp of the gipsies for ever. The King, then advancing towards him, spat upon him, and the circle which enclosed him simultaneously opened to admit of his retreating from among them, while they smote him with branches of trees, as he left the ground. The meeting then broke up, and the parties assembled went their different ways; some of them having come some considerable distance, in order to be present at the tribunal."

Early in November Mr. J. Simon, LL.B., was called to the

Bar, being the first Jewish barrister connected with the Middle Temple. A Hebrew bible had to be obtained, on which he could be sworn, and a difficulty having arisen, owing to the custom of Jews putting on their hats when taking an oath, the size of the wig rendering it impossible in this case, it was ruled that the head was sufficiently covered by the wig.

On 31 May, 1842, an Act (5 & 6 Vic., c. 22) was passed for the demolition of the Fleet prison, and on 30 Nov., the records, books, etc., and the remaining prisoners, seventy in number, were removed to the Queen's prison. The Marshalsea was also closed, and its three prisoners were also transferred. The Fleet had been a prison ever since the time of William the Conqueror.

Writing about the Fleet prison sets one thinking of the marriages solemnized within its rules, and there is an entry in one of the registers: "The Woman ran across Ludgate Hill in her shift." In the *Times* of 15 Dec., I find the following, copied from the *Boston Herald:*

"GEDNEY.—A most extravagant exhibition took place here on Friday. A widow, named Farrow, having four children, was married to a man named David Wilkinson; and the woman having been told that if she was married, covered by nothing but a sheet, her husband would not be answerable for her debts, actually had the hardihood to go to church with nothing on but a sheet, sewn up like a sack, with holes in the sides for her arms, and in this way was married." I have come across several instances of this vulgar error.

On the 3rd Dec. was tried a famous gambling case which ended in the discomfiture of a notorious gaming-house keeper, named Bond. It was a case in the Court of Exchequer— Smith *v.* Bond. At the gaming house kept by the latter, the game played was, usually, "French Hazard"; and persons of rank were in the habit of staking large sums against the "bank" held by Bond, to whom reverted all the profits of the game; in one evening they amounted to £2,000 or £3,000. Considerable losses were sustained, on various occasions, by

Mr. Bredall, Capt. Courtney, Mr. Fitzroy Stanhope, the Marquis of Conyngham, Lord Cantelupe and General Churchill. The action was brought under the Act 9th Anne, c. 14, to recover from Bond the sums alleged to have been unlawfully won. A verdict for the plaintiff was returned on five out of ten counts, with damages including the treble value of £3,508, the sum lost. Half the damages went to the parish.

CHAPTER XIX.

Murder of Mr. Drummond—Rebecca and her Daughters—Spread of the Movement through Wales—Its End—Rebecca Dramatised—Rebecca in London.

THE year opened badly, with the assassination of Edward Drummond, Esqre., the private secretary of Sir Robert Peel. Walking quietly down Parliament Street, he was suddenly fired at by a man named Daniel McNaughton. Poor Mr. Drummond did not die at once, but lingered for a few hours. It was believed by very many people, myself among the number, that it was a political assassination, the Secretary being taken for the Premier, but the man got off on a plea of insanity, a plea which was very fashionable in favour of criminals at that time, and highly conducive to their benefit.

An episode in the Social History of England, almost unknown to the rising generation, was the reappearance, in Wales, of " Rebecca and her daughters," a riotous mob, whose grievance was, at first, purely local—they resisted the heavy and vexatious tolls, to which, by the mismanagement and abuses of the turnpike system, they were subjected. Galled by this burden, to which they were rendered more sensitive by reason of their poverty, and hopeless of obtaining any assistance or relief by legitimate means, the people resolved to take the law in their own hands, and abate the source of so much annoyance and distress by the strong arm.

The first act of destruction of the toll gates occurred in 1839, and the gates then destroyed were particularly obnoxious to the people, who entertained doubts of the legality of their erection. They were broken down in open day, with no attempt at concealment, by a mob of persons rather in a spirit of mischievous frolic than otherwise. The proposal to re-erect these gates, on the part of the trustees, was overruled by a large body of magistrates and gentlemen, many of whom qualified for trustees expressly for the occasion. This decision gave strength and encouragement to the discontented, and, no doubt, prepared the way for further violence. The gate breakers had learned their power and though they did not immediately renew the exercise of it, the lesson was not forgotten, although it slumbered until the commencement of 1843, when it appeared in a systematic and organised form.

This organization was called " Rebecca and her daughters," their leader having taken this scriptural name from a misconception of the meaning of *Genesis* xxiv., 60 : " And they blessed Rebekah, and said unto her. . . . ' let thy seed possess the gate of those which hate them.' " This captain of the gate breakers in the guise of a woman, always made her marches and attacks by night, and her conduct of the campaign manifested no small dexterity and address. A sudden blowing of horns and firing of guns announced the arrival of the assailants at the turnpike selected for attack. They were mounted on horseback, and generally appeared in considerable force. The leader, who gave the word of command, and directed the motion of those whom she called her daughters, was attired in a female dress of some description, wearing, also, a bonnet, or head-dress, which served the purpose of disguise. Her bodyguard were dressed up in similar manner.

Immediately on arriving at the gate, they commenced the business of the night, and proceeded to raze gate, posts, and tollhouse, with an alacrity and perseverance which soon accomplished its purpose. They, generally, sawed off the gate posts close to the ground, broke the gate to fragments, and pulled down the toll-house to its foundations. To show that the abatement of the specific grievance was their only object, they, commonly, dealt very leniently with the toll-keeper, offering him, except in rare cases, no personal violence, and allowing him to remove his furniture and property, which they never attempted to destroy or plunder. The work was no sooner done than the mysterious assailants galloped off, firing their guns, and blowing their horns, as before. No trace nor clue was to be found of the quarter whence they had come, or of the retreats to which they dispersed themselves; nor did anything in the outward appearance of the country, by day, even when these nightly outrages were at their height, give sign of the extension and compact organization which evidently subsisted among the population.

The first notice I can find (in this year) of these riots is in

Rebecca and her Daughters.

[*Ill. Lon. News*, 11 Feb., 1843.

the *Times* of 10 Jan., in which is the following paragraph from the *Welshman*:

" The state of society in Wales may surprise some of our English readers, especially when we acquaint them with the fact, that there has been, for some months past, in the neighbourhood of St. Clear, a mob of lawless depredators, amounting to about 600, who assembled nightly, for the purpose of destroying the turnpike gates on the various lines of road in the neighbourhood of St. Clear. These ruffians are headed by a very tall man, dressed, for disguise, as a female, who goes by the name of Rebecca ; and, as many of his associates are likewise dressed as females, the whole gang have been christened ' Rebecca and her daughters.'   These men are nearly all ably mounted, and are a terror to the neighbouring country.   The Pwiltrap gate has been destroyed a great number of times and as frequently replaced by the trustees of the road ; but, immediately after its re-erection, the fellows have invariably assembled in greater force than before ; and, riding up to the gate, the following interesting colloquy has taken place.   The leader of the mob, addressing the others in Welsh, says, ' My children this gate has no business here, has it ? ' to which her children reply, that it has not ; the mother again asks, what is to be done with it, when the children reply, that it should be levelled with the ground. They then immediately break it down, and disperse in different directions.

" This system has continued for a length of time ; and, although a reward of £50 has been offered, not one of the offenders has been discovered.   About 100 constables have been sworn in, and three constables from London are down there ; but all precautions are ineffectual ; for so surely as the constables show the slightest diminution of their vigilance, Rebecca and her daughters appear, and level the gates.   A very short time ago, the policemen were after a fellow whom they suspected to belong to the gang and, while at a public house, baiting their horse, Rebecca and her daughters suddenly came in sight, and the affrighted officers of the law were obliged to fly for their lives.   The gates have now been re-erected, and no fresh act of violence has occurred since the 16th ult., but the organisation of the depredators still continues ; and, it is feared, will break out with fresh violence if the constabulary force be removed."

That this movement was serious and no joke, is evidenced by the fact that I have, in my notes, 45 paragraphs in the *Times* on the subject.

From Pembroke and Caermarthen, it gradually spread to Cardiganshire, on one side, and to Radnorshire and Glamorganshire, on the other.   Brecknockshire, alone of the South

Wales counties, enjoyed exemption from these disturbances. The destruction which the rioters effected in some of these districts was most extensive and unsparing. There were, at the time of the outbreak, between 100 and 150 gates, including side bars and chains, in the county of Caermarthen; of these, no less than between 70 and 80 were destroyed, the toll-houses, as well as the gates and posts, being, in many cases, razed to the ground; in some trusts not a single gate was left standing. In Pembrokeshire, and in one of the divisions of Cardiganshire, the destruction was carried on in the same wholesale manner. The trustees, at first, re-erected the gates which had been broken down, but they were again as speedily demolished by the rioters; again they were rebuilt, and again they were levelled with the ground. The trustees were, at length, compelled to desist, and the roads were left free of toll. None of these counties, except Glamorgan, possessed a paid constabulary, or any other force which could be of avail in checking the proceedings of the rioters; and the magistrates finding all local efforts unavailing, were obliged to appeal to Government for protection and support.

One of the boldest steps ventured on by the insurgents, whose confidence was, of course, much increased by their uninterrupted success, was an entry which was made, at mid-day, into the town of Caermarthen, by a large body of persons on the 10th of June. About noon, the rioters began to march into the town, through the Water Street gate, which they had destroyed some time before. They were headed by a band. The leading body consisted of some thousands on foot, many of whom were Chartists and rabble of the town; a large number of women was among the crowd, and men bearing inflammatory placards. They were followed by a man in disguise, representing Rebecca; some bearing brooms with which to sweep the foundations of the tollhouse and the work-house, and the rear was brought up by about 300 farmers on horseback. They paraded the town, passing the Hall and hooting the magistrates, and proceeded to the workhouse, which they attacked. They climbed over the high wall with which the building was surrounded, and then burst open the lodge gates and the porter's door; the horsemen rode into the yard, and surrounded the premises; and the rioters on foot soon forced an entrance into the building, and commenced their work of destruction. While the rioters were in the act of pulling down the inner doors and partitions of the Board Room, and other parts of the premises, and pitching the beds out of windows, the governor was ringing the alarm bell; and, in the midst of the tumult, came the military.

Representations of the excited state of the neighbourhood had been sent to the Home Office, and a troop of the 4th Light Dragoons had been ordered from Cardiff. An express from Caermarthen had met the Dragoons at four o'clock in the morning, just after they had passed through Neath, and were still 31 miles from their destination. They pushed on, riding the last 15 miles in an hour and a half, two horses dying from fatigue as they entered the town. They were met by one of the Magistrates, who led them to the Workhouse and read the Riot Act. The rioters were summoned to surrender; but they made an attempt to rush on the military. The Dragoons charged, using the flat of their swords, and soon put the rioters, outside the wall, to flight. Those within offered some resistance; and, for a moment, the edge of the sword was turned upon them, when they succumbed. Many escaped over the wall; but about 100 were taken prisoners, and several horses were abandoned by their riders. The disturbance which menaced so seriously the safety of the town, was thus happily put an end to, without any bloodshed or calamitous result.

As time advanced, the insurrection, which had at first been lightly thought of, and for which much allowance had been made, under the belief that the people had real grievances to complain of, assumed a more malignant and dangerous aspect. The farmers and peasantry, who in their impatience under the vexations of the tolls, had commenced it, soon fell into the hands of ill-disposed and designing men, who aggravated the excitement that prevailed, and availed themselves of the name and disguise of " Rebecca," in order to carry out their own evil and lawless purposes. Threatening letters were one of the means most freely resorted to; and great numbers, under the signature of " Rebecca," were sent about the country, conveying the most sanguinary menaces to those whose conduct had, in any way, given offence to the dastardly writers. Certain rules were laid down by conclaves of the disaffected, respecting the occupation of farms; and all who presumed to contradict the edicts of this invisible authority, were marked out, and denounced as victims to the just vengeance of Rebecca. The more active magistrates, as well as the tithe-owners and clergy, were made the special objects of this cowardly system of intimidation. In some instances, the rioters proved that their threats were not without meaning. Guns were fired into the houses of persons who had fallen under the popular displeasure. Some had their property fired, or otherwise injured; and a growing feeling of alarm and insecurity began to pervade the peaceable and well-disposed portion of the community. This feeling was further increased by a cold-blooded and shocking act of murder, committed on a poor old woman who kept a turnpike, called the Hendy gate, on the confines of Glamorganshire and Caermarthenshire. A party of rioters came to attack the gate at which she lived, and one of the number, actuated by some motive which was not distinctly accounted for, fired at her, and shot her dead. A coroner's inquest sat upon the body, and all the facts attending the revolting transaction were fully and clearly stated in evidence; but, such was the excitement of feeling then prevailing in the neighbourhood, or such the influence of fear exercised over the minds of the jurymen who investigated the case, that they actually brought in a verdict: " That the deceased died from suffusion of blood, which produced suffocation, but from what cause, is, to the jurors, unknown! "

By the continuance of these outrages, which threatened, 'ere long, to disorganise society, and render the tenure of life and property, in Wales, insecure, the Government were, at length, aroused to the necessity of adopting very vigorous measures for the enforcement and vindication of the law. A large body of troops was sent down to Wales, and a general

officer, of skill and experience, appointed to the command
of the disturbed districts. A strong body of London police
was imported, to exercise their skill in ferreting out the actors
in these lawless exploits, who had so long succeeded in elud-
ing detection. The districts most infested by the Rebeccaites
were closely occupied by parties of soldiers, some of whom
were quartered, at short intervals, in the villages and hamlets
wherein mischief was suspected to lurk, and in the neighbourhood of turnpike gates, which had, previously, been the
objects of attack. It was not, however, the policy of the
insurgents to place themselves in open collision with the
soldiers ; but the clandestine and shifting mode of warfare
which they had adopted with so much success, was but imperfectly counteracted by the presence of a military force.
Under cover of the night, and with the advantages afforded
by a knowledge of the country, and the sympathy of the
population, they could sweep down a gate, which was but
the work of a few minutes, with very little risk of interruption
or discovery. The presence of the police and soldiers, if it
could not entirely put an end to the attacks on the turnpikes,
prevented the disaffected from proceeding to further acts
of violence, and checked the growth of a conspiracy which
might, otherwise, have gone to the full length of open re-
bellion. From this, and other causes, the spirit of disturbance
in Wales began to decline, about the latter end of the
summer. The most obnoxious of the turnpike gates had
been swept away ; and, on some of the trusts, the trustees
had announced their determination not to re-erect those which
were most complained of as oppressive. Some of the more
active leaders of the riots were captured, in an affray with
the County police, on the borders of Glamorganshire, and the
terrors of a Special Commission impended over the Principality.

The movement was even dramatised, and on 20 Sep., at
the Royal Amphitheatre, Liverpool, was produced a new
play, called : " Rebecca and her Daughters ; or, Paddy the
Policeman " ; the programme of scenery etc., as described on
he play bill being : " Vigilance of the civil and military

authorities; £100 reward for the apprehension of Rebecca, and £10 for each of her daughters; False alarm; Invincible courage of the Yeomanry; Arrival of the London Police in disguise; Paddy Whack undertakes to capture the delinquents; Admonitions to the Constabulary; The inspection; Mysterious appearance of Rebecca and her daughters in the Glen of Llandilo, at midnight; Tried before the Justice of the Peace; Happy *denouement*."

I can find only one reference to Rebecca in connection with London—and that refers to a bar in Gower Street, which was taken down some few years since. It occurs in the *Times* of 30 Sep. : " During the last two or three days, considerable excitement has prevailed in the northern suburbs of the Metropolis, in consequence of rumours obtaining circulation that threatening notices had been posted about, signed, ' Rebecca,' intimating that it was the intention of that lady and her daughters to destroy the various turnpike and other gates. which they were pleased to term ' public obstructions.' It appears that these rumours were not altogether unfounded ; for, whether intended as a joke, or otherwise, the doings of the notorious Rebecca and her daughters in Wales, have, in reality, found persons foolhardy enough to follow their example in London. A few evenings since, Mr. Hill, the porter and keeper of the gate at the London University College, which crosses Gower Street, and prevents carriages from passing along the front of University College Hospital, received a letter, with the signature of ' Rebecca ' attached, declaring it to be the intention of herself and others to remove the ' obstruction called a gate ' on the following night. Mr. Hill, thinking the matter a joke, took no notice of the circumstance ; but, to his astonishment, early in the morning following the night on which the threatened attack was promised, he was awakened by the night porter, who informed him that the gate (a large wooden one, such as the ordinary toll bars) was gone. On examination, it was found that not only had the large padlock by which it was fastened, been broken and carried away, but the gate had absolutely been filed off its hinges, and conveyed by the depredators into the College grounds, and hidden behind some shrubs.   The gate has again been re-instated ; but, since the occurrence, Mr. Hill has received another threatening notice, informing him that it is the intention of Rebecca and her daughters, on Monday night next, to effect its entire destruction.   What is most extraordinary in connection with the affair is, that the gate should have been removed without the knowledge of the police, the beats of two constables joining close to the spot, or that of the night porters, either at the College, or the Hospital.   It is to be remarked that frequent complaints have been made at the erection of the gate in question, as it interrupts the otherwise direct communication between Holborn and Broad Street, Bloomsbury, with the Hampstead Road, and compels carriages, etc., to go considerably out of the way round Sussex and University Streets, before they can get into the New Road."

CHAPTER XX.

AT this time, Gretna Green marriages were in full blast (they were only made unlawful in 1856), and we learn from the *Carlisle Journal*, copied into the *Times* of 20 Feb., something about the Parsons : " We observe by announcement in some of the London papers, that some worthy gentlemen in London, are about to enlighten the public on the subject of Gretna Green marriages, by the publication of a book called *The Gretna Green Memoirs*, by Robert Elliott, with an introduction and appendix by the Rev. Caleb Brown. In addition to this information, we have been honoured with a copy of what Mr. Elliott calls a ' cercler,' which he is desirous we should publish as a paragraph for the benefit of our readers. From this ' cercler ' we learn that ' this interesting work contains an accurate account of remarkable elopements, pursuits, anecdotes, etc., never before published.' Then we are further informed that there is ' in the press,' to be published by subscription, *The Gretna Green Register*, containing the names of 7,744 persons married by Robert Elliott, the Gretna Green Parson. It is added, that ' the whole is being carefully printed from the original registers, written and kept by himself.' The Gretna Green Parson, we suspect, has fallen into dishonest hands, or he would not have suffered it to be said that he was about to publish registers which never had existence. The Gretna Green Parson is pretty well known in this neighbourhood. He married a grand daughter of old Joe Paisley,

the ' original ' blacksmith ; and, after the death of that worthy
' parson,' he set up an opposition shop, in the marriage line
to David Laing, who had acquired some notoriety in the
business.   This was in 1811, and he continued to ' trade ' until
1822, when it either fell away from him, or he from it.   His
reverence subsequently condescended to act as horsekeeper,
or hostler, at one of the inns in this city, and a few months
ago was sent for to London, as a witness, in some marriage
case, and is now set up as an author!   We suspect the whole
thing is an attempt to gull the public into the purchase of a
book of inventions.   If 7,000 were deducted from the names
of those to be inserted in the ' Register,' the number would
still exceed, by many a score, those who were actually ' married,' as it is called, by ' Robert Elliott, the Gretna Green
Parson.' "

The poor " Parson " could not stand this attack on his
veracity, and wrote a letter to the *Times*, which appeared in
its issue of 23 Feb., in which he does not deny the bulk of
the paragraph taken from the *Carlisle Journal*, but gives his
figures as to his matrimonial business : he says that in the
following years ; he married so many couples :

1811	...	58	1821	...	152	1831	...	168
1812	...	57	1822	...	178	1832	...	153
1813	...	59	1823	...	188	1833	...	100
1814	...	68	1824	...	196	1834	...	108
1815	...	87	1825	...	198	1835	..	124
1816	...	89	1826	...	187	1836	...	98
1817	...	96	1827	...	188	1837	...	55
1818	...	109	1828	...	186	1838	...	46
1819	...	121	1829	...	180	1839	....	42
1820	...	124	1830	...	179			

He says he married 7,744 persons, but, either his arith-
metic, according to the above account, is faulty, or there is
an inaccuracy in the *Times* figures.

On 3 March arrived, in London, the first instalment of the
Chinese indemnity—£1,000,000, all in silver.   I remember
seeing the dock wagons guarded by soldiers, and wondering,

until told, what they contained. Some more arrived on the 7th.

The Thames Tunnel was opened to the public on 25 March, with as much ceremony as a private company could manage. There were the Lord Mayor, the directors, and a host of scientific persons, who solemnly went in procession down the staircase on the Rotherhithe side, passed along the western archway of the Tunnel, ascended and descended the staircase at Wapping, and returned through the eastern archway. ·In the evening there was a grand dinner at the "London Tavern," where "Prosperity to the Thames Tunnel" was drunk in some wine which had been preserved from the commencement of the enterprise, to celebrate its completion.

As with motor cars, so with aeronautics, the time of which I write, was well in advance. We know of Sen. Santos Dumont's performances with his motor balloon, in connection with the Eiffel Tower, but Mr. Samuel Henson was before him in applying mechanical power in aeronautics. He took out a patent (No. 9,478), dated 29 Sep., 1842, for "Apparatus and machinery for conveying letters, goods and passengers, from place to place through the air."

It was an aeroplane. The car which contained passengers, engineer, engines, etc., was suspended in the centre of a frame-work, which combined strength with lightness, covered with a light, but close, woven fabric. It was started by descending an inclined plane, the impetus from which caused it to rise in the air, when the steam engine was put in action, to continue its motion. The area of the sustaining surface was some 4,500 square feet, and the weight to be borne by it, including the carriage, etc., was estimated at 3,000lbs., which was claimed to be considerably less per square foot than that of many birds.

In April, 1843—but on what exact date I do not know, an experimental voyage was made from the Hill of Dumbuck, near Glasgow, by Professor Geolls. He successfully nego-tiated the descent of the inclined plane, and rapidly rose in the air, until he reached an altitude of nearly 3 miles. Feeling giddy, he determined to descend to a mile and a half above the earth. " This I easily effected by depressing the tail of the machine, which, up to this moment, I had kept at an angle with the horizon of 9¾ degrees, to that of 45. My course I had not varied since leaving the hill ; it was, per compass, south-west, and by west, half-west, passing over Ayrshire, and in a direct line from Dumbuck to Ailsa Craig, whither, indeed, I was tending, with the view of landing, the latter being admirably suited for launching the machine in a similar way to that adopted at Dumbuck, on my return home again.

" Daylight had now broken, and the scene was most gorgeous. I passed many ships ; and, in particular, one steamer, but whose paltry speed, in comparison with mine, was nothing. Alas! however, this was not destined to last ; for, just as I had shot ahead of the steamer, something went wrong with the machinery, and the fanners stopped. This did not at all alarm me ; for, as described by Mr. Henson, these fanners are only necessary for propulsion, and not at all requisite for maintaining the machine in the air. Unfortunately, however, I perfectly forgot, in the hurry of the moment, to remove the weights from the safety valve, and the effects from this were disastrous in the extreme. The great accumulation of steam that took place was too much for the pipes ; and, consequently, bang went three of them, at the same instant. The machine, at this exact moment, feeling its equilibrium altered, surged considerably, and the remaining pipes necessarily followed the example of the others : fizz—bizz—whizz, away they went, one after the other, like pop guns. Unfortunately, one of these pipes, in flying off, struck a bamboo stretcher, and shattered it so, that the machine, losing bearance on one side, toppled over and became perfectly unmanageable ; she, in fact, whirled over and over in a way that may be imagined, but which it is altogether impossible to describe.

I, of course, was now descending with fearful rapidity, and nothing was left me to contemplate but death and destruction. I can only compare my sensations at this moment to those experienced in a nightmare, which, everyone knows, are not the most agreeable in the world. Sensibility now forsook me ; and, indeed, this was not to be wondered at, in consequence of the whirling of the machine. On coming to my senses again, I found myself in bed, with severe headache, nausea and vomiting, the usual accompaniments of such a flight through the air ; but, thanks to Providence, I am now in a fair way of recovery, and willing to perform the same feat again."

Luckily for the aeronaut, the accident was seen by the master of a steamer, who sent a boat to his assistance, but the machine was lost.

We often hear of " treasure trove," but seldom find the owner. However, here is a case : On 11 April, the magistrate at Clerkenwell Police Court had a man named Benjamin Thomas, and five other labourers, brought before him, under the following circumstances. It seems they had been recently engaged in grubbing up the roots of some trees in Tufnell Park, Holloway, when they found, buried in the earth, two jars full of sovereigns, supposed to have amounted to £400. They divided the money between them ; but it was claimed by Mr. Henry Tufnell, as Lord of the Manor ; and all of them consented to give up what they had, except Thomas, who said that his share was £51, but that he had spent, or lost it. The sum recovered only amounted to £231 17s. Thomas was remanded for a few days, but, in the interval, a new claimant appeared, in the person of Mr. Joseph Frost, of the firm of J. and J. Frost, brass founders in Clerkenwell. It appeared that, some time in August last year, in a temporary fit of mental delusion, he had carried the money out at night, and buried it. Mr. Tufnell waived his claim in favour of Mr. Frost, and Thomas was committed for trial, on the charge of feloniously appropriating the money to his own use.

A very curious accident happened to Brunel, the eminent engineer. He was playing with the child of a friend, pretending to swallow a half-sovereign, and bring it out at his ear, when it slipped, and stuck in his trachæa, whence it could not be disloged. This must have been in the latter part of April, for it is mentioned in the *Times* of 28 April, as having occurred some short time previously. All efforts of the surgeons could not reach the coin, even though they constructed a machine which suspended him by the heels, when he was shaken and thumped. On 27 April Sir B. Brodie performed trachæotomy on the unfortunate gentleman, but without avail; so they waited until he had somewhat recovered, and again hung him up by his heels. This was on 13 May, and, after a few gentle thumps, the half-sovereign quitted its place, and dropped out of his mouth, without causing him any pain or inconvenience.

In these days, millionaires, and multi-millionaires are exceedingly common, but not so in the time of which I write, and much astonishment was created at the sum of money which Mr. Richard Arkwright, son of Sir Richard, the inventor of the spinning jinny, left behind him. His will was proved, on 24 May, in Canterbury Prerogative Court, and his personal property was sworn to exceed £1,000,000; the stamp duty on the probate of which was £15,000, which was the highest duty then payable, when the testator's personal estate was £1,000,000 or upwards. In this case the deceased left behind him a fortune of nearly £3,000,000.

The 18th of May is memorable in the Presbyterian Church of Scotland, for the great secession of its members, and the foundation of the Free Church. This was the day appointed for the opening of the General Assembly, and Dr. Welsh, the Moderator of the former Assembly, took the Chair. As soon as business commenced, he read a protest from those who were dissatisfied with the then state of the Church. It was a very long document, and having read it, the Doctor, and those who were of the same opinion, quietly left the Hall, forming a procession and marching four abreast, to a Hall in Canon-mills, where they elected Dr. Chalmers as their Moderator.

A contemporary account of this movement is given in the *Observer* of 29 May: " The number of clergymen who have seceded from the Church of Scotland, is now 450; and it cannot be a question that, by the middle of the week, the number will be close on 500. This is nearly the half of the entire clergy, the number being under 1,200. Among the leaders will be found the name of almost every minister distinguished for talent, moral worth, or weight of character. Nearly the whole of the people have left the Establishment with their ministers—so that the Free Presbyterian Church, instituted by those who have left the Establishment, may be considered the Church of Scotland. The general impression in Scotland is, that the residuary church cannot long exist. About £240,000 have been raised in less than ten weeks, for the erection of new churches, and for the support of the seceding clergy; and there can be no question that, in a few weeks, the amount will considerably exceed £300,000. Among the contributors, are the Marchioness of Breadalbane, £1,000; a Colonel in the Army, whose name we do not remember, £6,000, in three yearly instalments of £2,000; Mr. Henry Paul, a private gentleman, £2,000; Mr. Nisbet, bookseller, London, £1,000; a Dissenter, £500; and there are various other subscriptions of £2,000 and £1,000 each. Mr. Fox Maule is to build and endow a church at his own expense; Mr. A. Campbell, member for Argyleshire, is to do the same. In Elgin, the pious and spirited inhabitants have raised £1,000 to build a church for the Rev. Alexander Topp, a young and popular minister; and they will also liberally contribute to his support. So that, in many instances, churches will be built, and ministers be provided for, solely by private munificence and local exertion, without requiring any aid from the general fund. The General Assembly of the Establishment is now sitting in Edinburgh, but its proceedings excite little interest. The General Assembly of the Free Church, which the people recognise as the Church of Scotland, is also sitting in Edinburgh, and its proceedings excite an intensity of interest hitherto unparalleled in the ecclesiastical history of Scotland."

About this time there arose an objectionable class of men, who tried to ape the gentleman, but could not, and they went by the generic term of " Gents." *Punch* was death upon them, and I give one of the satirist's onslaughts, as it reproduces the costumes and amusements of the day. First let us see the

"Gent," pictorially, and then, afterwards, read what manner of animal he was.

Punch, vol. IV., p. 142.

AN ACT

For amending the Public Deportment of certain individuals called " Gents," abiding in London and other places.

WHEREAS it having been represented that there are, at present existing in the Metropolis, as well as in the provincial districts, certain individuals known and spoken of as " Gents," whose bearing and manners are perfectly at variance with the characters, which, from a monomania, they appear desirous of assuming :

AND WHEREAS, in consequence of cheap clothes, imitative

dispositions, and intellectual poverty, this class is greatly on the increase, it has been thought necessary that this Act should be framed to control their vicious habits :

May it, therefore, please your Majesty, that it be enacted : AND BE IT ENACTED henceforth, that all Gents, not actually in the employ of the *Morning Post*, or Mr. Simpson, of the "Albion," be prevented from wearing white cravats at parties, the same being evidently an attempt of sixth-rate individuals to ape the manners of first-class circles. And that no Gent, who does not actually keep a horse, and is not in the Army, be allowed to strut up and down the Burlington Arcade, with a whip and moustachios, such imposition being exceedingly offensive, and amounting to a passive swindling of the spectators.

AND BE IT ENACTED, that all such things as light-blue stocks, large figured shawls, cheap primrose gloves, white Chesterfield coal sacks, half-guinea Albert boots ; in fact, all those articles ticketed in the shop windows as "Gent's last style," be considered the distinctive marks of the class, and condemned accordingly. And that every individual, moreover, smoking outside an omnibus, sticking large pins in his cravat, wearing fierce studs in his shirt, walking with others four abreast in Regent Street, reading slang publications, and adopting their language, playing billiards in public rooms, sporting dingy white gloves in the slips of the theatres, frequenting night taverns, and being on terms of familiarity with the singers and waiters, thinking great things of champagne, as if everything at a party depended upon it ; and, especially, wearing the hat on one side, be the signs of most unmitigated Gents, and shunned equally with hydrophobia.

AND BE IT FURTHER ENACTED that no Gent be, in future, allowed to cross a hired horse with a view to ten shillings worth of Sunday display in the Parks, the turnout being always detected ; nor shall be permitted to drive a gig, in a fierce scarf, under similar circumstances. Nor shall any Gent imagine that an acquaintance with all the questionable resorts of London is "knowing life" ; or that trousers of large check pattern are anything but exceeding Gentish.

SAVING ALWAYS that the Gents have not the sense to endeavour bettering their condition, which is exceedingly probable ; under which circumstances they had better remain as
they are, in ignorance of their melancholy position. But, on
the other hand, it is commanded that people of common intel-
lect, henceforth cease to designate any of their male friends
as " Gents," the word being one of exceedingly bad style, and
equally objectionable with "genteel," which is, possibly, de-
rived from it. And that if, after this, anyone speaks of a
" Gent," or " Party " he knows, it is ordered that such speaker
be immediately set down as one of the unfortunate class in
question.

The Shakspere autograph which was sold on 24 May, 1841,
came again into the market, and was bought on 19 May, for
£145, by the Corporation of the City of London. The *Patres
Conscripti* of the Common Council were not of one mind as
to the eligibility of the purchase. On the motion " that the
Court agree to the report, and that the Chamberlain be instructed to pay the sum," Mr. Warton rose to move, as an
amendment, that the report should lie upon the table. (A
laugh, and loud cries of " Hear, hear.") He had, he said, done
all he could in the Committee, to prevail upon the members
that the purchase of the autograph was a most wasteful and
prodigal expenditure. (" Hear, hear," and " No, no.") The
precedent was a most mischievous one. If the Court sanctioned such a proceeding as that which the report had described, by and by the autographs of archbishops and bishops,
and other individuals who had, in times long past, distinguished themselves, would supply apologies for wasting the
City cash, in order to gratify gentlemen who were afflicted
with that description of mania. (Laughter.) He hoped the
Court would not catch the infection, but second his rational
effort to check it, by condemning the report to its proper
station on the table. After all, the document was doubtful ;
but there was no doubt at all as to the profligacy of the expenditure. (Laughter, and cries of " Hear, hear," and " No,
no.") Mr. Knott said it was quite ridiculous to think for a

moment, of voting £145 for a few doubtful, illegible, almost obliterated scratches of a pen.   (Laughter, and cries of " Hear, hear.")   He defied any man on earth to say what those scratches represented.   On a division there were, for the motion 41 ; for the amendment 31.

CHAPTER XXI.

Exhibition of cartoons—A duel—A monster—Gambling—The " Albert Hat "—
Nelson's statue—Fun thereon—Soldiers' savings banks—A post boy and
Lord Mayor's show—M. Jullien and his orchestra—Prince Albert as a
farmer—George IV.'s Statue—Ojibbeway Indians.

THE public exhibition of Cartoons for the frescoes for the
new Palace of Westminster, took place in Westminster Hall,
on 3 July. There were 140 subjects altogether, varying in
size from 15ft. to 10ft. square, none being admitted over, or
under those standards. Prizes of £300 each were awarded to
Armitage, Watts and Cope; of £200 to Calcott, Bell and
Townsend; of £100 to Frost, Harris, Selous, Bridges and
Severn; the judges being the Marquis of Lansdowne, Sir
R. Peel and Messrs. S. Rogers, Westmacott, Cook and Etty.
The Cartoons remained in Westminster Hall for 6 months;
and, in Nov. were removed to the Suffolk Street Gallery.
They were finally adjudicated upon by the Royal Commission
of Fine Arts, on 12 July, 1844, and the successful artists chosen
to execute frescoes were Cope, Horsley, Dyce, Maclise, Red-
grave, and Cave Thomas.

The practice of duelling was fast dying out, and I give
the following case as being nearly one of the last, and one
in which the seconds and surgeon were tried for being accessory to murder. Two brothers-in-law—Lt.-Col. Fawcett of
the 55th Regiment and Lt. Munro of the Royal Horse Guards
—quarrelled, and on the morning of the 1st July fought a
duel with pistols in a field at the back of the " Brecknock Arms
Tavern," in Camden Road. Lt.-Col. Fawcett fell, mortally
wounded, and died on the 3rd July. The Coroner's jury
found Lt. Munro, and the two seconds, guilty of wilful murder,

and the surgeon as guilty in the second degree only, as it
was believed he was present only as medical attendant. Lieut.
Munro and his second got out of the way, but Lt.-Col. Fawcett's second and the surgeon were tried at the Central
Criminal Court on 25 Aug. No evidence was tendered against
the surgeon, and he was at once discharged, and the jury
found the second "Not Guilty." Lt. Munro's second surrendered himself, was tried on 14 Feb., 1844, and acquitted.
Lieut. Munro was cashiered from the Army for being absent
without leave ; he afterwards surrendered, and was tried, 18
Aug., 1847, found guilty, and sentenced to death ; which
sentence was commuted to 12 months' imprisonment in Newgate.

The *Times* of 30 June, quoting the *Reading Mercury*, has
the following : " A MONSTER.—A day or two since, a gentleman travelling along the road near Colnbrook, had his attention attracted to the screams of a child in the care of a
tramping woman, who had with her, two other children totally
blind. The cries of the child were so distressing, that he insisted on knowing the cause ; but, not getting a satisfactory
answer, he forcibly removed a bandage from its eyes, when,
horrid to relate, he found these encased with two small per-
forated shells, in which were two live black beetles, for the
purpose of destroying the sight. The woman was instantly
seized, and given into custody ; and, at the magistrate's meeting, at Eton, on Wednesday last, committed for trial. There
is too much reason to fear that the wretch produced the blind-
ness of the other two children, by similar means." This was
rendered into a street ballad.

A correspondent pointed out that it was well known to
all who pass through the parish of St. James's, at night, that
the district absolutely swarmed with gaming houses ; there
was, in fact, no concealment about the matter, as the keepers
vied with each other in illuminating their doors and windows
to attract the notice of their victims. How was it that this
disgrace was permitted to exist from season to season? The
police seemed satisfied with the occasional conviction of one
or more minor delinquents from the neighbourhood of Leices-

ter Square, but the Leviathans in crime were allowed to continue their nightly course of profligacy and plunder with impunity. The French authorities, by a law which was strictly enforced, entirely swept away this nuisance from their capital, notoriously, for years, the very hotbed of the vice of gaming; but we were lamentably behind our neighbours; for, while we boasted of a Court pure in morals, and strict in the performance of every religious duty, we allowed the Sabbath to be desecrated, and the Palace of the Sovereign to be contaminated by the close vicinage of houses expressly open for the practice of this demoralising habit.—Are we much better now?

At the latter end of October, a new headdress for the infantry was proposed, and Prince Albert was universally credited as being its godfather—but public opinion was so unequivocally expressed against it, that it was never likely to be popular. It was neither soldier-like, nor appropriate, and bore a strong resemblance to the old Hessian cap, which was introduced into the German service. This headgear was covered with black cloth, the crown and brim being of black-varnished leather; the band was of white worsted, as was the tuft, which was placed on a ball of red worsted. Beneath this ball was a royal crown, underneath which was a Maltese cross, in the centre of which was inscribed the number of the regiment.

Punch was especially severe upon the Albert hat—and with the pictorial satire of " Prince Albert's Studio " (by the way the hat is in no ways exaggerated), is the following : " Ever since the accession of Prince Albert to the Royal Husbandship of these realms, he has devoted the energies of his mind, and the ingenuity of his hands to the manufacture of Infantry caps, Cavalry trousers, and Regulation sabretaches. One of his first measures was to transmogrify the pantaloons of the Eleventh Hussars ; and, as the regiment alluded to is " Prince Albert's Own," His Royal Highness may do as he likes with his own, and no one can complain of his bedizening the legs of the unfortunate Eleventh, with scarlet cloth and gold door leather. When, however, the Prince, throwing the whole

of his energies into a hat, proposed to encase the heads of
the British soldiery in a machine which seemed a decided

Prince Albert's Studio.

[*Punch*, vol. V., p. 179.

cross between a muff, a coal scuttle and a slop pail, then
Punch was compelled to interfere, for the honour of the
British Army. The result has been that the headgear has

been summarily withdrawn, by an order from the War Office, and the manufacture of more of the Albert hat has been absolutely prohibited.

"Greatness of mind is shown in various ways by different

Nelson's Statue.

individuals. Hannibal was a great cutter out, for he cut a passage through the Alps; but Prince Albert cuts out Hannibal, inasmuch as His Royal Highness devotes his talent to the cutting out of coats, and 'things inexpressible.' The Prince's studio could not fail to be an object of interest to the readers of *Punch*. We have, therefore, at an enormous sacrifice of time and specie, obtained a view of it."

On the morning of Nov. 3, at 4 a.m., the raising of a portion of the colossal statue of Nelson, on the pillar in Trafalgar Square, commenced. This figure is 17 feet high from its base to the top of the hat, and is made of stone from the Granton quarry, belonging to the Duke of Buccleugh. It weighs nearly 18 tons, and, needless to say, is made in segments. These were put together before it was raised, to show the public—and during the two days it was on view, it was visited by 100,000 persons.

The building this column had seemed slow, but that was nothing compared to its completion; the bas reliefs were long in being placed, and it was not till 31 Jan., 1867, that Landseer's four couchant lions were exposed to public gaze. Of the progress of its building, *Punch* (25 Nov., 1843) has some very fine fooling.

"THE NELSON COLUMN DRAMA.

The earliest announcement of the late Covent Garden management, was a piece entitled 'Trafalgar Square, or the Nelson Monument.' We have obtained the following slight information respecting it. The drama is described as 'a grand architectural and historical burletta,' in two acts; and the prologue was to have been spoken by Mr. Widdicomb, as *Time*. The two acts comprise the commencement and completion, and a lapse of twenty years is supposed to take place between them, in which time 'the boy,' who is the principal character, becomes a middle-aged man. The following speech is very fine. The boy enquires of the mason when the column will be finished, who replies, in an interval of the steak banquet, which they are enjoying together:

> *Mason.*—I've asked that fearful question of the stars,
>   Who wink responding—of the Board of Works,
>   Whose works have bored us—of the misty moon,
>   Towards whose lodgings, after years of toil,
>   We rise no nearer. All were still, but now,
>   Whilst gazing on that steak of beef,

15

Sent up to form our capital repast,
And cheer us in our lonely solitude,
I hope the best—the best can hope no more.
'Twill rise, like College honours, by degrees,
And to our limbs a pillar be, of ease :
Our hearts are warm—although upon the frieze.

The following duet is also introduced by the man and the boy in the second act :

BOY.

I remember, I remember,
　When I was a little boy,
On the column, in November,
　I was given some employ.

I helped the man to build it,
　And we labour'd hard and long,
But the granite came up slowly,
　For we were not very strong.

　I remember, I remember,
　　How we raised its form on high,
　With one block in December,
　　And another in July.

BOTH.

I remember, I remember,
　When St. Martin's bells were rung,
In the laying of the first stone, for
　We both were very young.

But weary years have past, now,
　Since we our work begun ;
We fear we shall not last now,
　To see our labour done.

　We remember, we remember,
　　But we heard it on the sly,
　'Twon't be finished next November,
　　Nor the subsequent July."

Very early in November, a War Office circular (dated 31 Oct.) was issued, to regulate and establish regimental savings banks, which have done so much to encourage thrift among our soldiers. The maximum of each soldier's deposit was limited to £30 in any one year, and to £200 in the whole. The rate of interest on deposits was fixed at £3 15s. per cent. per annum, but no interest was to be allowed upon less than 6s. 8d. and 13s. 4d., nor upon any sums that had not remained on deposit for at least one month, to be reckoned from the last monthly muster day.

In the *Times* of 10 Nov. is the following : " A rather amusing scene took place in Cheapside, yesterday, shortly before the Lord Mayor's procession to Westminster. Whilst the streets were blocked up against the passage of vehicles and horses, one of those sharp little urchins, known by the generic title of the ' twopenny cavalry,' who rattle through the streets with Her Majesty's suburban mails, was stopped, opposite Bow Church, by a party of police, who told him they acted under the orders of the Lord Mayor. The post-boy, with all the dignity of Her Majesty's representative, assuming an air of great condescension, assured the police that he had the highest possible respect for the Lord Mayor, but, being express upon Her Majesty's business, he was determined to proceed. The police persisted in stopping him, a crowd collected, and it was clear their sympathies sided with the post-boy, who carried himself, throughout the controversy, with great courage, calmness, and self-possession. The police had, by this time, seized the bridle, whilst the boy endeavoured to force his way forward, backed by the strenuous exertions of his steed, who also appeared as if inspired by the authority of a Royal Commission. The post-boy, finding physical force insufficient, tried what authority would do, and threatened them with the vengeance of the Home Secretary, for attempting to stop Her Majesty's mails. This had the desired effect of bringing the police to a parley ; and, as the post-boy was backed by popular applause, he gained momentarily in the discussion, but did not complete his advantage until he took out a memorandum book, and began, coolly, to note down the numbers of the constables. This stroke was decisive ; they, at once, capitulated, merely stipulating that they should have his address in return. To this, he readily assented, and searched diligently for his cardcase, but that mark of gentility was not at hand.   He, however, made a page from his memorandum book serve his purpose, and took his leave amid the loud congratulations of the applauding crowd, with the following pithy address to the constables : ' I can't well see what use you are.   A hundred years ago there were no police, and Lord Mayor's shows went off better than they do now. For my part, I can't see what you do here at all, for you know '—he added with a significant grin—' you know you don't look so very well in a procession.'   Shouts of laughter followed the post-boy's brief speech, as he rode on triumphantly."

It was about this time that M. Louis Antoine Jullien, to whom we owe so much for the popularisation of good music, and for the improvement of our orchestras, came into notoriety as a caterer for the public's amusement, and for his promenade concerts.   These had been popular in the open air at Vauxhall, Ranelagh, Marylebone, and other public gardens ; but the first, under cover, was given in 1838 at the Lyceum Theatre, or, as it was then called, The English Opera House, when the pit was boarded over, and an orchestra erected on the stage exactly as we are now so familiar with.   Jullien, in 1838, had been unlucky in Paris, was bankrupt, and came to London, where, in 1840, he was assistant to Eliason, the violinist and conductor of an orchestra of 100 performers, and a small chorus.   Next year Jullien was the conductor ; and, in 1842, on 2 Dec., he started for himself, at the English Opera House, the series of promenade concerts with which his name will always be associated.

He always would have the very best musicians that he could find for his orchestra, and in this year (1843) among them were Barrett, Baumann, Harper, Kœnig, Richardson, Hill, Lazarus, Patey, Howell and Jarrett, and in after years he had such soloists as Ernst, Sivori, Bottesini, Wieniawski and Sainton.   In 1857 he came, financially, to grief ; he then went to Paris, was imprisoned for debt in Clichy, in 1859, and died in a lunatic asylum on 14 March, 1860.

In his later years he became much stouter than he is here represented, and, as a conductor, posed a great deal too much.

Those of my readers who recollect him will acknowledge the
truth of the following description of him, when conducting
his British Army Quadrilles, taken from his biography in
Grove's History of Music and Musicians : " With coat thrown
widely open, white waistcoat, elaborately embroidered shirt
front, wristbands of extravagant length, turned back over his

M. Jullien.

[*Ill. Lon. News*, 25 Nov. 1843, p. 348.

cuffs, a wealth of black hair, and a black moustache—itself
a striking novelty—he wielded his baton, encouraged his
forces, repressed the turbulence of his audience with indescribable gravity and magnificence, went through all the panto-
mime of the British Army or Navy Quadrilles, seized a violin
or a piccolo at the moment of climax, and, at last, sunk
exhausted into his gorgeous velvet chair. All pieces of
Beethoven's were conducted with a jewelled baton, and in

a pair of clean kid gloves, handed him, at the moment, on a silver salver."

Prince Albert took a great interest in Agriculture, and his Flemish Farm at Windsor was a model; but it was hard to make the average Englishman believe that a foreigner could ever do any good as a Farmer, and John Leech drew a fancy

Prince Albert, the British Farmer.

portrait of the prince in *Punch*, 25 Nov., where it illustrates a portion of a speech of Sir Robert Peel at Tamworth: "Prince Albert has turned his attention to the promotion of agriculture; and, if you have seen, as most probably you have, an account of the sale of Prince Albert's stock, and the price they fetched, I have not the slightest doubt you will give one cheer more to Prince Albert, as a British Farmer."

In the beginning of December the bronze equestrian statue

of George IV. was set up on a pedestal at the north-east corner of Trafalgar Square. It is the work of Chantrey, and was intended to be mounted on the Marble Arch, which was, originally, the gateway to Buckingham Palace, until its removal to Cumberland Gate, Hyde Park, in 1851.

In the very early part of December, some of Her Majesty's subjects, Canadian Indians, from the north-eastern shores of Lake Huron, came to visit England. They were of the Ojibbeway tribe, and were nine in number, two old chiefs, four warriors, two women, and a little girl, 10 years old. On the 20 Dec. they were presented to the Queen at Windsor, and received from Her Majesty a cheque for £20, and a quantity of gorgeous plaid, with which to astonish the other natives, on their return. They afterwards exhibited themselves, danced war dances, etc., at the Egyptian Hall, at an admission fee of half-a-crown.

CHAPTER XXII.

THE *Times* of 19 Jan. copies the following from the *Worcester Chronicle*: "A CHILD FOR SALE.—The following extra-ordinary letter was received, a short time ago, by a gentleman in the neighbourhood of Tewkesbury, from a person residing here. The letter is dated from a certain court in this town, but we omit the precise locality, and the writer's name, hoping that, without pursuing the exposure to that extent, it will be sufficient to teach him that natural affection is not to be made a matter of bargain and sale, and that it is the duty of a parent himself to cherish the child which he has been the means of bringing into the world:—' Sir,—Having heard that you expressed a wish to have a child and did not mind giving a sum of money as an inducement i flatter myself that I have it in my power to furnish you with one to answer your purpose in every respect it is a boy 2 years old a good looking healthy spirited child and sound in wind and limb and that you can rair him up to suit your inclination you can send word by the bearer and appoint any time to inspect the child.'"

With every wish, in this book of Gossip, to steer as clear of politics as possible, yet it would belie its name were the famous trial of Daniel O'Connell not to be mentioned. "Repeal of the Union" was his watchword and perpetual cry, and with it he stirred up the Irish people to a pitch when he found it difficult to manage and restrain them. On 16 March, 1843, was held at Trim the first of great public meetings which he designed, but did not carry out; and on 15 Aug. was a monster meeting on the Hill of Tara; but the one to be held at Clontarf on 8 Oct. was to have eclipsed its predecessors. But this was forbidden by the Government, and, a week later, warrants were issued for the arrest of O'Connell, his son John, and his chief colleagues, on a charge of conspiring to create discontent and disaffection among the liege subjects of the Queen, and with contriving, " by means of intimidation, and the demonstration of great physical force, to procure and effect changes to be made in the government, laws, and constitution of this realm." O'Connell was allowed bail, but on 8 Nov. a true bill was found by the jury, yet the trial did not take place till the 15th Jan. of this year. On the 12th Feb., the jury returned a verdict of guilty of unlawful and seditious conspiracy, but judgment was not delivered till 30 May, when he was sentenced to imprisonment for twelve months, a fine of £2,000, and to find surety to keep the peace for seven years. He had to go to prison, where he was well treated and allowed to see his friends ; his sentence was appealed against, and reversed in the House of Lords, on 4 Sep., 1844, when he was instantly liberated.

During all this time there was great excitement, people wearing Repeal buttons, one of which is here delineated, and

other emblems, while the uncrowned King of Ireland was presented, at Mullaghmast, with a velvet cap surmounted with shamrocks, and having a green tassel ; the cap, in fact, with which readers of *Punch* are so familiar.

Of course, his release from prison was an occasion to be made the most of. An amphitheatrical triumphal car was provided, and, upon it, were mounted O'Connell, his son, and the Rev. Dr. Miley, and this gimcrack piece of property was drawn by six horses ridden by postillions. The following is an account by an eye witness :

"The ovation commenced at two o'clock. First came the trades of Dublin, each preceded by the banner of its body, and a band playing such music as only temperance bands can play, and, generally, with much discrimination, selecting rather difficult pieces for their performance, and eschewing all national airs. The banners were usually displayed from coaches, intended to hold four, but contriving to allow from sixteen to eighteen to fit into, and hang on by them. Thus they came on: Bricklayers (with a painting of the Bank of Ireland, and the superscription of 'Our Old House at Home'); slaters, woollen operatives (in a small open car); nailors (with a picture of Brian Boroihme 'nailing' the Danes

O'Connell's Cap.

at Clontarf); coach makers, tailors (with a very gorgeous equipage, six horses, postillions and outriders); tinplate workers, displaying as their sign, a man with a tin helmet on his head, and a dish cover of the same metal on his arm—otherwise unassumingly attired in a blue coat and white trousers; and other bodies of tradesmen too numerous to mention, with their appropriate emblems and banners.

"Next came a number of Repeal wardens, bearing wands, and occupying respectable-looking coaches and carriages. After them drove the committee of the political trades' unions; the members of it attired in green sashes and scarves, and bearing wands with green flags in their hands. Next in order were the various members of the Corporation, aldermen, town councillors, and officers, dressed in their robes of office and cocked hats, glittering with chains, and furred from head to foot. The majority of these gentlemen were in their own carriages, into each of which were packed as many of the owner's friends as could find standing room, several private vehicles being mixed up through the order of procession. Then came the private carriages of the Lord Mayor, who was in full dress; and then, preceded by a confused mass of wand bearers, the triumphal chariot itself, surrounded by a mob so dense that it was with great difficulty that the six splendid dappled greys could force the cumbrous vehicle along, which, every instant, seemed to become a second Car of Juggernaut, and crush some of its adorers. More vehicles, a few horsemen, multitudes of hack cars and pedestrians, a tail of old women and little boys, followed; and so the monster procession, after winding its slow length along through the greater part of Dublin, and causing a total cessation of business in the line of its progress, terminated."

In February appeared, in London, at the Princess's Theatre, "General Tom Thumb," the most popular of modern dwarfs—thanks to the advertising qualities of his exhibitor, P. T. Barnum. The real name of this mite was Charles S. Stratton, and he was said to have been born on 11 Jan., 1832, but this, as with all data connected with him, must be accepted with caution. It was said of him, that, at his birth, he weighed 9 lbs. 2 oz., somewhat more than the average weight of a newly born infant. At about 5 months old, he weighed 15 lbs., and measured 25 inches in height; since which time he never increased in stature; and, at the time of his arrival in England, he weighed but 15 lbs. 2 oz. He had, previously, been exhibited in New York and the principal cities of America, where his miniature palace, furniture and equipage excited considerable curiosity. When he embarked from New York for England, he was escorted to the packet by not less than 10,000 persons.

On 1 April, he appeared, by command, before Her Majesty at Buckingham Palace, when the Queen presented him, *with her own hand*, with " a superb souvenir, of the most exquisite handicraft, manufactured of mother of pearl, and mounted with gold and precious stones. On one side are the crown and Royal initials, V.R., and, on the reverse, bouquets of flowers in enamel and rubies. In addition to this splendid gift, Her Majesty subsequently presented the General with a beautiful gold pencil case, with the initials of Tom Thumb, and his coat of arms, engraved on the emerald surmounting the case."

Anent this, *Punch* is exceedingly satirical: "Her Majesty

Tom Thumb.

[*Ill. Lon. News*, 24 Feb., 1844, p. 124.

has again commanded 'the performances of *Tom Thumb*, the Yankee Dwarf.' This, indeed, was to have been expected. We have only to reflect upon the countless acts of patronage towards the Arts and Sciences—had only to remember a few of the numerous personal condescensions of the Queen towards men of letters, artists and philosophers—to be assured that even TOM THUMB would be welcomed with that graceful cordiality which has, heretofore, made Buckingham Palace and Windsor Castle the homes of Poetry and Science. *De minimis curat Regina!* Continental monarchs stop short in their Royal favours at full-grown authors and artists; but the enthusiasm of Her Majesty QUEEN VICTORIA, not content with showering all sorts of favours and rewards upon the literary and artistic spirits of her own country and age, lavishes, with prodigal hand, most delicate honours upon an American TOM THUMB, whose astounding genius it is, to measure, in his boots, five-and-twenty inches!   To this, how small is VICTOR HUGO at the Tuileries; to this, how mean and petty Göthe at the Court of Saxe-Weimar!

      *   *   *   *   *

" TOM THUMB being—according to the biography published by his showman, BARNUM—the son of a Yankee carpenter, we should much like to know the General's arms.   Did Her Majesty, before the ' performance,' send to learn them, that they might be duly engraved? or were they, as MATHEW'S French Shoemaker made his little boot, struck off in ' a moment of enthusiasm ' ? "

About this time came to us " that sweet boon," THE POLKA. Originally a Bohemian Peasant dance, it was imported into fashionable saloons of Berlin and St. Petersburg.   It was, at this time, the rage in Paris, as the *Times* observes : " The Paris papers are destitute of news.   Our private letters state that ' politics are, for the moment, suspended in public regard, by the new and all-absorbing pursuit—the Polka—a dance recently imported from Bohemia, and which embraces in its qualities the intimacy of the waltz, with the vivacity of the Irish jig.   You may conceive how completely is ' the Polka ' the rage, from the fact that the lady of a celebrated ex-minister, desiring to figure in it at a *soirée dansante*, monopolised the professor, *par excellence*, of that *spécialité*, for three hours, on Wednesday morning last, at 200 francs the hour.' "

On its first importation into England, it was used as a *ballet*, on the stage, with very fancy Bohemian costume, as we may see in the three following illustrations of Mdlle. Carlotta Grisi and M. Perrot, dancing their idea of it at Her Majesty's Theatre in 1844.

Madlle. Carlotta Grissi and M. Perrot, in The Polka at Her Majesty's
Theatre.—No. 1.

[*Ill. Lon. News*, 27 April, 1844, p. 280.

The Polka.—No. 2.   The Polka.—No. 3.

But it soon became a Drawing-room dance, and it is edify-
ing to know exactly how it was danced then.   It was found
too elaborate, and the number of steps had to be reduced in
quantity, and curtailed in quality.   But this is the dance as
given in the *Illustrated London News* of 11 May :

"THE DRAWING-ROOM POLKA.

We are much gratified in being enabled to lay before our
readers an accurate description of the *véritable*, or *Drawing-
room Polka*, as danced at Almack's, and at the halls of the
nobility and gentry of this country.

La Polka having appeared amongst us under so many different guises, we determined to spare no pains to procure a true
description of its *danse;* for which we are indebted to Mrs.
James Rae, who has been fortunate enough to secure the
details from M. Coralli, fils, the instructor of the young noblemen and gentry in Paris.

La Polka, like its predecessors, the waltz and galop, is
a *danse à deux*, couples following each other in the *salle
de danse*, commencing at pleasure, and adopting, of the
following figures, that which pleases them most at the
moment.   All those anxious to shine in *La Polka*, will dance
the whole of them, returning from time to time, by way of
rest, to the first figure.

The measure, or time, is 2-4 ; but, to facilitate our defini-
tion, we subdivide each measure, or bar, into one—two—three
—four ; the accent on the two, etc., to be played not so fast
as the galop.

The steps are two, and the following description may, in
some measure, convey them to our readers ; we commence
with the first, and most general.   At the one, hop on the
right leg, lifting, or doubling up your left leg at the same
moment ; at the two, put your left leg boldly forward on the
ground ; at the three, bring your right toe up to your left heel ;
at the four, advance your left foot a short step forward :
now, at the one, in the next measure, or bar of the time,
hop on the left leg, doubling, or lifting up your right leg, and

so on, proceeding in this step, with your arm encircling your partner's waist, round the room. This may be termed the first figure.

Figure 2.—Still adopting the same step, with your right arm round your partner's waist, and her right hand in your left, you place your lady exactly before you, and back all

The Drawing-room Polka.—Figure 2.

[*Ill. Lon. News*, 11 May, 1844, p. 301.

round the room, your lady pursuing you (as shown in the sketch); you then reverse this figure, and let your partner do the back step, whilst you pursue her, and, at the same time, carefully guide her round the room.

In backing, the leg which in figure one, you put boldly forward on the ground, you now fling boldly backward, and are thus enabled to effect your progress round the room.

Figure 3.—With the same step you waltz round the room —in other words, you perform the Galop waltz, substituting the Polka step as described.

Figure 4.—This is also a waltz with the second step, which we will now describe as "the Heel and Toe step." At the one, make a little hop on the right leg, dropping your left heel close to your right foot; at the two, another little hop on the right leg, pointing your left toe (not forward, but as close to your right foot as possible); at the three, another little hop on the right leg, advancing one step forward with

The Drawing-room Polka.—Figure 5.

the left foot; at the four, bring up the right foot, turning at the same instant, and passing your partner over to your left arm from your right arm; in your next measure, return your lady to your left arm, and so on.

Figure 5.—This is termed the back waltz. The step adopted in it by yourself and partner, is the back step described in figure two, and you turn in this waltz exactly the contrary way to that in which you turn in all other waltzes— hence its name.

In *La Polka*, before commencing the figures we have just
described, there is a short introduction (of which we give
a sketch), consisting of four measures, danced thus ; leading
your partner from her seat, and giving her her place in the
circle, and placing themselves *vis-à-vis*, you take her left
hand in your right, and make the first step four times—
first forward, then backward, forward again, and then back-

The Drawing-room Polka.—Introduction.

ward, taking care to gain ground in the forward steps ; you
then start with the first figure.

There was a furore about the Polka ; not only in dancing
it, but there was an absolute mania for naming articles of
dress after it. Ladies wore Polka hats, Polka jackets and
Polka boots, and men had Polka ties. Jullien published a
new Polka about every fortnight, and the whole people were
Polka mad. Here is a street ballad on the subject :

" JULLIEN'S GRAND POLKA.

Oh ! sure the world is all run mad,
The lean, the fat, the gay, the sad—
All swear such pleasure they never had,
Till they did learn the Polka.

Chorus.

First cock up your right leg—so,
Balance on your left great toe,
Stamp your heels, and off you go
To the Original Polka.   Oh !

There's Mrs. Tibbs, the tailor's wife,
With Mother Briggs is sore at strife,
As if the first and last of life
Was but to learn the Polka.

Quadrilles and waltzes all give way,
For Jullien's Polkas bear the sway,
The chimney sweeps, on first of May,
Do, in London, dance the Polka.

If a pretty girl you chance to meet,
With sparkling eyes and rosy cheek,
She'll say, young man, we'll have a treat,
If you can dance the Polka.

A lady who lives in this town,
Went and bought a Polka gown,
And for the same she gave five pound,
All for to dance the Polka.

But, going to the Ball one night,
On the way she got a dreadful fright,
She tumbled down and ruined quite
The gown to dance the Polka.

A Frenchman has arrived from France,
To teach the English how to dance,
And fill his pocket—" what a chance "—
By gammoning the Polka.

Professors swarm in every street,
'Tis ground on barrel organs sweet ;
And every friend you chance to meet
Asks, if you dance the Polka.

16*

Then over Fanny Ellsler came,
Brilliant with trans-Atlantic fame ;
Says she, I'm German by my name,
So best I know the Polka.

And the row de dow she danced,
And in short clothes and red heels pranced,
And, as she skipped, her red heels glanced
In the Bohemian Polka.

But, now, my song is near its close,
A secret, now, I will disclose,
Don't tell, for it's beneath the rose,
A humbug is the Polka.

Then heigh for humbug France or Spain,
Who brings back our old steps again,
Which John Bull will applaud amain,
Just as he does the Polka."

CHAPTER XXIII.

As the length of time between this date, and the present
writing is great, and our social habits have somewhat changed,
it may be interesting to some of my readers to hear a Frenchman's account of an upper-class dinner. It is taken from the
Constitutionel, the organ of M. Thiers :

" Madeira wine has been out of fashion, in England, for
some time. Sherry and Port (to which are occasionally added
Bordeaux and Champagne, Rhenish wines and Hermitage)
are, now, the only wines to be seen on the tables of the
rich. As for beer (the national drink), it only makes its appearance at a banquet, for remembrance sake, and in very
small quantity. Port wine is held in especial favour by the
English, because, while it is more impregnated with alcohol
than any other, it is, at the same time the least irritating, and
facilitates, more than all the rest, the important operations of
the digestive organs. In order, however, to be possessed of
all the requisite qualities, it must not only be of the finest
growth, or have been eight or nine years in the cellar, but
the regular connoisseurs insist that it must cross the line
several times, in order to be first-rate. Five or six servants,
with powdered wigs, in silk stockings and knee breeches,
hover about the table. The covers are always changed at
every successive course, and there is no fear of eating off the
dirty plate of one's neighbour, or using his knife or fork, the

sideboard being laden with piles of plates and conveniences of every description.   After fish, which always constitutes the first course, the host invites one of his guests to drink a glass of wine with him, desiring him to help himself to that which he likes best.   You take that which is offered you. Your host then pours out a glass for himself, and sends you the bottle by a servant.   You fill your glass, you raise it to your lips with a half bow, and drink as much of it as you feel inclined.   The same ceremony is repeated among the other guests.   It should be mentioned that, if you ask a lady to take wine, you always fill her glass before your own ; but, if you invite a gentleman so to do, you never fail to help yourself first.   This custom was, formerly, very inconvenient to strangers, it being, then, absolutely necessary to empty one's glass ; at present, you need only drink a portion, and ladies may satisfy the rules of etiquette by merely moistening their lips.   After fish, come roast meats, boiled vegetables, and various delicate sauces, with which you make your *cuisine* upon your own plate ; puddings and game of all sorts follow, amongst which there is, always, to begin with, one dish, especially appropriate to the season.   It is to the former article of diet (puddings), that English children are indebted, it is said, for their excellent health, and their magnificent rosy complexions.   The cloth is at length removed, and the mahogany table shines forth in all its splendour.   Dessert follows, consisting of a few sweetmeats, or *confitures*, but abounding in fruits from all five parts of the world, and the produce of all the four seasons, and including superb pine-apples, Portugal grapes, almonds, red nuts of a delicious flavour, dates, figs, rich juicy oranges, etc., etc.   The wine is brought on in glass decanters, ticketed and placed in silver stands.   These stands glide along the shining table, which is as smooth as ice, in the midst of silver, or crystal vases filled with fruit, etc.   The host, after helping himself to wine, pushes about the whole ' battery ' of decanters, which, going the round of the table, soon regain their original situation.   A quarter of an hour elapses, when the mistress of the house rises and retires, followed by all the ladies.   It is then that

the *séance de vin* begins.   The subject of conversation soon
changes, and political questions are discussed.   The conversation, without getting stormy, acquires that degree of warmth
and animation, which a good dinner, when one is blessed with
a strong head and a good digestion, generally inspires.   Hard
drinking has, generally speaking, fallen into desuetude.   It is
only foxhunters and country gentlemen who remain faithful,
nowadays, to that ignoble custom.   A gentleman who has
any self-respect, never so far forgets himself as to get tipsy,
for he would certainly be looked upon with an evil eye, by
the company, if he were to enter the drawing-room with an
indistinct articulation, or with trembling legs.   Dinner is over
about half-past nine.   The gentlemen then rejoin the ladies
to take tea and coffee, and the conversation turns, as before,
upon the news of the day."

On 8 April, Consols rose to par, or £100 for £100 stock,
for the first time for nearly a century.   The last time they
were at £100 was in 1749, the year after the peace of Aix la
Chapelle ; at which period the public debt was rather more
than £78,000,000.   The highest price the Three per Cents.
ever rose to, previously, was in June, 1737, and again, in
May, 1739, when they attained the high price of £107.   In
September, 1797, they fell to 47⅜, which is the lowest price
to which they have ever fallen.

On 23 May, the Derby was won by a horse called *Running Rein*, which was the occasion of an Action in the Court
of Exchequer, on 1 July, before Baron Alderson.   It was
alleged that the horse had not been truly described, that he
was not of the age which qualified him to run for the Derby,
and that he ought not, therefore, to be deemed the winner of
the race.   Colonel Peel, the owner of Orlando, the second
horse, claimed the stakes, on the ground that Running Rein
was not the horse represented ; and Mr. Wood, the owner
of Running Rein, brought this action against the Colonel.

Mr. Cockburn, who conducted the plaintiff's case, gave the
pedigree of Running Rein, and his whole history.   Among
other things, Mr. Cockburn mentioned that, in October, 1843,

Running Rein won a race at Newmarket; that he was objected to on the score of age; but, eventually, the stewards
had decided in his favour. The horse was, originally,
the property of Mr. Goodman; and, Mr. Cockburn said,
it was because suspicion attached to some transactions of
Goodman, and because certain persons had betted heavily
against Running Rein, that opposition was raised against Mr.
Wood receiving the stakes. He made a severe attack on
Lord George Bentinck, who, he asserted, was the real party
in the cause. Witnesses for the plaintiff described the horse
at various periods of its career; it was of a bay colour, with
black legs, and a little white on the forehead; its heels were
cracked, and, in 1842, it broke the skin on one leg, which
left a scar. George Hitchcock, a breaker of colts, employed
to break Running Rein in October, 1842, was cross-examined
to this effect:

"I know George Dockeray, the trainer. I never said to him,
'Damn it, this colt has been broken before; here is the mark
of the pad on his back.' I showed him the mark, but I never
said those words, or any words to that effect. I don't know
why I showed him the mark. It was not big enough for the
mark of a pad, and it was not the place for the saddle to
make it. I told Lord George Bentinck the same. The mark
of the pad never wears out. I recollect being asked, in the
presence of Mr. Smith, what I had there? and I recollect
answering, a four-year-old. I have not the slightest doubt
of it. Mr. Smith struck me for it. I did not say, afterwards,
that I had forgotten all about the horsewhipping, and that
the marks of the pad had worn out. I never said, either, that
somebody had behaved very well to me."

At an early period of the examination of witnesses, Mr.
Baron Alderson expressed a wish that he and the jury should
see the horse; and Mr. Cockburn said he had no objection.
On the cross-examination of William Smith, a training groom
residing at Epsom, it came out that the horse had been
smuggled out of the way, that it might not be seen by the
defendant's agents. The judge, animadverting on this, and
on the evident perjury of the witness, said it would be better

that the horse should be seen by him and other parties. The
Solicitor-General, who appeared for the defendant, was
anxious that the horse should be seen by veterinary surgeons.
To which the other side objected, maintaining that the mark
of mouth, by which, alone, those surgeons could judge of the
age of a horse, was a fallible criterion.

On the conclusion of the evidence for the plaintiff, the
Solicitor-General, in addressing the jury for the defence, denounced the case as a gross and scandalous fraud on the part
of the plaintiff. The case for the defendant was, that the
horse was not Running Rein at all, but a colt by Gladiator,
out of a dam belonging originally to Sir Charles Ibbotson ;
and that it had the name, Running Rein, imposed upon it,
being originally called Maccabeus, and having been entered for
certain stakes under that designation. But his allegations
were against Goodman, not against Mr. Wood ; the former
had entered into a conspiracy with other persons to run horses
above the proper age. The Gladiator colt had been entered
for races, under the name of Maccabeus, before Goodman
purchased him ; and to run these races while the colt was
in training for the Derby, for which he was entered as Running
Rein, Goodman hired an Irish horse, which he disguised as
Maccabeus, though a year older than that horse. The
Gladiator colt, the *soi-disant* Running Rein, when he ran
for the Derby, in 1844, was four years old, the race being
for three-year-old horses. After hearing some evidence in
support of these statements, the case was adjourned till the
following day.

The next day, when Mr. Baron Alderson took his seat
upon the Bench, a conversation ensued between Mr. Cockburn
and the Judge, respecting the production of the horse. Mr.
Cockburn asserted that it had been taken away without Mr.
Wood's knowledge, and thus it was out of his power to
produce it ; he felt it would be vain to strive against the
effect which must be felt by the non-production of the horse,
after the remarks of the learned Judge on that point. After
some conversation, however, the case proceeded, and two
witnesses for the defence were examined, whose evidence ,

went to prove that Running Rein was, in fact, the Gladiator colt. Mr. George Odell, a horse dealer at Northampton, said he could swear to that fact; the colt had two marks on one leg.

Mr. Baron Alderson remarked: " Now, if we could see the horse, that would prove the case. Who keeps him away? It is quite childish to act in this manner."

Mr. Cockburn now stated that Mr. Wood was convinced that he had been deceived, and gave up the case.

Mr. Baron Alderson then briefly addressed the jury with much warmth, and in a most emphatic manner; directing them to find a verdict for the defendant, observing :

" Since the opening of the case, a most atrocious fraud has proved to have been practised ; and I have seen, with great regret, gentlemen associating themselves with persons much below themselves in station. If gentlemen would associate with gentlemen, and race with gentlemen, we should have no such practices. But, if gentlemen will condescend to race with blackguards, they must expect to be cheated."

The jury found for the defendant, and the effect of their verdict was, that the Derby Stakes went to Orlando, and that Crenoline should be considered the winner of the Two-Year-Old Plate at Newmarket, run the previous year.

Punch, in commenting upon Mr. Baron Alderson's remarks, says : " They " (the gentlemen) "go among these knaves and swindlers, these low-bred ruffians, reeking of gin and the stables, *to make money of them.* They associate with boors and grooms, Jew gambling-house keepers, boxers and bullies, for money's sake to be sure. What other motive could bring such dandies into communication with such scoundrels, any more than he would willingly incur an infection, unless he had some end in view. And the noble patrons of the Turf *have* a great end in view—that of money."

This ought to have been sufficient roguery, one would think, for one race, but it was not. A horse, named Rattan, was so evidently " nobbled," that two men connected with it, Rogers and Braham, were warned off all the Jockey Club's premises.

And yet another case. A horse, named Leander, ran in this race, and so injured its leg, that it was shot. Shortly afterwards, it was suspected that it was four, instead of three years old ; and, on its being exhumed, *the lower jaw was missing*. The resurrectionists, however, cut off the head, and veterinary experts confirmed the previous suspicions. For this, the owners, Messrs. Lichtwald, were, for ever, disqualified from racing. This case occupied much time before the Select Committee of the House of Lords.

The Select Committee on Gaming, in the Commons, in 1844, report that : " Your Committee have some evidence to show that frauds are, occasionally, committed in Horse Racing, and in betting on the Turf ; but they feel difficulty in suggesting any remedy for this evil, more stringent, or more likely to be effectual, than those already in existence."

On June 1, two Royal visitors arrived here, the Emperor of Russia and the King of Saxony. They had to pay the usual penalty of hard labour for a week.

In the House of Commons, on 14 June, Mr. T. Duncombe presented a petition from W. J. Linton, Joseph Mazzini, and two others, complaining of their letters being opened before delivery, and praying that " The House would be pleased to grant, without delay, a Committee to inquire and give immediate redress to the petitioners, and prevent the recurrence of so unconstitutional and infamous a practice." Sir James Graham (Home Secretary) replied that " the House must be aware that from as early a period as the reign of Queen Anne, power existed in the hands of the Principal Secretary of State, to detain and open letters passing through the Post Office ; and the House would also be aware that this power had come under the review of Parliament, at so late a period as the year 1837, and by the Act of 1 Vic., this power of issuing warrants to open and detain letters, continued still vested in the Secretaries of State. He must, for fear of creating misapprehension by his answer, state that the circumstances mentioned in the petition were, to a great extent, untrue. As to three of the petitioners, he doubted if their letters had ever been detained, and no warrant as to them had been issued; but, as to one of the petitioners, he had to state, that, on his responsibility, a warrant had been issued as to the correspondence of that person, which warrant was no longer in force."

On 2 July, a Committee of Secrecy was appointed "to inquire into the state of the Law in respect to the detaining and opening of Letters at the General Post Office, and into the mode under which the authority given for such detaining and opening has been exercised, and to report their opinion and observations thereupon to the House." The Committee met, took evidence, and duly reported, when it being shewn that the privilege was not often exercised (the total number of warrants issued between 1799 and 1844 being only 372), and that, of late years, the average of warrants had decreased, the public were satisfied, and the subject dropped.

Chantrey's equestrian statue of the Duke of Wellington, which stands in front of the Royal Exchange, was uncovered, amidst much cheering. It cost £9,000 besides the metal.

On 23 Sept. Barry, a clown at Astley's, fulfilled his promise

Barry, the Clown, on the Thames.

of sailing in a washing-tub drawn by geese, from Vauxhall to Westminster. He successfully accomplished his voyage, and repeated it on Oct. 11, from the Red House, Battersea (where now is Battersea Park), to Vauxhall.

On 8 Oct. Louis Philippe, the King of the French, landed at Portsmouth on a visit to the Queen. He was made a Knight of the Garter, and generally fêted, and should have returned to France, from Portsmouth on the 12th, but the sea was too rough, and he had to cross from Dover, instead ; but even this trip was delayed by a great conflagration at New Cross Station, so that he really did not depart until the 13th.

I meet with the first mention of that eminent fertiliser, Guano, in a commercial point of view, in the *Times* of the 18 Oct., where it says that on 16th were put up for sale, at Liverpool, in lots of 10 tons each, 180 tons of the best African guano.   But one lot of five tons was sold, and that fetched £5 12s. 6d.   The next lot was not sold, in consequence of the price offered being under that, and the whole of the re-maining lots were withdrawn, there being no probability of the reserved price being realised.   It was then being fetched from Ichaboe, an island off the south-west coast of Africa— but it was afterwards procured in large quantities from the Chincha Islands, off the coast of Peru.

On 28 Oct. the Queen opened the New Royal Exchange, with great State, and the Lord Mayor (W. Magnay, Esq.) was made a baronet ; the reading-room at Lloyd's was made into a Throne room for the occasion, and a sumptuous *déjeuner* was served in the Underwriters' room.   It was a very im-posing pageant and pretty sight ; but, although the Exchange was formally opened, no merchants assembled within its quad-rangle until the first of the following January.

Whilst on matters civic I must mention the very rare fact of Sir William Magnay's successor in the office of Lord Mayor (Mr. Alderman Gibbs), being hooted and yelled at, on 9 Nov., whilst going to Westminster, and returning thence.   He had been churchwarden of St. Stephen's, Walbrook, and the popu-lar mind was imbued with the idea that something was wrong with his accounts, so they virtuously insulted him.   He had a hard enough time of it both by land and water, when going, what his returning was, is best told by a contemporary :

" The ceremony within the Court of Exchequer having ter-minated, similar uproarious shouts to those which had hailed the arrival of the new Lord Mayor, now marked his embarca-tion for the city ; and, in his passage down the Thames, with but here and there a solitary exception, the civic barge was

the target of repeated vollies of yells and groans, levelled by
no unskilful, or ineffective voices at it, from the banks and
bridges of the river.   The landing at Blackfriars was attended
with a more concentrated attack of ' public execration,' for,
there, an immense multitude was wedged together, anxious
to be spectators of the scene, though not inactive ones.   On
the procession passed amid the continued manifestations of
public disapprobation of the present, and respect for the retiring Lord Mayor.   Many interrogations of a searching nature
were repeatedly bawled forth, not that they could reach the
right honourable ear, but they were exercises in that peculiar
art, styled ' talking at folks.'   The same description must apply
to Ludgate Hill, St. Paul's Churchyard, and Cheapside, in
which place some merriment was created by a party chanting
in appropriate style :

> ' Oh, Alderman Gibbs,
> Pray dub up the dibbs ! '

   " It was somewhat after 4 o'clock, when the cortège arrived
at the bottom of King Street, where, immediately before
Guildhall Yard, about 2,000 persons had collected, and others
pressing out of the several streets, caused a dense mass to
be formed.   This was the place where a parting salutation
was to be presented to the new Lord Mayor, by his pitiless
persecutors, and a very good view of the scene was attainable
from an upper window at the western angle of Gresham
Street.   Hearty and continued cheering announced the progress of Sir William Magnay ; but, as soon as the State coach
with the new Lord Mayor arrived, the yells and groans which
broke forth, were perfectly stunning.   Never was the manner
in which the two Lord Mayors had been received throughout
the day, marked with stronger contrast.   The accumulation
of carriages in Guildhall Yard, caused the detention of the
State coach for some minutes, during which a real tempest
of execration was poured forth upon the unfortunate gentleman ; and many persons did not hesitate to testify their dis-
like to him in a manner to be condemned, by spitting at the
carriage, their distance from which, however, defeated their

intention.   In truth, Mr. Gibbs had to endure a perpetual and pitiless storm of hisses, yells, groans, gibes, sneers and jeers ; and at every stoppage where the crowd was in close proximity to his carriage, unusually furious bursts of indignation broke forth ; yet no missile was thrówn during any portion of the day."

CHAPTER XXIV.

Murder by Tawell—Curious story—King William IV.'s Statue—Visits by the
Queen—Testimonial to Rowland Hill—Breaking the Portland Vase—Sad
end of William Austin—Sale of Van Amburgh's stud—Hungerford Suspension bridge—Accident at Yarmouth—An Excise case—Beginning of the
Railway Mania—Sailing of Sir J. Franklin.

THIS year begins badly—with a murder—which I should not
chronicle, were it not that it was the first case in which the
electric telegraph lent its services for the detection of a crime.
A man named John Tawell, a member of the Society of
Friends, and who occupied a decent position in life, poisoned
a poor woman at Salt Hill. A Quaker who seemed much
confused had been met close by her house, and he went by
train from Slough to Paddington. Suspicion being aroused,
a message was sent from Slough, giving a description of him,
and asking that he should be shadowed on his arrival. This
was done, and, next day, he was arrested. He was tried,
found guilty, and duly executed. The case, at the time,
created an immense sensation, mainly because the villain was
a member of the Society of Friends. *Apropos* of this, the
Observer of 23 March is responsible for the following:

" THE MURDERER TAWELL.—The following strange statement has been made by a person, who is a Quaker, living
near Berkhampstead, and who is acquainted with Tawell:
About a year ago, the stillness and decorum of the Quakers'
meeting at Berkhampstead, at which Tawell attended, was
disturbed by one of the male members, who suddenly rose
from his seat and exclaimed, with frantic earnestness, that
there was then present, a person who was, at that very moment,

meditating a most fearful crime. His conviction was so strong, that he passionately besought this individual, whoever, he might be, to reflect upon the wickedness of his intention, and to implore his Maker's pardon for his murderous thoughts. As may be imagined, the Friends were thrown into great consternation by this strange and impetuous appeal, and the meeting broke up in alarm and confusion. Tawell was present at the time."

Early in January the statue of King William IV., by Samuel Nixon, was placed on its pedestal, fronting London Bridge; but, as far as I know, there was no public ceremony at its inauguration, for the *Times* of 1 Feb. says: " That workmen are now actively employed in cleansing down the colossal figure of King William IV., preparatory to the hoarding being removed, and the statue thrown open to the view of the public. The base will present a very novel and pleasing appearance, it being ornamented with numerous naval trophies. The four cross footpaths leading to the figure will be lighted by four gas lamps, on massive granite pillars. In a few days the whole work will be completed, when it will be inspected by Her Majesty, the Queen Dowager, and His Royal Highness Prince Albert, those illustrious personages having intimated their desire to view it when finished."

On 15 January the Queen paid a visit to the Duke of Buckingham, at Stowe, and the magnificence of her reception had much to do with the financial collapse of the too generous Duke. On leaving Stowe she went to Strathfieldsaye to stay with the Duke of Wellington. It was on this occasion that the old Duke gave a lesson to the gentlemen of the Press; which the interviewers of our times might well take to heart: " Field-Marshal the Duke of Wellington presents his compliments to Mr. ——, and begs to say he does not see what his house at Strathfieldsaye has to do with the public press."

On 21 Jan. a National Testimonial was presented to Rowland Hill for his labours in connection with the introduction of the Penny Post, and Mr. Larpent, the Chairman of the City of London Mercantile Committee on Postage, handed him a cheque for £10,000, which handsome sum had been raised by a public subscription, which was not confined to the mercantile community alone, persons of every rank, and of both sexes, contributing amounts varying from large sums to a few pence.

Just before the closing of the British Museum at 4 p.m. on 7 Feb., a crash was heard, and the famous Barberini, or Portland Vase, was found in pieces on the floor. A man, named Lloyd, in a fit of delirium produced by drink, had smashed it out of pure wantonness. The vase was valued at £1,000 by the Museum authorities, but, of course, that sum was purely nominal, as the vase was unique. It was deposited in the British Museum in the year 1810 by the Duke of Portland, and was considered as his property ; hence the name of the " Portland Vase." It was found about the middle of the 16th century, about two and a half miles from Rome, on the road leading from Frascati. At the time of its discovery it was enclosed in a marble sarcophagus, within a sepulchral chamber, under the mount called Monte di Grano. The material of which it is made is glass, the body being of a beautiful transparent dark blue, enriched with figures in relief, of opaque white glass. For more than two centuries it was the principal object of admiration in the Barberini Palace. It came into the possession of Sir William Hamilton, from whom it was purchased by the Duchess of Portland.

On 11 Feb. the delinquent was brought before Mr. Jardine, at Bow Street, and the Museum authorities electing to prosecute him for the minor offence of breaking the glass case which held the vase, and which was under the value of £5, he was convicted of that offence, and sentenced to pay £3, or two months' hard labour in the House of Correction. He could not pay, and was committed to prison, in default, but on 13 Feb., someone paid the money, and the man was released.

An employé of the British Museum, named Doubleday, undertook, and effected, the restoration of the Vase, and it may now be seen in the Gold Room of the British Museum, but, alas! " all the King's horses, and all the King's men," can never make it as it was.　Wedgwood feebly reproduced it in ceramic ware, copies of which are now worth £200 each, and one copy, if not more, was made in silver.

I come across a curious paragraph in the *Morning Post* of March 13: "WILLIAM AUSTIN.—This person, whose name must be familiar to all who have had any acquaintance with the history of the Parliamentary proceedings in the case of the late Queen Caroline, or the eventful life of that unhappy Princess, arrived in London, last week, from Milan, where he has been residing for several years, for the most part, in a state of fatuity, the inmate of a lunatic asylum.　We understand that he has been removed to this country through the intervention of the British Government, under an authority from the Lord Chancellor, in whose care, his person, and some considerable property, left to him by the late Queen, have been placed by certain proceedings on the part of his relations. He was conveyed hither from Milan under the charge of a medical and two other attendants; and immediately on his arrival, was visited by two London physicians, who, after an interview with him of some duration, at the hotel where he stopped, signed the necessary certificate for his detention in a private asylum, where he now remains.　Austin is a very good-looking man, apparently about 40 years of age; and though, beyond doubt, mentally enfeebled, has no betrayal of such imbecility in the expression of his face.　He has been in his present unfortunate condition since the year 1830; and, for a great part of that time, he has maintained an immovable taciturnity.　No ingenuity has been able to extract a syllable from him.　He answers no questions, nor asks any—enters into no conversation—and, even during the whole journey from Milan to London, he never spoke a word to his attendants, or any one else.　Neither could the medical gentlemen who waited upon him here induce him to reply to any of their inquiries; and no doubt, this fact, of itself, formed no inconsiderable ingredient in the judgment at which they arrived. The unhappy man is extremely docile, has no disposition to violence, and readily understands and obeys any signs made to him."

17*

Van Amburgh's stud, lions, etc., were sold at Manchester on 17 March, and fetched high prices; a fine black maned lion, £350; another, 6 years old, £310; two lion cubs, eight months old, male and female, sold, the one for £12 10/-, the other for £35. An elephant realised £750, and a giraffe £400.

Hungerford Suspension Bridge, the first of its kind over the Thames, was opened on 1 May, and, although a toll was demanded, it was calculated that, before dusk, some 25,000 persons had crossed from one side of the Thames to the other. It was taken down in July, 1862, to make room for the Charing Cross Railway Bridge. It was transferred to Clifton, and there opened, on 8 Dec., 1864, and it now spans the Avon.

On the next day (2 May) a terrible accident occurred at the Suspension bridge at Great Yarmouth. A clown was to emulate Barry's folly, and cross the river in a washing-tub drawn by geese; and thousands of people assembled to see him, of whom a great number (accounts vary from 300 to 600), containing very many children, were on the bridge. Some of the suspension rods snapped, and the crowd fell into the water. Every assistance was rendered, but the number of recovered dead bodies, nearly all children, or young persons, was 77, and many are supposed to have been swept away by the current.

On the 2nd of May, the famous Excise trial at Bar, *i.e.*, before twelve judges, the Attorney General *v.* Smith, came to an end, after lasting eight days. Mr. George Smith was a distiller, in a large way of business, at Whitechapel, and the premises of his brother James, who was a rectifier, adjoined his. The law forbids the junction of the businesses of distilling and rectifying, or any communication between premises carrying on such businesses; and, in this case, it was presumed that all spirit would be conveyed from one to the other by means of the highway. But the contention of the prosecution was, that the Excise officers, finding a great deficiency in the spirits ostensibly produced, as compared with the "wash," had detected holes in a large receiver, and found, moreover, that they could themselves convey spirits from the distillery to the rectifying house, through pipes under ground, which were mixed up with those which supplied water, and so escaped detection. This the defendants denied, and brought forward evidence that the pipes were obsolete and disused. In the end, the verdict of the jury was, " We find for the Crown ; but we are anxious to express our opinion that there has not been any evidence adduced before us which shows that the pipe has been fraudently used by the defendant." The amount of damages claimed by the Crown was £150,000 ; but, by agreement, this was reduced to £76,000 ; and, finally, after an appeal from Mr. Smith, the Government were content with a cheque for £10,000.

About this time commenced what is well termed " The Railway Mania," or, rather, public attention was particularly called to it, as it was becoming a crying scandal. So much so, that it attracted the notice of the legislature ; and, if we look at a " Return to the Order of the Honourable the House of Commons, dated 8th April, 1845, for an alphabetical list of the Names, Description, and Places of Abode, of all Persons subscribing to the Amount of £2,000 and upwards to any Railway Subscription Contract deposited in the Private Bill Office during the present Session of Parliament," we shall see that amongst the names will be found many of the leading nobility, large manufacturing firms, names well known in commerce and literature, mingled together in a most heterogeneous manner. The same column shows a combination of peers and printers, vicars and vice-admirals, spinsters and half-pay officers, Members of Parliament and special pleaders, professors and cotton spinners, gentlemen's cooks and K.C.'s, attorneys' clerks and college scouts, waiters at Lloyd's, relieving officers and excisemen, editors and engineers, barristers and butchers, Catholic priests and coachmen, dairymen and dyers, braziers, bankers, beer sellers and butlers, domestic servants, footmen and mail guards, and almost every calling under the sun.

And these, it must be remembered, were subscribers for £2,000 and upwards ; those who put down their names for less were supposed to be holders of £21,386 6s. 4d. in Stock.

Of course, *Punch* could not overlook this mania for speculation, and we find the following in the number for 31 May:

"The night was stormy and dark.　The town was shut up in sleep;　Only those were abroad who were out on a lark, Or those, who'd no beds to keep.

"I pass'd through the lonely street,　The wind did sing and

"How many hundred shares have you wrote for?"

Railroad Speculators.

blow;　I could hear the policeman's feet　Clapping to and fro.

"There stood a potato-man　In the midst of all the wet; He stood with his 'tato can　In the lonely Haymarket.

"Two gents of dismal mien,　And dank and greasy rags, Came out of a shop for gin,　Swaggering over the flags:

"Swaggering over the stones,　Those shabby bucks did walk;　And I went and followed those needy ones,　And listened to their talk.

"Was I sober, or awake? Could I believe my ears? Those dismal beggars spake Of nothing but railroad shares.

"I wondered more and more; Says one, 'Good friend of mine, How many shares have you wrote for In the Diddlesex Junction Line?'

"'I wrote for twenty,' says Jim, 'But they wouldn't give me one'; His comrade straight rebuked him For the folly he had done:

"'Oh, Jim, you are unawares Of the ways of this bad town; *I* always write for five hundred shares, And *then*, they put me down.'

"'And yet you got no shares,' says Jim, 'for all your boast'; 'I *would* have wrote,' says Jack, 'but where Was the penny to pay the post?'

"'I lost, for I couldn't pay That first instalment up; But, here's taters smoking hot, I say Let's stop, my boy, and sup.'

"And at this simple feast, The while they did regale, I drew each ragged capitalist Down on my left thumb nail.

"Their talk did me perplex, All night I tumbled and tossed, And I thought of railroad specs, And how money was won and lost.

"'Bless railroads everywhere,' I said, 'and the world's advance; Bless every railroad share In Italy, Ireland, France; For never a beggar need now despair, And every rogue has a chance.'"

And yet another extract. Who does not remember Thackeray's *Diary of C. Jeames de la Pluche, Esqre.?* but few know how the idea was started. It was by W. M. T. himself in *Punch* of Aug. 2:

A LUCKY SPECULATOR.

Considerable sensation has been excited in the upper and lower circles in the West End, by a startling piece of good fortune which has befallen JAMES PLUSH ESQ., lately footman in a respected family in Berkeley Square.

One day, last week, MR. JAMES waited upon his master, who is a banker in the City; and, after a little blushing and hesitation, said he had saved a little money in service, and was anxious to retire, and invest his savings to advantage.

His master (we believe we may mention, without offending delicacy, the well-known name of SIR GEORGE FLIMSY, of the firm of FLIMSY, DIDDLER AND FLASH) smilingly asked MR. JAMES what was the amount of his savings, wondering considerably how—out of an income of thirty guineas, the main part of which he spent in bouquets, silk stockings and perfumery—MR. PLUSH could have managed to lay by anything.

MR. PLUSH, with some hesitation, said he had been *speculating in railroads*, and stated his winnings to have been thirty thousand pounds.   He had commenced his speculations with twenty, borrowed from a fellow-servant.   He had dated his letters from the house in Berkeley Square, and humbly begged pardon of his master, for not having instructed the railway secretaries, who answered the applications, to apply at the area bell.

SIR GEORGE, who was at breakfast, instantly arose, and shook Mr. P. by the hand; LADY FLIMSY begged him to be seated, and partake of the breakfast which he had laid on the table; and has, subsequently, invited him to her grand *déjeuner* at Richmond, where it was observed that MISS EMILY FLIMSY, her beautiful and accomplished seventh daughter, paid the lucky gentleman *marked* attention.

We hear it stated that Mr. P. is of very ancient family (HUGO DE LA PLUCHE came over with the Conqueror); and the new Brougham which he has started, bears the ancient coat of his race.

He has taken apartments at the Albany, and is a director of thirty-three railroads.   He purposes to stand for Parliament at the next general election, on decidedly conservative principles, which have always been the politics of his family.

Report says that, even in his humble capacity, MISS EMILY FLIMSY had remarked his high demeanour.   Well, "none but the brave," say we, "deserve the fair."

This we may call the commencement of the mania; in their proper places will be noticed its culmination and collapse.

On 18 May sailed from Greenhithe the two Arctic discovery ships, the *Erebus* and *Terror*, under the command of Sir John Franklin, whose instructions were "to push to the westward, without loss of time, in the latitude of about 74¼ degrees, till you have reached the longitude of that portion of land on which Cape Walker is situated, or about 98 degrees west. From that point we desire that every effort be used to endeavour to penetrate to the southward and westward, in a course as direct towards Behring's Straits as the position and strength of the ice, or the existence of land, at present unknown, may admit. We direct you to this particular part of the Polar Sea, as affording the best prospect of accomplishing the passage to the Pacific."

They were provisioned for three years, but when, in 1850, Captain Ommanney discovered, on Beechey Island, traces of the expedition having spent their first winter there, he found large stacks of preserved meat canisters, which, there is little doubt, contained putrid filth, and had been condemned by survey.

As nothing was heard of the expedition, another was organised, in 1847, to start, for search and relief, from Hudson's Bay ; and, indeed, no one can say that the two exploring vessels were forgotten ; for, from that date, till 1857, *thirty-nine different expeditions were sent to look after them.* The first to find traces of them was that of Capt. Ommanney, in 1850 ; then, in April, 1854, Dr. Rae heard, from the natives, of a party of white men having been seen, four winters previously, and that their bodies had afterwards been seen. From these Eskimo, Rae obtained some silver spoons and other small articles which left no doubt but that they had belonged to the ill-fated expedition. But it was the *Fox* yacht, which was fitted out by Lady Franklin, and commanded by Capt. McClintock, which settled the question of their fate. Early in 1859, a boat, a few skeletons, chronometers, clothing, instruments, watches, plate, books, etc., were discovered ; and, towards the end of May, a written paper was found, which gave news of them up to 25 Apl., 1848, and told that " Sir John Franklin died on 11 June, 1847, and the total losses by deaths in the expedition has been, to this date, nine officers and 15 men; we start on, to-morrow, 26th, for Back's Fish River." From the Eskimo was learned how one of the ships sunk in deep water, and the other was wrecked, after which they all perished miserably, some "falling down and dying as they walked," as an old woman told Capt. McClintock.

CHAPTER XXV.

THE Queen gave a Costume Ball, at Buckingham Palace, on 6th June, which was a magnificent affair, and gave plenty of food for conversation. Every guest had to appear in a costume appropriate to the period of English history between 1740 and 1750; but, with the exception of the minuet, the dances were modern.

I have only space for the dresses of the Queen and Prince Albert. Her Majesty's dress was composed of gold tissue, brocaded in coloured flowers, green leaves and silver, trimmed round the top, bottom and sides (the upper dress being open in front) with point lace over red ribbon; the dress looped up with red satin ribbons, and two large bows, in each of which was a diamond bow and tassel. The stomacher was composed of two large diamond bows, and a diamond point; the sleeves, which were tight, finished with point lace ruffles, and trimmed with red ribbon; on the left arm, the Garter in diamonds, and, on the right, a diamond rosette. She wore the blue ribbon and diamond George as usual. The under petticoat was of white and silver tissue, trimmed with a deep flounce of rich point lace (which had belonged to Queen Charlotte), headed by a quilling of red satin ribbon and bows; above, a narrower flounce of point lace, trimmed like the other; in each ribbon bow, a diamond rosette.

Prince Albert wore a suit of the richest crimson velvet

(of Spitalfields manufacture); the coat lined with white satin,
edged throughout with gold; and the buttons were of gold.
On his left breast His Royal Highness wore a most splendid
star of the order of the Garter, composed of diamonds, with
the exception of the cross, which was formed of rubies. The
badge of the Order was confined at the shoulder by an
epaulette composed of large brilliants, and a most splendid
George was suspended from the ribbon, wholly formed of
brilliants. The Prince also wore the insignia of the Golden
Fleece, formed of opals and diamonds. The Garter was set
in brilliants, and the hilt of His Royal Highness's sword was
covered with diamonds. The waistcoat was of white satin,
richly and elegantly embroidered with gold, the buttons being
of gold. Shoe buckles of diamonds. Hat, three cornered,
edged with gold lace, with handsome diamond ornament in
the cockade in front.

The Earl of Cardigan could not masquerade as Bayard,
but "he excited no little attention. He wore the uniform
of the 11th Dragoons at Culloden; and, with the costume,
which became him extremely, he contrived to assume the
portentous bearing, and the true jack-boot stride and swagger."

The *Morning Chronicle* is answerable for the following:
"For some time past the copper coinage of William IV. has
been eagerly purchased by persons who are stated to be Jews,
and a report has, in consequence, gained ground that gold is
contained in it. What reason there may be for this it is
impossible to say; but it is a well-known fact, that agents
have been at work for the last two months buying up those
particular coins in Westminster, and they now fetch double
the price of their legal issue. The mania has extended eastward, and twopence for a penny piece, and a penny for a
halfpenny, etc., are now asked for the 'precious issue.'"

On 9 June, the new street connecting Holborn with Oxford
Street, and now called New Oxford Street, was thrown open
for carriages.

Messrs. Christie and Manson sold, at the Egyptian Hall,
Piccadilly, on 23 June, the first portion of the "Napoleon
Museum," collected by Mrs. Sainsbury, and which had long

been on exhibition. The prices fetched were ridiculously low, as the following examples will show. Among the bronzes, an infantine bust of the King of Rome, formerly in the possession of Josephine, at Malmaison, cost 20 guineas, sold for £1 10s. A drawing in sepia, by Debret, of Napoleon visiting the wounded on the field, after the battle of Eylau, £5 5s. The pictures illustrative of the principal events in the life of Napoleon, were almost given away; the highest price obtained, being £12 for one by the great French painter David, of Napoleon, with the crown raised in both his hands, to place on the head of Josephine, at the Coronation in Notre Dame. Twenty beautiful enamels by Lienard, of Napoleon, Ney, Berthier, Junot, Joseph, Lucien, Louis and Jerome Bonaparte, Murat, Caroline, the youngest sister of Napoleon, Cardinal Fesch, Marie Louise, etc., fetched but £76, and, on the other days' sales, the lots went for far under their value.

My readers may possibly remember how, on 8 Dec., 1900, a number of Nelson relics in the Painted Hall, at Greenwich Hospital, were stolen, during the night, by a burglar, who escaped; and may like to know the story of Nelson's coat. The *Times* of 9 July, copies the following from the *Spectator* :

" An interesting relic of Nelson has been discovered; and some interest also attaches to the manner in which it has been secured to the nation. Sir Harris Nicolas, in his laborious researches for editing the hero's Despatches, had satisfied himself that the coat and waistcoat which Nelson wore when he fell at Trafalgar, were carefully preserved. In pursuance of the Admiral's directions, they were given, with several other things, by Sir Thomas Hardy, his captain, to Lady Hamilton; by her, they were transferred, under peculiar circumstances, to a late alderman of London, and they remained in the possession of the alderman's widow. The lady is not rich, and she asked £150 for the relic. This sum being beyond his own means, Sir Harris determined to raise it by subscription, in order that the coat and waistcoat might be deposited, like the coat which Nelson wore at the battle of the Nile, in Greenwich Hospital. With that view, he put the proposition in writing, and had it printed as a circular. Before issuing this circular, however, he sent a copy to Prince Albert, who immediately desired that the purchase might be made for himself, as he should feel 'pride and pleasure' in presenting the precious memorials to Greenwich Hospital. Sir Harris Nicolas took them to the Royal purchaser on Wednesday; and we understand that the Prince manifested a very fine feeling on the occasion. There is kind and generous wisdom in this act; for nothing could so help to identify the Queen's husband with the British people, as such little tributes to their maritime pride. The coat is thus described in Sir Harris Nicolas's circular, and it will be seen that it has an historic value: 'The coat is the undress uniform of a vice-admiral, lined with white silk, with lace on the cuffs, and epaulettes. Four stars—of the Order of the Bath, St. Ferdinand and Merit, the Crescent, and St. Joachin—are sewn on the left breast, as Nelson habitually wore them; which disproves the story that he purposely adorned himself with his decorations on going into battle! The course of the fatal ball is shewn by a hole over the left shoulder, and part of the epaulette is torn away; which agrees with Dr. Sir William Beattie's account of Lord Nelson's death, and with the fact, that pieces of the bullion and pad of the epaulette adhered to the ball, which is now in Her Majesty's possession. The coat and waistcoat are stained in several places with the hero's blood."

Further confirmatory evidence is given in the *Globe*, copied into the *Times* of 22 July. "It will scarcely be believed that the coat of the great naval hero, together with his cocked hat, and an immense quantity of his property, was, as it were, mortgaged for the sum of £120, yet such was the fact. The late Alderman Jonathan Joshua Smith was executor of Lord Nelson with Lady Hamilton; and, prior to his death, goods sufficient to fill six crates (amongst which were the coat, hat, breeches, etc.), were placed in the Town Hall, Southwark, under the care of Mr. Kinsey, the chief officer, and who now attends the aldermen at the Central Criminal Court. Kinsey was Alderman Smith's confidential servant for a number of years, and to whom £120 was owing at his master's death. Application was made to the Court of Aldermen, by some members of the Nelson family, for the restitution of the property; and, after a long discussion, Alderman Lucas consented to act as arbitrator between the family and Kinsey, and £30 was paid to the latter, in satisfaction of his claim, upon which, the things were repacked, and sent to Mrs. Smith, at Heron Court, Richmond, in whose possession they remained, until the purchase of the coat was made by Prince Albert."

The King of the Netherlands paid the Queen a visit on 24 July, and the good man must have thought well of us, inasmuch as he was very much let do as he liked. In London he stopped at Mivart's Hotel, went to the Opera, paid a few visits, was a guest of the Duke of Richmond for Goodwood Races, was made a Field Marshal, held a review in Hyde Park, and went back again; a far lighter sentence than is usually passed on Royalty when visiting this country.

We now find the inflation of Railway speculation attracting attention; and, in the *Times* of Aug. 1 is a letter, a column in length, of which I give the following extract, referring to the inquiry into the Dublin and Galway Railway:

"The next case is that of letters addressed to 1, Park Place, Devonshire Street, Mile End Road. So great is the number of letters delivered here, that additional assistance has been given in the duty. Upwards of 1,000 letters have been delivered here within nine months; only last week 120 were taken in on one day, of which, at one time, no less than 16, and, at another, 30, letters were delivered. This No. 1, Park Place, is up an obscure court, consisting of three small houses, of about 5/6 rent per week. No. 1 is occupied by a man and woman, and the next door by their daughter. The proceedings of these persons have been closely watched. Directly a packet of letters has been received in the morning, off starts the old man and woman, and, sometimes, the daughter, to the places appointed to meet the receiver. On the first occasion, the old woman, who had received 16 letters, evidently wanted to deposit her treasure at Crosby Hall Chambers; for, opposite to them, she halted, carefully looking about her; but, unfortunately, she found she was watched; and, escaping through the Excise Office, hid herself somewhere, till her pursuer lost her. The next morning, another packet was received, with which the old man was intrusted; he started immediately, and, after a most circuitous route, to avoid detection as to where he deposited his treasure, he was seen to enter the King's Arms Tavern, Bishopsgate Churchyard, where he was seen to deliver his despatches to a smart, dapper Jew, well known, who, after a few moments' deliberation, left the house, and was speedily joined by several confederates at the top of the churchyard, who, after dividing the letters, dispersed as instantaneously as can be imagined. The next day, it became necessary to augment the detective force, for the old people became more wary; the old man went out before post time, and the daughter was selected as the messenger with despatches; she was fleet of foot, but she had been carefully identified, therefore that did not avail her much, as the detective force was divided, and stationed at such places as were likely to succeed. She took a most circuitous route, but, eventually, found herself opposite the Auction Mart, evidently looking out anxiously for someone; she saw she was watched, and away she started, and, after a long round, found shelter in Maidenhead Court, Aldersgate Street, in a little smith's shop—which turned out to belong to the identical party who resides at No. 1, Park Place, where the letters were first delivered. Here the pursuit was given up. No further attempt to trace the receiver was made, the inquiry before the select committee coming on; but sufficient is shown to exhibit the system existing to this hour. How, it may be asked, do they procure the signatures to the deed, one party holding so many letters of allotment? The system is this : one party signs the deed as often as disguise will shield him from discovery; then the practice is resorted to of procuring persons, from 15 years to 60, to accompany the holder of the banker's receipt to the Railway Office, to sign the deed in such name as he may direct; for which, when done, he receives remuneration, varying from one shilling to ten, according to the premium the scrip may bear in the market."

There were several police cases as to writing and forging these bogus names, and prudent people were beginning to look shy at railway scrip.

Here is a case which we can hardly understand nowadays. As long as Newspapers were stamped, it was a misdemeanour to allow anyone to read them, unless they purchased them, as it was considered a fraud upon the Revenue. On 23 Aug., in the Court of Requests, Kingsgate Street, a case came before the Commissioners for adjudication, in which a newsvendor summoned a person for a small sum, for "reading" the various newspapers. The plaintiff, in stating the case, said the defendant had been in the habit of seeing the papers daily, for which a penny a day was charged, and the present proceedings were taken to recover a balance due on that account. The Commissioners said that he could not recover, as he had been guilty of a gross fraud upon the Stamp Office in letting newspapers out for hire. The plaintiff : But he was in the habit of coming to my shop, and seeing them. The Commissioner : That don't matter ; it is a fraud upon the Stamp Office, and you render yourself liable to an information being laid against you for it.

Here is a little anecdote chronicled in the *Annual Register* (6 Sep.) : "REVERSE OF FORTUNE.—Edward Riley, living with his family in Hadley Street, Burton Crescent, having been proved next of kin to Maj.-Gen. Riley, who recently died at Madras, leaving property to the amount of £50,000, to the whole of which he has become entitled, has greatly amused the neighbourhood by his conduct. From having been but a workman in the dust-yard in Maiden Lane, he has, now, become a man of independence. Some days after his sudden acquisition of wealth, he called, in his cab, on a tailor in Seymour Street, and, taking him to the dust yard, desired him to measure the whole of the men in the yard for a suit of clothes, which being accomplished, he ordered them to go to a bootmaker, where they were all served. On the following Sunday, he ordered a butcher to supply each of them with a joint of meat. Riley has taken a house in Argyle

Square ; and, upon entering it, purposes to give a dinner to all the dustmen in London, and illuminate the front of his house."

We have seen, in 1843, *Punch's* idea of Prince Albert as a farmer, and we next hear of him, in connection with this business, as refusing to pay parish rates for the Flemish Farm ; so at a vestry meeting held at Windsor, on 18 Sep., the subject was brought forward. It appeared that the estimated rental of the property was £450, and that the last rate, at 8d. in the pound, amounting to £15, had not been paid. It was stated that the Prince had refused to pay the rates on two grounds, first, that he had no " beneficial occupation," and, secondly, that " the property belonged to the Queen." The reply to this was, that the Prince certainly had a beneficial occupation in the farm, for the two prize oxen sold by him, last year, at £70 and £80, were fatted on this farm, to say nothing of the crops and agricultural produce, from which His Royal Highness received great profits, and it was thought there was no reason why he should be let off, and the poorer farmers made to pay the rates. It was settled that the collector should make application for the arrears, amounting to over £200.

Punch drew a harrowing picture, of the brokers being put into Windsor Castle, and of a paragraph which might appear in the *Court Circular :* " Yesterday, Her Gracious Majesty visited Prince Albert at her own Bench." But matters did not go so far, for on 14 Jan. next following, the Prince vouch-safed an answer to the Vestry, in which he denied his liability *in toto*, acting on the advice of the Attorney and Solicitor General, and Sir Thomas Wilde ; and, after crushing the poor vestry, the letter winds up thus : " And His Royal Highness feels himself at liberty to take the course which is most satis-factory to his own feelings, and to pay, as a voluntary contribu-tion, a sum equal to the rate which would have been annually due, had the legal liability of His Royal Highness been estab-lished. It is also His Royal Highness's intention that the payment of the sum referred to should commence from the year 1841."

And so it has continued to the present day, if we may credit the authority quoted in the accompanying cutting from the *Globe* of 8 June, 1901 : " HOW THE KING PAYS TAXES.—It is not generally known (says the *Free Lance*) that the King pays taxes under protest—that is to say, His Majesty, like Queen Victoria, claims to be exempt from impost, and yet is willing to contribute, without prejudice, to the rates.   For instance, part of the Windsor farm land lies within the radius of the borough.   The municipal authority issues demand notes for the rates.   The Royal officials respond by paying a sum just under the amount requested, and the collector is satisfied. There is no question of going to law, for how can the King be summoned in his own Courts ? "

On 31 Oct. Lieut. Waghorn practically demonstrated the feasibility of his " Overland Route " to India.   The regular Mail and his Express arrived at Suez by the same steamer on 19 Oct.   The Express was given to a man on a dromedary, who, stopping nowhere, entered Alexandria on the 20th.   The Express was delivered to Mr. Waghorn, who started at 11 o'clock.   He had been waiting on board an Austrian steamer, which had remained in quarantine, so that he arrived at Trieste in free *pratique*.   He landed, however, at Divina, twelve miles nearer London than Trieste, and hurried through Austria, Prussia, Baden, and Bavaria, with a passport ready *viséd* by the representatives of those countries.   He reached Mannheim in 84 hours, proceeded by a steamer to Cologne, thence by special train to Ostend, by boat to Dover, to London by railway, and arrived at 4.30 in the morning of the 31st.   The news from India thus brought, was published in all the London papers, which were in Paris before the Mail from Marseilles was on its way to London.

CHAPTER XXVI.

The Railway Mania—Deposit of plans.

THE accompanying illustration from *Punch* (18 Oct.) justly holds up to ridicule the Railway Mania, which might then be said to have been at its height. It is called "THE MARCH OF SPECULATION.—'This is the young Gent. as takes my Business, Mem. I'm agoin' into the Railway—Director Line myself.'"

As a proof of this Madness, see this paragraph : "Oct. 25. During the past week there were announced, in three newspapers, eighty-nine new schemes, with a capital of £84,055,000 ; during the month, there were 357 new schemes announced. with an aggregate capital of £332,000,000."

On 17 Nov. the *Times* published a table of all the railway companies registered up to the 31st October, numbering 1,428, and involving an outlay of £701,243,208. "Take away," it said, "£140,000,000 for railways completed, or in progress, exclude all the most extravagant schemes, and divide the remainder by ten, can we add, from our present resources, even a tenth of the vast remainder? Can we add £50,000,000 to the railway speculations we are irretrievably embarked in ? We cannot, without the most ruinous, universal and desperate confusion."

Here is a Parody on the situation, 1 Nov. :

> "There was a sound, that ceased not day or night,
>   Of speculation. London gathered then
> Unwonted crowds, and moved by promise bright,
>   To Capel Court rushed women, boys and men,

All seeking railway shares and scrip ; and when
The market rose, how many a lad could tell
  With joyous glance, and eyes that spake again,
'Twas e'en more lucrative than marrying well ;—
When, hark, that warning voice strikes like a rising knell.

Nay, it is nothing, empty as the wind,
  But a " bear " whisper down Throgmorton Street ;
Wild enterprise shall still be unconfined ;
  No rest for us, when rising premiums greet
  The morn, to pour their treasures at our feet ;—
When, hark ! that solemn sound is heard once more,
  The gathering bears its echoes yet repeat—
'Tis but too true, is now the general roar,
The Bank has raised her rate, as she has done before.

And then, and there were hurryings to and fro,
  And anxious thoughts, and signs of sad distress,
Faces all pale, that, but an hour ago
  Smiled at the thought of their own craftiness ;
  And there were sudden partings, such as press
The coins from hungry pockets, mutual sighs
  Of brokers and their clients.   Who can guess
How many a " stag " already panting flies,
When upon times so bright, such awful panics rise ? "

Mr. Francis, in his *History of the English Railway*, says :
" The daily press was thoroughly deluged with advertisements ; double sheets did not supply space enough for them ;
double doubles were resorted to, and, then, frequently, in-
sertions were delayed.   It has been estimated that the receipts of the leading journals averaged, at one period £12,000
and £14,000 a week, from this source.   The railway papers.
on some occasions, contained advertisements that must have
netted £700 to £800 on each publication.   The printer, the
lithographer, and the stationer, with the preparation of prospectuses, the execution of maps, and the supply of other
requisites, also made a considerable harvest.

" The leading engineers were, necessarily, at a great premium.   Mr. Brunel was said to be connected with fourteen
lines, Mr. Robert Stephenson with thirty-four, Mr. Locke with
thirty-one, Mr. Rastrick with seventeen, and other engineers
with one hundred and thirteen.

"The novelist has appropriated this peculiar portion of commercial history, and, describing it, says gravely and graphically : ' A colony of solicitors, engineers and seedy accountants, settled in the purlieus of Threadneedle Street. Every town and parish in the Kingdom blazed out in zinc plates over the doorways. From the cellar to the roof, every fragment of a room held its committee. The darkest cupboard on the stairs contained a secretary, or a clerk. Men, who were never seen east of Temple Bar before, or since, were, now, as familiar to the pavement of Moorgate Street,* as the stockbrokers ; ladies of title, lords, Members of Parliament, and fashionable loungers thronged the noisy passages, and were jostled by adventurers, by gamblers, rogues and imposters.'

"The advantages of competition were pointed out, with the choicest phraseology. Lines which passed by barren districts, and by waste heaths, the termini of which were in uninhabitable places, reached a high premium. The shares of one company rose 2,400 per cent. Everything was to pay a large dividend ; everything was to yield a large profit. One railway was to cross the entire Principality without a single curve.

"The shares of another were issued, the company formed, and the directors appointed, with only the terminal points surveyed. In the Ely railway, not one person connected with the country through which it was to pass, subscribed the title deed.

"The engineers who were examined in favour of particular lines, promised all and everything in their evidence. It was humourously said of them, ' they plunge through the bowels of mountains ; they undertake to drain lakes ; they bridge valleys with viaducts ; their steepest gradients are gentle undulations ; their curves are lines of beauty ; they interrupt no traffic ; they touch no prejudice.'

"Labour of all kinds increased in demand. The price of iron rose from sixty-eight shillings to one-hundred-and-twenty

---

* From Moorgate Street 83 prospectuses, demanding £90,175,000, were sent out. Gresham Street issued 20, requiring £17,580,000.

per ton.   Money remained abundant.   Promoters received
their tens and twenties of thousands.   Rumours of sudden
fortunes were very plentiful.   Estates were purchased by those
who were content with their gains ; and, to crown the whole,
a grave report was circulated, that Northumberland House,
with its princely reminiscences, and palatial grandeur, was to
be bought by the South Western. Many of the railways
attained prices which staggered reasonable men. The more
worthless the article, the greater seemed the struggle to obtain
it.   Premiums of £5 and £6 were matters of course, even
where there were four or five competitors for the road.   One
company, which contained a clause to lease it at three-and-a-
half per Cent., for 999 years, rose to twenty premium, so
mad were the many to speculate.

"Every branch of commerce participated in the advantages
of an increased circulation.   The chief articles of trade met
with large returns ; profits were regular ; and all luxuries which
suited an affluent community, procured an augmented sale.
Banking credit remained facile ; interest still kept low ;
money, speaking as they of the City speak, could be had for
next to nothing.   It was advanced on everything which bore
a value, whether readily convertible, or not.   Bill brokers
would only allow one-and-a-half per cent. for cash ; and what
is one-and-a-half to men who revelled in the thought of two
hundred ? The exchanges remained remarkably steady. The
employment of the labourer on the new lines, of the operative
in the factory, of the skilled artisan in the workshop, of the
clerk at the desk, tended to add to the delusive feeling, and
was one of the forms in which, for a time, the population was
benefitted. But, when the strength of the Kingdom is wasted
in gambling, temporary, indeed, is the good, compared with
the cost. Many, whose money was safely invested, sold at
any price, to enter the share market. Servants withdrew their
hoards from the savings banks. The tradesman crippled his
business. The legitimate love of money became a fierce lust.
The peer came from his club to his brokers ; the clergyman
came from his pulpit to the mart ; the country gentleman forsook the calmness of his rural domain for the feverish excite-

ment of Threadneedle Street. Voluptuous tastes were in-
dulged in by those who were previously starving. The new
men vied with the old, in the luxurious adornments of their
houses. Everyone smiled with contentment ; every face wore
a pleased expression. Some, who, by virtue of their un-
abashed impudence, became provisional committee-men, supported the dignity of their position in a style which raised the
mirth of many, and moved the envy of more. Trustees, who
had no money of their own, or who had lost it, used that
which was confided to them ; brothers speculated with the
money of sisters ; sons gambled with the money of their
widowed mothers ; children risked their patrimony ; and it
is no exaggeration to say, that the funds of hundreds were
surreptitiously endangered by those in whose control they were
placed."

But Railways had been projected, and, in order to carry
them through, the plans must, by law, be deposited with the
Board of Trade, before, or on 30 Nov. ; and, on this occasion,
there was a scene, which is very well told in the *Annual
Register* :

"An extraordinary scene occurred at the office of the Railway Department of the Board of Trade on this day (Sunday,
30 Nov.), being the last day on which the plans of the new
projects could be deposited with the Railway Board, in order
to enable Bills to authorise them to be brought before Parliament, in compliance with the Standing Orders.

"Last year, the number of projects, in respect of which
plans were lodged with the Board of Trade, was 248 ; the
number, this year, is stated to be 815. The projectors of the
Scotch lines were mostly in advance, and had their plans duly
lodged on Saturday. The Irish projectors, too, and the old-
established companies, seeking powers to construct branches,
were among the more punctual. But upwards of 600 plans
remained to be deposited. Towards the last, the utmost exertions were made to forward them. The efforts of the litho-
graphic draughtsmen and printers in London were excessive ;
people remained at work, night after night, snatching a hasty
repose for a couple of hours, on lockers, benches, or the floor.

Some found it impossible to execute their contracts; others did their work imperfectly. One of the most eminent was compelled to bring over four hundred lithographers from Belgium, and failed, nevertheless, with this reinforcement, in completing some of his plans. Post horses and express

Deposit of Railway Plans with the Board of Trade, 30 Nov., 1845.
[*Ill. Lon. News*, 6 Dec., 1845, p. 358.

trains, to bring to town plans prepared in the country, were sought in all parts. Horses were engaged days before, and kept, by persons specially appointed, under lock and key. Some railway companies exercised their power of refusing express trains for rival projects, and clerks were obliged to make sudden and embarrassing changes of route, in order to travel by less hostile ways. A large establishment of clerks

were in attendance to register the deposits ; and this arrangement went on very well, until eleven o'clock, when the delivery grew so rapid, that the clerks were quite unable to
keep pace with the arrivals. The entrance hall soon became
inconveniently crowded, considerable anxiety being expressed
lest twelve o'clock should arrive 'ere the requisite formalities
should have been gone through. This anxiety was allayed
by the assurance that admission into the hall before that
hour, would be sufficient to warrant the reception of the documents.

As the clock struck twelve, the doors of the office were
about to be closed, when a gentleman with the plans of one
of the Surrey railways arrived, and, with the greatest difficulty,
succeeded in obtaining admission. A lull of a few minutes
here occurred ; but, just before the expiration of the first
quarter of an hour, a post chaise, with reeking horses, drove
up, in hot haste, to the entrance. In a moment, its occupants
(three gentlemen) alighted, and rushed down the passage,
towards the office door, each bearing a plan of Brobdingnagian
dimensions. On reaching the door, and finding it closed, the
countenances of all drooped ; but one of them, more valorous
than the rest, and prompted by the bystanders, gave a loud
pull at the bell. It was answered by Inspector Otway, who
informed the ringer it was now too late, and that his plans
could not be received. The agents did not wait for the conclusion of the unpleasant communication, but took advantage
of the door being opened, and threw in their papers, which
broke the passage lamp in their fall. They were thrown back
into the street. When the door was again opened, again went
in the plans, only to meet a similar fate.

" In the whole, upwards of 600 plans were duly deposited."

CHAPTER XXVII.

ALTHOUGH the collapse of the Railway Mania really began
in 1845, its effects were not fully felt until the commencement
of this year, when 10 per cent. on Railway Capital had to
be lodged with the Accountant General, within seven days
from the assembling of Parliament, which in this case meant
the 29th Jan. It really received its first serious wound when
the Bank of England rose its rate of discount on 16 Oct.,
but it was only when the calls had to be paid, that it was
found how rotten the whole concern was, as the Marquis of
Clanricarde, in a speech, plainly exposed. Said he: " One
of the names to the deed, to which he was anxious to direct
their attention, was that of a gentleman, said to reside in
Finsbury Square, who had subscribed to the amount of
£25,000 ; he was informed no such person was known at that
address. There was, also, in the Contract deed, the name
of an individual who had figured in the Dublin and Galway
Railway Case, who was down for £5,000, and who was understood to be a half-pay officer, in the receipt of £54 a year,
but who appeared as a subscriber in different railway schemes
to the amount of £41,500. The address of another, whose
name was down for £12,200, was stated to be in Watling
Street, but it appeared he did not reside there. In the case
of another individual down for £12,500, a false address was
found to have been given. Another individual, whom he
would not name, was a curate in the parish in Kent ; he might

be worth all the money for which he appeared responsible in various railway schemes, but his name appeared for £25,0co in different projects, and stood for £10,000 in this line. Another individual, who was down for £25,000, was represented to be in poor circumstances. A clerk in a public company was down for upwards of £50,000. There were several more cases of the same kind, but he trusted he had stated enough to establish the necessity of referring the matter to a Committee. There were, also, two brothers, sons of a charwoman, living in a garret, one of whom had signed for £12,500, and the other for £25,000; these two brothers, excellent persons, no doubt, but who were receiving about a guinea and a half between them, were down for £37,000."

The story of the collapse is so admirably told by Mr. Francis, that I prefer giving his version than writing of it myself :

" Money was scarce, the price of stock and scrip lowered ; the confidence of the people was shaken, and a vision of a dark future on every face. Advertisements were suddenly withdrawn from the papers, men of note were seen no more as provisional committeemen ; distrust followed the merchant to the mart and the jobber to the Exchange. The new schemes ceased to be regarded ; applications ceased to be forwarded ; premiums were either lowered, or ceased to exist. Bankers looked anxiously to the accounts of their customers ; bill brokers scrutinised their securities ; and every man was suspicious of his neighbour.

" But the distrust was not confined to projected lines. Established railways felt the shock, and were reduced in value. Consols fell one and a half per cent. ; Exchequer bills declined in price, and other markets sympathised. The people had awoke from their dream, and trembled. It was a national alarm.

" Words are weak to express the fears and feelings which prevailed. There was no village too remote to escape the shock, and there was, probably, no house in town some occupant of which did not shrink from the morrow. The Statesman started to find his new Bank Charter so sadly and so suddenly tried ; the peer, who had so thoughtlessly invested, saw ruin opening to his view.   Men hurried with bated breath to their brokers ; the allottee was uneasy and suspicious, the provisional committeeman grew pale at his fearful responsibility ; directors ceased to boast their blushing honours, and promoters saw their expected profits evaporate.   Shares which, the previous week, were a fortune, were, the next, a fatality, to their owners.   The reputed shareholders were not found when they were wanted ; provisional committeemen were not more easy of access.

" One Railway advertised the names and addresses of thirty —none of whom were to be heard of at the residences ascribed to them.   Letters were returned to the Post Office day after day.   Nor is this to be wondered at, when it is said that, on one projected line, only £60 was received for deposits, which should have yielded £700,000.

" It was proved in the Committee of the House of Commons, that one subscription list was formed of ' lame ducks of the Alley ' ; and that, in another, several of the Directors, including the Chairman, had, also, altered their several subscriptions to the amount of £100,000, the very evening on which the list was deposited, and that five shillings a man was given to anyone who would sign for a certain number of shares.

" Nothing more decidedly marked the crisis which had arrived, than the fact that everyone hastened to disown railways.   Gentlemen who had been buried in prospectuses, whose names and descriptions had been published under every variation that could fascinate the public, who had figured as Committeemen, and received the precious guineas for their attendance, were eager to assure the world that they were ignorant of this great transgression.   Men who, a month before, had boasted of the large sums they had made by scrip, sent advertisements to papers denying their responsibility, or appealed to the Lord Mayor to protect their characters. Members of Parliament who had remained quiet under the infliction, while it was somewhat respectable, fell back upon their privileges, when they saw their purses in danger.   There is no doubt that an unauthorised use of names was one feature of fraudulent companies, and that, amidst a list of common names, it was thought a distinguished one might pass unnoticed. The complaints, therefore, of those who were thus unceremoniously treated, were just ; but the great mass of denials emanated from persons who, knowingly, encountered the risk, and, meanly, shrunk from the danger.

" It is the conviction of those who were best informed, that no other panic was ever so fatal to the middle class. It reached every hearth, it saddened every heart in the metropolis. Entire families were ruined. There was scarcely an important town in England but what beheld some wretched suicide. Daughters, delicately nurtured, went out to seek their bread ; sons were recalled from academies ; households were separated, homes were desecrated by the emissaries of the law. There was a disruption of every social tie. The debtors' jails were peopled with promoters ; Whitecross Street was filled with speculators ; and the Queen's Bench was full to overflowing. Men, who had lived comfortably and independently, found themselves suddenly responsible for sums they had no means of paying. In some cases, they yielded their all, and began the world anew ; in others, they left the country for the continent, laughed at their creditors, and defied pursuit. One gentleman was served with four hundred writs ; a peer, when similarly pressed, when offered to be relieved from all liabilities for £15,000, betook himself to his yacht, and forgot, in the beauties of the Mediterranean, the difficulties which had surrounded him. Another gentleman who, having nothing to lose, surrendered himself to his creditors, was a director of more than twenty lines. A third was Provisional Committee-man to fifteen. A fourth, who commenced life as a printer, who became insolvent in 1832 and a bankrupt in 1837, who had negotiated partnerships, who had arranged embarrassed affairs, who had collected debts, and turned his attention to anything, did not disdain, also, to be a Railway promoter, a Railway director, or to spell his name in a dozen different ways."

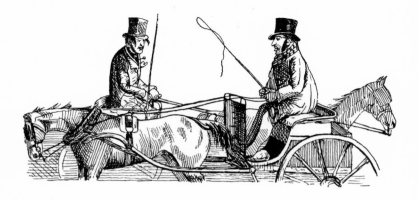

The Sheriff's Officers had a busy time of it, and *Punch*, in "GOING OUT ARRESTING," gives the following colloquy between two of the fraternity:

" 'Vell, Aaron, my tear, have yer 'ad any sport?'
" 'Pretty vell, I've bagged four Allottees, and two Provisionals!' "

But a notice of the Railway Mania would be very incomplete without a mention of George Hudson, the Railway King. He was born at Howsham, a village near York, in March, 1800; was apprenticed to a draper in York; and, subsequently, became principal in the business; thus, early in life, becoming well off, besides having £30,000 left him by a distant relative. In 1837, he was Lord Mayor of York; and, the same year, was made Chairman of the York and North Midland Railway, which was opened in 1839. In 1841, he was elected Chairman of the Great North of England Company; and, afterwards, held the same position in the Midland Railway Company. He speculated largely in railways, and, in the Parliamentary return, already alluded to, his subscriptions appear as £319,835.

He came to London, and inhabited the house at Albert Gate, Knightsbridge (now the French Embassy), where he entertained the Prince Consort, and the aristocracy generally.

He was elected M.P. for Sunderland in Aug., 1845, and again served as Lord Mayor of York in 1846. The Railway smash came; and, year by year, things went worse with him, until, early in the year 1849, he had to resign the Chairmanship of the Eastern Central (now Great Eastern), Midland, York, Newcastle and Berwick, and the York and North Midland Railway Companies. He went abroad, where he lived for some time, and tried, unavailingly, to retrieve his fortune. In July, 1865, he was committed to York Castle for Contempt of the Court of Exchequer, in not paying a large debt, and was there incarcerated till the following October.

He fell so low, that, in 1868, some friends took pity on him, and raised a subscription for him, thus obtaining £4,800, with which an annuity was purchased. He died in London, 14 Dec., 1871."

We have been so accustomed to have nigger minstrels with us that I suppose very few of us know when they began. Of course, I do not mean the solitary minstrel like Rice of " Jump Jim Crow " fame, who was the first, coming over here in 1836; but the first troupe. I find it in the *Illustrated News* of 24 Jan., 1846, whence also comes this illustration:

The Ethiopian Serenaders.

" A party of American minstrels, under the above designa-tion, commenced on Wednesday night (21 Jan.), at the Hanover Square Rooms, a series of concerts, for the avowed

19

purpose of affording an accurate notion of Negro character and melody. These artists are remarkably clever, and admirably ' made up.' They are painted jet black, with ruddy lips, and large mouths ; and, being capital actors, the deception created is so great, that wagers have been offered that they are really ' darkies.' They dress in dandy costume, *à la Jullien*—that is, white waistcoated and wristbanded, turned up in the most approved D'Orsay fashion. Of course, it is impossible to come to any right conclusion as to the authenticity of the African airs, especially as they have arranged the compositions of the great European masters in such a grotesque manner. The executants are five in number ; one plays the tambourine, Mr. Germon, who is the leader ; another the bone castanet ; the third, the accordion ; and the two others, the banjo, or African guitar. The castanet player does not sing ; but his four colleagues have good voices, and, in glees, harmonize charmingly. In a quartet, the parody on the Phantom Chorus, from Bellini's ' Sonnambula ' ; and in a glee, ' You'll See Them on the Ohio,' nothing can be more effective than the skilful blending of the parts. It is, perhaps, the *buffo* exhibition which will create the greatest sensation, and in this quality they are inimitable. The tambourine performer affects a ludicrous air of pompous sentiment, while the castanet sable hero indulges in all kinds of buffoonery and antics. He is a wonderful player—nc Spaniard can rival him in rapidity, delicacy and precision. A scene called a ' Railway Overture,' causes an explosion of laughter ; they seem to be endowed with perpetual motion ; and the scream of the whistle, at the same time as the noise of the engine, beggars all description. The entertainment is quite a novelty, and will, no doubt, be attractive. They have been provided with letters of recommendation from President Polk, and some leading persons in America, who must be better able to appreciate the accuracy of their African delineations than Europeans."

They *were* popular, with a vengeance—for every little street arab had beef bones for castanets, and every new song was roared out in the streets until it nauseated. *Punch* drew policemen and dustmen as Ethiopian Serenaders, and even suggested that Lablache, Mario and Tamburini should adopt the style.

The Queen opened Parliament on 19 Jan., and in her speech, whilst deprecating "the very frequent instances in which the crime of deliberate assassination has been, of late, committed in Ireland," she went on: "I have to lament that, in consequence of a failure of the potato crop in several parts of the United Kingdom, there will be a deficient supply of an article of food which forms the chief subsistence of great numbers of my people. The disease by which the plant has been affected, has prevailed to the utmost extent in Ireland. I have adopted all such precautions as it was in my power to adopt, for the purpose of alleviating the sufferings which may be caused by this calamity; and I shall confidently rely on your co-operation in devising such other means for effecting the same benevolent purpose, as may require the sanction of the Legislature."

On 13 March, Parliament talked somewhat about the matter, and Sir James Graham, the Home Secretary, confessed that distress "pervades the whole of Ireland. It is to be found in every province, in every county, in every union; nay, almost in every parish in Ireland. The course Her Majesty's

19*

Government has taken, has been this. We have, in particular parts of Ireland, established depôts, where food can be bought at an easy price, at the very lowest price, and, thinking that eleemosynary relief ought to be avoided as much as possible, we propose to afford, to the utmost possible extent, either by means of public works to be undertaken, or by works already established, the means by which the people may be enabled to earn wages, and so to purchase food at the moderate cost at which it will be supplied."

But, in spite of all the Government could do, with the very best intentions, gaunt famine was stalking through the land, and the hungry folk could not be quiet, with the sight of food before them. They were not going to starve when they saw the bakers' shops full of bread, and the butchers', of meat. Human nature and a hungry belly could not stand it—so we can scarcely wonder at the famine riots which ensued. The shops were wrecked, the food was taken ; they even laid their hands on a boat proceeding from Limerick to Clare with relief, and plundered it of its cargo of corn and maize flour. But, alas! this was only the commencement of the sad story.

There was an alternative, open to those who had the money —to emigrate—and this they did—see the following, from the *Cork Reporter*, copied into the *Times* of 18 April : " For the last fortnight our quays have been daily thronged with the fine and stalwart peasantry of this and the adjoining counties, preparing to emigrate to various parts of the trans-Atlantic world. Perhaps, upon no former occasion, even before the hope of railway employment was held out to the people, and when " Government grants " for their relief were never heard of, did the number of emigrants from this quarter exceed the proportion of this present year. Besides the various large and full-freighted vessels, which have left the quays of Cork, direct for America, several ships were despatched to the west of the county, and had no difficulty in obtaining their full complement of passengers. Two large ships went round to Berehaven, a few days ago, and have, since, left the shores of that bleak district, with over 200 passengers. Several other vessels have proceeded, or are about to proceed, for Baltimore and Berehaven, localities in which the destitution of the present year has been severely felt. Three hundred persons have been ready, for the last fortnight, to embark from Dingle ; but, not being able to get a ship to visit them, sufficiently commodious for their accommodation, have been obliged to make the best of their way to Cork. Several vessels, now lying at Passage, will sail this day, these taking five hundred and fifty passengers. . . . . . At a moderate computation, about 9,000 emigrants have, or, within the next month, will have, left this port for America. It is to be hoped their anticipations will be realised. There can be little fear, however, that their condition could be worse, or their prospects more disheartening than those which the 'potato famine' in this country, little mended by the promise of Indian corn, had occasioned. *La faim chasse le loup hors du bois.* To starve, or emigrate, are the only alternatives of the people."

The *Waterford Chronicle* thus comments : "There will have gone, after the season is over, upwards of 3,000 people, from this country, by this port alone. Not to talk of the rearing of these people—the trouble and expense of bringing up a healthy man, woman, or child, and, especially, leaving out the irreparable loss to society, in this country, of their affections, hopes, and family ties—all, now, sundered and destroyed—not to talk of the countless living deaths of wholesale emigration from a feeling and warm-hearted mother country—the amount of capital taken by these 3,000 is immense. Assuming that each individual spends £10 in his passage, and before he settles, and that he has £10 more to establish himself, here is direct taking away, in hard cash, of £60,000 gone out of the bleeding pores of Ireland, to increase the misery which is left behind. We are in possession of facts which show that many cunning landlords are sending away their people yearly, but by degrees, and not in such a manner as to subject themselves to a 'clearance notice.' If this system be continued, we shall be tempted to give names. After these things, who will blame the people for outbreaks

occasioned by famine? There is nothing plentiful in the
land but ruin! Employment is scarce—money is scarce—the
people are being thinned—farms are being consolidated—
bullock land is progressing—

> " Ill fares the land, to hastening ills a prey,
> Where cows accumulate, and men decay."

For some long time there had been a conflict of opinion
as to the merits of different sized gauges for railways. Brunel,
the magnificent, advocated a width of seven feet, and practised
it on the Great Western; others wished for something far
more modest. Great was the wrangling over this "battle of
the gauges," and a Royal Commission was appointed to inquire into the matter. They gave in their Report on 30 May,
and the question was settled by "An Act for regulating the
Gauge of Railways" (9 and 10 Vic., c. 57—passed 18 Aug.,
1846) by which it was settled that, in future, all Railway lines
in England were to be 4 feet 8 ½ in. wide, and in Ireland, the
width was to be 5 ft. 3 in.

By the way, Railway surveyors were paid well, and almost
everyone that had ever dragged a chain posed as a surveyor.
As a sample—on 23 Ap. is reported the case of White v. Koe
and Maun—where a witness said "Levellers are always well
paid. I have received, before this £10 a mile, and I could
level from seven to eight miles a day. These are not extraordinary terms. I had to find hands to help me. I had three
men at 7s. a day each."

On 22 June poor Haydon, the painter, committed suicide.
He was extremely egotistical, and nothing could persuade him
that he was not the best painter of his time. His fixed idea
was that he was without a peer—but no one else thought so.
His diary is very sad reading. Here is an entry (Ap. 13)
relative to the exhibition of his picture, "The Banishment
of Aristides": "Receipts £1 3s. 6d. An advertisement of a
finer description could not have been written to catch the
public; but not a shilling more was added to the receipts.
They rush by thousands to see Tom Thumb. They push—
they fight—they scream—they faint—they cry 'Help!' and

'Murder!' They see my bills and caravans, but do not read them; their eyes are on them, but their sense is gone. It is an insanity—a *rabies furor*—a dream—of which I would not have believed Englishmen could have been guilty." He even wrote to the *Times* about it : " GENERAL TOM THUMB, last week, received 12,000 people, who paid him £600; B. R. HAYDON, who has devoted 42 years to elevate their taste, was honoured by the visits of 133 ½, producing £5 13s. 6d., being a reward for painting two of his finest works, 'Aristides and Nero.' HORACE VERNET, LA ROCHE, INGRES, CORNELIUS, HESS, SNORR, and SCHEFFER, hasten to this glorious country of fresco and patronage, and grand design, if you have a tender fancy to end your days in a Whig Union."

CHAPTER XXVIII.

The last Post Office Bellman—The "Corn Law" Act—Sir Walter Scott's monument—The Irish famine—The Duke of Wellington's statue—Gun cotton—Introduction of ether—Model dwelling houses—Baths and Washhouses—Smithfield Cattle market—" The Bull Fight of Smithfield "—The first submarine telegraph.

The Illustrated London News, of 27 June, gives us " THE LETTER CARRIER'S LAST KNELL.—We have just lost another of what poor Thomas Hood called, ' Those evening bells.' The Postmaster General having issued his fiat for the abolition of ' ringing bells ' by the Letter Carriers, the last knell was rung out on the evening of Wednesday last ; and, as a memorial of the departure of what appeared to most persons, a very useful practice, our artist has sketched a Letter Carrier, on his last evening call at our office ; and another hand has appended the following lament :

    *   *   *   *   *

> The Dustman was first to forego his brass clapper,
>   The Muffinboy speedily followed his shade ;
> And, now, 'tis the Postman—that double-tongued rapper—
>   Must give up his Bell for the eve's promenade.
> " *Tantæ Animis ?* ' sage Legislators !
>   Why rage against trifles like these ? Prithee tell,
> Why leave the solution to rude commentators,
>   Who say, that at home, you've enough in one *Belle ?* "

On 26 June the Royal Assent was given to an Act (9-10 Vic., c. 22), called " An Act to amend the Laws relating to the Importation of Corn." This regulated the duty on corn by a sliding scale of prices, which was to be in force until

1 Feb., 1849, when it was fixed at 1s. per quarter. The passing of this Act caused general rejoicing throught the country,
and put an end to a great deal of political rancour.

The inauguration of Sir Walter Scott's Monument, at Edinburgh, took place on 15 Aug., the anniversary of his birth.
It was erected in 1840-44, after designs by Mr. George M.

The last Post Office Bellman.

[*Ill. Lon. News*, 27 June, 1846

Kemp, at a cost of £15,650. It is cruciform, with a Gothic
spire, chiefly modelled on the details of Melrose Abbey; and
includes, beneath its basement arches, a Carrara marble sitting
statue of Scott, with his dog *Maida*, by his side, which is the
work of Mr. Steel, and cost £2,000.

The potato crop utterly failed again in Ireland, and the
outlook there was indeed black. In the *Times* of 2 Sep., its
correspondent, writing from Dublin, on 31 Aug., says: "As it
is now an admitted fact, on all sides, that the destruction of
the early potato crop is complete, there can be no earthly use

in loading your columns with repetitions of the sad details, as furnished day after day in the accounts published by the Irish newspapers. It will, therefore, nearly suffice to say that, according to the reports from all quarters, the crisis of deep and general distress cannot be much longer averted, and that it will require all the energies of both Government and Landlords to mitigate the inevitable consequences of a calamity, of which both parties have been duly forewarned. In the meantime, the following statement in a Limerick paper of Saturday, is another curious illustration of the Irish ' difficulty ' :

" ' In the Corn Market, this day, there appeared about 4,000 bushels of oats, and about an equal quantity of wheat. All this grain was purchased up, principally for exportation, whilst the food of the people, as exhibited this day in the Potato Market, was a mass of disease and rottenness. This is an anomaly which no intricacies of political economy—no legal quibbles, or crochets—no Government arrangements can reconcile. In an agricultural country which produces the finest corn for the food of man, we have to record that the corn is sold and sent out of the country, whilst the individuals that raised it by their toil and labour, are threatened with all the horrors of starvation.'

" From a multiplicity of concurrent statements respecting the pestilence, I shall merely subjoin one, which appears in the last *Tralee* paper : ' A man would hardly dig in a day, as much sound potatoes as himself would consume. But that is not the worst of it. Common cholera has set in among the people of the town, owing to the use of potatoes, which contain a large quantity of poisonous matter. A professional gentleman in this town, of considerable experience and unquestioned integrity, assures me, that he has attended, within the last fortnight, in this town and neighbourhood, more than 12 cases of common cholera, and that he would think a person as safe in consuming a certain quantity of arsenic, as in using the potatoes now exposed for sale.' "

This is how the Famine of 1846-7 began, and what followed is a matter of history, which everyone ought to know, and

ponder well over, but it can hardly come under the name of
Gossip.   There were, naturally, a few food riots in different
parts of the country, but everyone tried to do their best, even
in a blundering way, to alleviate the distress.   The Archbishop
of Canterbury composed a Special Form of Prayer, to be used
on Sunday, 11 Oct.

On 29 Sep. the gigantic equestrian statue of the Duke of
Wellington, which used to crown the arch opposite Apsley
House, and which was taken down 24 Jan., 1883, and then
set up at Aldershot, was moved from the artist's (Wyatt)
studio, in Harrow Road, to Hyde Park.   It was 27 feet high,
and weighed about 40 tons, being made of brass guns taken
by the Duke in various victories.   Being of so great a weight,
the appliances to remove it were on an equally massive scale,
the carriage and framework in which it was placed weighing
about 20 tons.   It took 100 soldiers to haul the statue out
of the studio ; and, when mounted on its carriage, it took 29
huge dray horses, lent by Mr. Goding, of the Lion Brewery,
Waterloo, to drag it to its destination.   It was escorted by
soldiers and military bands, and did the distance in about an
hour a half.   The next day was spent in preparing to hoist
it ; the day after, it was lifted some 50 feet, and there remained
all night—and the next day was safely landed and put in
position.   From that time, until it was taken down, it was
the butt of scoffs and jeers, and no one regretted its departure.

Gun cotton was brought into public notice by some experiments by its inventor, Professor Schönbein, of Basel, before
the chairman of the East India Company, and a number of
scientists.   Professor Brande had previously lectured upon
it, at the Royal Institution, on 15 Jan., when he stated that,
about fifteen years before, Braconnot had ascertained that sawdust, wood shavings, starch, linen and cotton fabrics, when
treated with concentrated nitric acid, produced a gelatinous
substance, which coagulated into a white mass, on the addition of water ; this substance, which he called " xyloidine," was
highly inflammable.   Schönbein, however, made his explosive
from purified cotton, steeped in a mixture of equal parts of

nitric and sulphuric acids, which when carefully washed, and dried, kept its appearance of cotton wool. In the *Times* of 4 Nov., is a notice of Gun sawdust (a powder now much used), made by Mr. George Turner of Leeds.

Whilst on the subject of Chemicals, I may as well mention, what was much talked of at the time—the discovery of sulphuric ether, when inhaled, being an anæsthetic. Previous to this, Nitrous Oxide, or, as it was called, "Laughing Gas," somewhat inadequately performed the same function. This latter was discovered by Dr. Priestley, in 1776, and its use, as an anæsthetic, recommended by Sir H. Davey in 1880, was put into practice by Mr. Wells, in America, to lessen the pain in extracting teeth in 1844.

The first notice of the inhalation of sulphuric ether that I know of, is in No. XLV. of the *British and Foreign Medical Review*, which says: "Just as our last proof was passing through our hands, we received from our medical friends in Boston, the account of a matter so interesting to surgeons, and, indeed to everyone, that we take the opportunity of introducing it here. We know nothing more of this new method of eschewing pain than what is contained in the following extracts from two private letters, kindly written to us by our excellent friends Dr. Ware and Dr. Warren, of Boston—both men of the highest eminence in their profession in America—and, we may truly say, in Europe also. It is impossible, however, not to regard the discovery as one of the very highest importance, not in the practice of operative surgery only, but, also, as Dr. Ware suggests, in practical medicine. We trust our friends will forgive us for putting into print their private communications. The importance of the subject, and the necessity of authenticating the statements, are our excuses. The authors of the discovery are Dr. C. T. Jackson and Dr. Morton.

Dr. Warren writes, under date of 24 Nov., that "In six cases, I have had it applied with satisfactory success, and no unpleasant sequel." And Dr. Ware (29 Nov.) says: "It was brought into use by a dentist, and is, now, chiefly employed by that class of practitioners. He has taken out a patent for the discovery, and has despatched persons to Europe to secure cne there also ; so you will soon hear of it, and, probably, have an opportunity of witnessing its effects."

Then follows a long list of operations performed in America —wound up with this postcript : " Dec. 22. Yesterday, we had, ourselves, this new mode of cheating pain put in practice by a master of chirurgery, on our own side of the Atlantic. In the theatre of University College Hospital, Mr. Liston amputated the thigh of a man, previously narcotized by the inhalation of ether vapour. Shortly after being placed on the operating table, the patient began to inhale, and became apparently insensible in the course of two or three minutes. The operation was then commenced, and the limb was removed in, what seemed to us, a marvellously shcrt time —certainly less than a minute ; the patient remaining during the incisions and the tying of the arteries, perfectly still and motionless. While the vessels were being secured, on being spoken to, he roused up partially (still showing no signs of pain), and answered questions put to him, in a slow, drowsy manner. He declared to us that at no part of the operation had he felt pain, though he seemed to be partially conscious ; he had heard some words, and felt that something was being done to his limb. He was not aware, till told, that the limb was off ; and, when he knew it, expressed great gratification at having been saved from pain. The man seemed quite awake when removed from the operating room, and continued so. Everything has since proceeded as usual, and very favourably.

" Mr. Liston afterwards performed one of the minor—but most painful operations of surgery—the partial removal of the nail, in *onychia*, on a man similarly narcotised, and with precisely the same result. The patient seemed to feel no pain ; and, upon rousing up, after the operation, declared that he had felt none."

Punch found another and more domestic use for this anæsthetic.

Wonderful effects of Ether in a case of a scolding wife

Patient: "This is really most delightful—a most beautiful dream."

Not only was there advance in medicine, but, also, in social science—people began to think that the condition of the working classes might be ameliorated by giving them better dwellings. As yet, little or nothing had been done, in this way, in London, but a grand opportunity occurred at Liverpool, in the building of Birkenhead, and an extensive range of model dwellings were erected, four-storied, with ornate exterior, the rents varying from 3s. to 5s. per set of rooms, according to position; but this included a constant supply of water, and the use of one gas burner in each set of rooms, and all rates and taxes; with, moreover, two iron bedsteads, a grate with an oven, and convenient fixtures; and they were found to answer financially.

The Queen's consent was given on 26 Aug. to an "Act to Encourage the Establishment of Public Baths and Wash-houses" (9-10 Vic., c. 74). How it was appreciated by the animals called "Vestrymen" may be seen by the fact that at a Vestry meeting of the inhabitants of St. Leonard's, Shoreditch, held 26 Oct., the subject was brought forward, when an amendment was moved " that it be taken into consideration that day six months." For the amendment, 28 ; against 20!

The dangers of Smithfield Market were becoming too apparent, as we see by a letter in the *Times* of 26 Nov. :

" Sir,—Your paper of this morning again gives an account of more accidents arising in consequence of cattle being driven along our crowded streets, and we may expect to hear of

The Bull Fight of Smithfield.

numerous, probably some fatal, injuries being sustained during the short, and, often, very dark days, which are common for some months in the winter. Everyone, whose avocations call him into the city, has to complain of the delay arising from the over-crowded state of the leading thoroughfares ; and, on Smithfield Market days, the obstruction is greatly increased by the droves of cattle and sheep which, in a bewildered, and frequently infuriated state, are being forced by crowds of men, boys, and dogs, along the streets, to the great annoyance, and, often, danger, of the passengers. I do not here dwell on the revolting scenes of cruelty to the animals, which everyone has to witness and deplore ; but, on the ground of danger to human life, and, also, because of the seriously increased obstruction to the general traffic, which is caused by having the cattle market in the heart of the metropolis, I would urge the removal of Smithfield Market to some more appropriate place. When this has been effected—when *abattoirs* have been constructed, where, alone, all the larger animals are permitted to be slaughtered, and when cattle are allowed to be driven through the streets only at hours before the business of the day has commenced—then, and not before, will London be, in reference to its cattle market and slaughter houses, what is required in the middle of the nineteenth century."

Punch gives us the following lyric on the subject :

THE BULL FIGHT OF SMITHFIELD.

There's trampling feet in Goswell Street, there's row on Holborn Hill,
There's crush and crowd, and swearing loud, from bass to treble shrill ;
From grazier cad, and drover lad, and butcher shining greasy,
And slaughter men, and knacker's men, and policemen free and easy.

'Tis Monday morn, and onward borne to Smithfield's mart repair
The pigs and sheep, and, lowing deep, the oxen fine and fair ;
They're trooping on from Islington, and down Whitechapel road,
To wild halloo of a shouting crew, and yelp, and bite, and goad.

From combs of distant Devonshire, from sunny Sussex wold,
From where their Durham pastures the stately short-horns hold ;
From Herefordshire marches, from fenny Cambridge flat,
For London's maw they gather—those oxen fair and fat.

The stunted stocks of Cambria's rocks uneasily are lowing,
With redder blaze of wild amaze their eyes around them throwing ;
And the unkempt stot of Galloway, and the Kyloe of the Mearns,
Whose hoof, that crush'd the heather tuft, the mild MACADAM spurns.

They may talk of *plaza mayors*, of *torero's* nimble feat,
Of MONTEZ, the famed *matador*, of *picadors* so fleet ;
But what is Spanish Bull fight to deeds which we can show,
When through the street, at all they meet, the Smithfield oxen go ?

See there, see there, where, high in air, the nurse and nurseling fly !
Into a first-floor window, see, where that old gent, they shy !
Now they're bolting into parlours, now they're tumbling into cellars,
To the great disgust and terror of the peaceable indwellers.

Who rides so neat down Chiswell Street ?   A City Knight, I ween ;
By girth and span an alderman, nor less by port and mien.
Look out, look out ! that sudden shout ! the Smithfield herd is nigh !
Now turn, Sir Knight, and boldly fight, or, more discreetly, fly.

He hath eased round on his saddle, all fidgetty and fast ;
There's another herd behind him, and the time for flight is past.
Full in his front glares a rabid runt, thro' tears of pain that blind him,
For the drover's almost twisted off the tail that hangs behind him.

All lightly armed for such a shock was stout SIR CALIPEE,
But he couched his new umbrella, and " Police " aloud cried he !
Crash—smash—slap-dash !   The whalebone snaps, the saddle seat is bare,
And the Knight, in mazy circles, is flying thro' the air !

The runt tears on, the rout is gone, the street is calm once more,
And to Bartlemy's they bear him, extended on a door ;
Now, gramercy, good SIR CALIPEE, to the turtle and the haunch,
That padded out thy civic ribs, and lined thy stately paunch.

No ribs are broke, but a shattering stroke thy system has sustain'd ;
Any other than an alderman had certainly been brained.
And, soon as he had breath to swear, the Knight right roundly swore
That, straight, he'd put down Smithfield, and set up an *abattoir*.

In this year there were sold at Smithfield 226,132 beasts,
1,593,270 sheep and lambs, 26,356 calves, and 33,531 pigs—
to deal with which there were about 160 salesmen.   Things
went on very much in the same style as described in *Punch*
until 1851, when the contracted space of the market, the
slaughtering places adjoining, and many other nuisances, gave
grounds for general dissatisfaction, and after an investigation,
an Act (14-15 Vic., c. 61) was passed on 1 Aug. " For providing
a Metropolitan Market, and conveniences therewith, in lieu
of the Cattle Market at Smithfield."   A suitable site was
found in Copenhagen Fields, Islington ; the last market at
Smithfield was held on 11 June, and the first at the new one
on 13 June, 1855.

The *Hampshire Guardian*, copied into the *Times* of 12
Dec., gives us the story of the first submarine Telegraph :
" We are enabled to supply the following additional particulars
respecting the submarine Telegraph laid down across our
harbour.   It is now about three years since the telegraph

20

from the Nine Elms terminus to the terminus at Gosport was first established. Subsequently, from the inconvenience experienced at the Admiralty Office here, because of the distance to the telegraph station, the wires were continued from that place to the Royal Clarence Yard. With this addition, although the inconvenience was lessened, it was far from being removed, the harbour intervening, leaving a distance of upwards of a mile, to the Admiral's house, unconnected ; and, notwithstanding the wish of the authorities, both here and in London, that the telegraph should be carried to the Dockyard, no attempt has, hitherto, been made to do so, because it has been considered almost impossible to convey it under water.   An offer, indeed, was made to the Admiralty, to lay down a telegraph enclosed in metallic pipes, which were to be fixed under the water by the aid of diving bells. This scheme, having been found to be impracticable, has been very prudently abandoned.   Whatever difficulties may have hitherto interfered to prevent the establishment of submarine telegraphs, appear, now, to have been entirely overcome, for the time occupied from the commencement of carrying the telegraph from shore to shore, and transmitting signals, did not occupy a quarter of an hour.   The telegraph, which has the appearance of an ordinary rope, was coiled into one of the dockyard boats, one end of it being made fast on shore, and, as the boat was pulled across, the telegraphic rope was gradually paid out over the stern, its superior gravity causing it to sink to the bottom immediately. . . .   Independently of the simplicity of this submarine telegraph, it has an advantage which even the telegraphs on land do not possess— in the event of an accident, it can be replaced in ten minutes. The success of the trial here has, we understand, determined the inventors to lay down their contemplated line across the Channel, from England to France, under the sanction of the respective Governments."

Such was the germ of the multitudinous cables which now span every ocean.

CHAPTER XXIX.

Medals for Army and Navy—Grenville library—Day of fasting—" Binding of Satan "—Suspension of transportation—New House of Lords—Jenny Lind —*Bunn v. Lind*—" Jenny Linden "—Death of O'Connell—Story of the Duke of Buccleugh—Abolition of Eton " Montem."

AT this time, at all events, we did not plaster our soldiers with medals for every trifling deed of duty, and it was not until January of this year, that a Commission was appointed to decide upon the medals which were to be presented to the officers and men who served in the Peninsula, under Wellington and other commanders. And it was not till the 1st of June, that an Order was issued from the Horse Guards, that claims might be sent in by those who were present in battles from 1793 to 1814—or, rather, the list began with Maida, 1806, and ended with Toulouse, 1814. The medals for naval service began with the " Glorious First of June," 1794, and ended with the fight between the Endymion and President on 25 Jan., 1815. The Medal for Waterloo was granted some long time afterwards.

In January, the British Museum received the splendid bequest of the Library of Thomas Grenville, Esqre., who died 17 Dec., 1846. This magnificent library of over 20,000 volumes, valued at the very low estimate of £50,000, contains two copies of the Mazarin bible, one on vellum, a first folio of Shakespere, Caxton's " Reynard the Fox," and countless other literary treasures and rarities. He had intended to leave this library to the Duke of Buckingham—but, reflecting that as most of the books had been paid for with the proceeds of a sinecure office (Chief Justice in eyre, south of the Trent)

20*

of £2,000 a year, which he had held from 1800 to 1817, when it was abolished, he felt it only just that they should be given to the nation, who had virtually paid for them. With them came, as curator, his valet, Mr. Holden, who remained with his master's beloved books until three or four years since.

On 9 March a Royal Proclamation was issued for a day of Fasting and humiliation on account of the famine and distress in Ireland, and it was duly kept on the day set apart for it, 24 March.

There is a curious paragraph in the *Times* of 23 March : " BINDING OF SATAN.—During the past two or three weeks, a number of persons have been going round the streets, on the Surrey side of the water, wearing belts, like those worn by the fire brigade, on which passages from the Scriptures are painted, carrying with them an inkhorn and long sheets of paper, soliciting signatures to what they pretend to be a petition to Heaven, for the binding of Satan, the Prince of darkness.   So eager are those persons to get the paper signed, that men, women, and children are stopped indiscriminately, and requested to sign.   Those who are too young to sign, or unable to write their names, have the same done for them by the men, who do not attempt to disguise the fact of belonging to the followers of Joanna Southcote.   Upon several occasions, a great deal of confusion has been created by the parties, for they generally manage to go about with knots of forty or fifty persons ; and, occasionally, discussions ensue, which are calculated to bring the Scriptures into perfect ridicule.   One person, more intelligent than the persons who are hawking the petitions about, inquired who it is that will present the petition ? when the man replied, with the greatest coolness, that as soon as a sufficient number of names are attached to the petition, it will be presented to the Throne of Mercy by Joanna Southcote herself.   Surely it is high time that such exhibitions were put down by the police."

Early in April a circular from the Home Secretary was forwarded to the magistrates at the various gaols, telling them that, in consequence of the suspension of transportation of male convicts to Van Diemen's Land, it would be requisite for them to make immediate provision for the confinement and employment, in this country, of a great number of such offenders.

On the 14th of April the Queen paid a visit of inspection to the New House of Lords, and, on the next day, the Peers took possession of it, and transacted business there for the first time.

Talk of Gossip, was there ever such food for it as the arrival of Jenny Lind—it was a furore, a madness. She arrived in London late on the afternoon of Ap. 17, and was present in the evening at the performance at Her Majesty's Theatre. On May 4 she made her first appearance on the Stage in England—in this Theatre—where she played in " Robert le Diable," and, from that moment, until the end of the season, nothing else was thought of—nothing else talked of—but Jenny Lind, and it was no short-lived fit of enthusiasm, for she was *the* favourite of the public until her retirement; her beautiful voice and simplicity of manner charming everyone, from Royalty downwards. Unfortunately her début was somewhat marred by a pecuniary squabble between her and Bunn, the operatic poet, a rival *impresario*, Lumley, having secured her services. Here is Punch's version of the squabble :

" JENNY-LINDEN.

A DREADFUL ENGAGEMENT BETWEEN THE SWEDISH NIGHTINGALE AND THE POET BUNN.

On LIND, when Drury's sun was low,
And bootless was the wild-beast show,
The lessee counted for a flow
    Of rhino to the treasury.

But JENNY LIND, whose waken'd sight
Saw Drury in a proper light,
Refused, for any sum per night,
    To sing at the Menagerie.

With rage and ire in vain display'd,
Each super drew his wooden blade,
In fury half, and half afraid
    For his prospective salary.

BUNN in a flaming frenzy flew,
And speedily the goose quill drew,
With which he was accustomed to
    Pen such a deal of poetry.

He wrote the maiden to remind
Her of a compact she had signed,
To Drury Lane's condition blind,
    And threatened law accordingly.

Fair as in face, in nature, she
Implored the man to set her free,
Assuring him that he should be
    Remunerated handsomely.

Two thousand pounds she offered, so
That he would only let her go ;
BUNN, who would have his bond, said No !
    With dogged pertinacity.

And, now, his action let him bring,*
And try how much the law will wring
From her to do the handsome thing,
    Who had proposed so readily !

The Swedish Nightingale to cage,
He failed ; she sought a fitting stage,
And left him to digest his rage,
    And seek his legal remedy.

Then shook the House, with plaudits riven,
When JENNY's opening note was given,
The sweetest songstress under heaven
    Forth bursting into melody.

But fainter the applause shall grow,
At waning Drury's wild-beast show,
And feebler still shall be the flow
    Of rhino to the treasury.

---

  * The case of *Bunn v. Lind* came on, in the Court of Queen's Bench, on 22 Feb., 1848. Damages laid at £10,000. The jury found a verdict for the plaintiff, and the case was ultimately settled by a payment of £2,000.

The Opera triumphs ! LUMLEY brave,
Thy bacon thou shalt more than save ;
Wave, London, all thy 'kerchiefs wave,
    And cheer with all thy chivalry.

'Tis night ; and still yon star doth run ;
But all in vain for treasurer DUNN,
And Mr. HUGHES, and poet BUNN,
    And quadrupeds, and company.

For Sweden's Nightingale so sweet,
Their fellowship had been unmeet,
The sawdust underneath whose feet
    Hath been the Drama's sepulchre.''

Died on 15th May, at Genoa, on his route to Rome, aged 72, Daniel O'Connell, the erst " uncrowned King of Ireland," who, during his lifetime, had been a thorn (and a very trouble-some one) in the side of every English government. His heart was forwarded to Rome, but his body was embalmed, and, in due time, was sent to Ireland for interment.

The *Liverpool Albion,* quoted in the *Times* of 14 May, is responsible for the following story : " Some time ago, the Duke of Buccleugh, in one of his walks, purchased a cow from a person in the neighbourhood of Dalkeith, and left orders to send it to his palace on the following morning. According to agreement, the cow was sent, and the Duke, who happened to be *en déshabille,* and walking in the avenue, espied a little fellow ineffectually attempting to drive the animal to its destination. The boy, not knowing the Duke, bawled out to him : ' Hi ! mun, come here an' gi'us a han' wi' this beast.' The Duke saw the mistake, and determined to have a joke with the little fellow, Pretending, therefore, not to understand him, the Duke walked on slowly, the boy still craving his assistance. At last, he cried in a tone of apparent distress : ' Come here, mun, an' help us, an' as sure as ony-thing, I'll give ye half I get.' This last solicitation had the desired effect. The Duke went and lent a helping hand. ' And now,' said the Duke, as they trudged along, ' how much do you think you will get for this job ? ' ' Oh, dinna ken,' said the boy, ' but I am sure o' something, for the folk up at the house are good to a' bodies.' As they approached the house, the Duke darted from the boy, and entered by a different way. He called a servant, and put a sovereign into his hand, saying, 'Give that to the boy that has brought the cow.' The Duke returned to the avenue, and was soon rejoined by the boy. 'Well, how much did you get?' said the Duke. 'A shilling,' said the boy, 'an' there's the half o't to ye.' 'But, surely, you got more than a shilling,' said the Duke. 'No,' said the boy, with the utmost earnestness, 'as sure's death, that's a' I got—an' d'ye not think it's a plenty?' 'I do not,' said the Duke; 'there must be some mistake; and, as I am acquainted with the Duke, if you return, I think I'll get you more.' The boy consented; back they went. The Duke rang the bell, and ordered all the servants to be assembled. 'Now,' said the Duke to the boy, 'point out the person who gave you the shilling.' 'It was that chap, there, with the apron,' pointing to the butler. The delinquent confessed, fell on his knees, and attempted an apology; but the Duke interrupted him, indignantly ordered him to give the boy the sovereign, and quit his service instantly. 'You have lost,' said the Duke, 'your money, your situation, and your character, by your covetousness; learn, henceforth, that honesty is the best policy.' The boy, by this time, recognised his assistant, in the person of the Duke, and the Duke was so delighted with the sterling worth and honesty of the boy, that he ordered him to be sent to school, kept there, and provided for at his own expense."

Eton "Montem" was abolished this year. It was a triennial custom, and had for its purpose the presentation of a sum of money to the Captain of the school on his departure to the University. Every third year, on Whitsun Tuesday, some of the Eton boys, clad in fancy costume (as is here given from the Montem of 1844), went to Salt Hill, and the neighbourhood generally, and levied contributions, or "Salt," from all passers-by. The custom led to grave abuses, and the Provost and Head Master determined that it should end, but, that the boy who benefited by it should not be a loser, the latter, Dr. Hawtrey, gave him £200 out of his own pocket.

The following is an account of the death and burial of Eton "Montem":

"Tuesday, 25 May.—This being the day on which the triennial festival of 'Montem' would have been celebrated at Eton and Salt Hill, had it not been abolished by the Provost and the authorities of Eton, considerable excitement prevailed in the vicinity of the College from an early hour this morning, in consequence (from rumours which had been in circulation for some time past) of its being apprehended

Dresses, Eton "Montem." 1844.

that some 'demonstration' would be made by the boys, assisted by several old Etonians from Oxford and Cambridge (who are strongly opposed to the abolition of the ceremony), which might lead to a breach of the peace. With the exception of about a thousand small squares of glass being demolished in the vicinity of the lower school, and similar breakages, but to a much smaller extent, at the houses of parties who were supposed to be in favour of the determination which had been come to by the Provost, we have heard of no demonstration of a riotous character on the part of the boys. This being a 'whole holiday,' several of the head boys had permission to proceed in boats, up the Thames, for the day, as far as Cliefden. Between 100 and 200 have, also, left for the Whitsun holidays; thus thinning the number remaining at College to a considerable extent.

"As soon as 'absence' had been called by the head master, the Rev. Dr. Hawtrey, shortly after 12 o'clock, the boys, numbering between 200 and 300, formed in procession in the playing fields, and marched across the fields, preceded by a black flag, to the celebrated mount at Salt Hill. They were joined by a great many of the old Etonians from the Universities of Oxford and Cambridge, who arrived at Eton this morning. Each wore, on his left arm, a band and rosette of black crape, and many had white hatbands and scarves. As they were seen wending their way towards Salt Hill, they had all the appearance of mourners (merry though they might be) in a funeral procession. Upon their arrival at the Mount, the black flag was waved in solemn silence, and, afterwards, placed on the summit, drooping on the ground, typical of the lost glories of Montem. The large party then proceeded to Botham's, at the Windmill Hotel, whence, after partaking of a luncheon, they again returned to the Mount, and, with the flag, retraced their steps back to College.

"A match at cricket was played during the day, between the Oxonians and the present Etonians, in the shooting fields attached to the College. A splendid cold collation was provided, in the evening, for the players, by Mr. Clarke, of the Christopher Inn. The waiters who attended upon the guests were compelled to wear black crape around their arms, 'in keeping,' as it was observed, 'with the solemnity of the occasion.' Such were the fears entertained by some of the College authorities that a disturbance might take place in the course of the day, that a strong body of the Metropolitan A division of police was stationed at Slough, in plain clothes (as we are informed), to be in readiness to assist the local authorities, in the event of their services being required, it being expected that a mob, composed of the idle and lazy of the two towns, might, in the course of the evening, show some disposition to create a disturbance. The abolition of Montem is not only considered to be a most unpopular proceeding on the part of the old and present Etonians ; but, also, by the tradesmen of Eton and Windsor, amongst the former of whom a large sum of money was triennially circulated, both before and during the festival."

Punch has a lament on it, of which I reproduce three verses :

> " Say, Hill of Salt, for thou hast seen
>   Full many a noble race
>   Do what might be considered mean
>   In any other case—
>   With cap in hand, and courtly leg,
>   Waylay the traveller, and beg ;
>   Say, was it not a pleasing sight
>   Those young Etonians to behold,
>   For eleemosynary gold,
>   Arrest the passing wight.
>
>   Whilst some, of more excursive bent,
>   Their vagrant arts to ply,
>   To all the various places went,
>   That in the neighbourhood lie ;
>   To Datchet, Slough, or Horton they,
>   Or e'en to Colnbrook, took their way,
>   Or ancient Windsor's regal town ;
>   Stopp'd every body they could meet,
>   Knocked at each house, in every street,
>   In hopes of half a crown.
>
>   Gay clothes were theirs, by fancy made ;
>   Some were as Romans drest,
>   Some in the Grecian garb array'd,
>   Some bore the knightly crest ;
>   Theirs was attire of every hue,
>   Of every fashion, old, or new,
>   Various as Nathan's ample store.
>   Angelic beings !   Ladies ! say
>   Will ye let these things pass away ?
>   Must Montem be no more ? "

From this, to the Accession of the Queen, there is no more Gossip to chronicle.